HISTORY, HOMAGES AND THE HIGHLANDS

AN OUTLANDER GUIDE

VALERIE ESTELLE FRANKEL

Other Works by Valerie Estelle Frankel

Henry Potty and the Pet Rock: An Unauthorized Harry Potter Parody

Henry Potty and the Deathly Paper Shortage: An Unauthorized Harry Potter Parody

Buffy and the Heroine's Journey

From Girl to Goddess: The Heroine's Journey in Myth and Legend

Katniss the Cattail: An Unauthorized Guide to Names and Symbols in The Hunger Games

The Many Faces of Katniss Everdeen: Exploring the Heroine of The Hunger Games

Harry Potter, Still Recruiting: An Inner Look at Harry Potter Fandom

An Unexpected Parody: The Unauthorized Spoof of The Hobbit Movie

Teaching with Harry Potter

Myths and Motifs in The Mortal Instruments

Winning the Game of Thrones: The Host of Characters and their Agendas

Winter is Coming: Symbols, Portents, and Hidden Meanings in A Game of Thrones

Bloodsuckers on the Bayou: The Myths, Symbols, and Tales Behind HBO's True Blood

The Girl's Guide to the Heroine's Journey

Doctor Who and the Hero's Journey

Doctor Who - The What, Where, and How: A Fannish Guide to the TARDIS-Sized Pop Culture Jam

Choosing to Be Insurgent or Allegiant: Symbols, Themes, and Analysis of the Divergent Trilogy

Sherlock: Every Canon Reference You May've Missed in BBC's Series 1-3

Women in Game of Thrones

Symbols in Game of Thrones

How Game of Thrones Will End: The History, Politics, and Pop Culture Driving the Show to its Finish

Joss Whedon's Names: The Deeper Meanings behind Buffy, Angel, Firefly, Dollhouse, Agents of S.H.I.E.L.D., Cabin in the Woods, The Avengers, Doctor Horrible, In Your Eyes, Comics and More LitCrit Press.May 2014.

Pop Culture in the Whedonverse

History, Homages and the Highlands: An Outlander Guide is an unauthorized guide and commentary on *Outlander* (book and show) and its related universe. None of the individuals or companies associated with the books or television series or any merchandise based on this series have in any way sponsored, approved, endorsed, or authorized this book.

ISBN-13: 978-0692328071 (LitCrit Press)

ISBN-10: 0692328076

LitCrit Press

Contents

Introduction

Outlander offers a dazzling world of mingled magic and history as Claire Beauchamp Randall plunges into the standing stones and finds herself on the edge of the Jacobite Rebellion. But who was Bonnie Prince Charlie historically? What was life really like among the bagpipes, kilts, cattle raids, and Gaelic of the Highlands? And what of the books – what are their sources? This book explores Scottish life of the 1740s and 1940s, together with the people and places Claire encounters on her adventures.

Learn the difference between Scottish and English pounds, customs of Highland weddings and funerals, and all the delightful expressions of the Scottish dialect. From Louis XV to George VI, it's a tour through European history before Claire travels on to meet the Founding Fathers of America.

There's also magic and mystery: standing stones, selkies, the fair folk, witchcraft, and always the mystery of Loch Ness. The Sun Feasts and Fire Feasts of Imbolc, Beltane, and Samhain are still celebrated today as people bind on protective charms and pray to Jesus and Mary along with the older Celtic gods of Lugh and Bride.

With over 20 million copies sold and now a Starz cable show, the series is a historical, romantic, fantastical adventure not to be missed!

OUTLANDER COMPANION

VALERIE ESTELLE FRANKEL

Salutes, Homages, and Influences

Doctor Who

While first inspired, Gabaldon was watching a *Doctor Who* rereun, specifically "War Games" with Patrick Troughton and his companion, Jamie MacCrimmon. The latter, a kilted Highlander recruited from just after the Battle of Culloden, was one of the most popular characters on the fifty-year show. She notes that she found his gallantry "endearing" and his kilt "rather fetching," so she began the book in his era. As Gabaldon goes into more detail about the *Doctor Who* scene:

> In this particular scene, Jamie McCrimmon and Lady Jennifer, a WWI ambulance driver (hence demonstrably no one's delicate blossom) are somewhere with the TARDIS, but without the Doctor, who was presumably in considerable danger elsewhere/when. Jamie declares that he must go rescue the Doctor, tells Lady Jennifer to wait there, and heads for the TARDIS - followed closely by Lady Jennifer. When he perceives that she plans to come, too, he insists that she must stay behind, ostensibly because someone needs to tell their other companions what's going on. Lady Jennifer greets this piece of feeble persuasion with the scorn it deserves, demanding, "You just want me to stay behind because I'm a woman, isn't that right?" To which our courageous young Scotsman (who is considerably shorter than Lady Jennifer) replies, "Well, no, I - that is... you... I... well... yes!" Now, I found this demonstration of pig-headed male gallantry riveting.
>
> ...

9

Jamie McCrimmon, from the eighteenth century and a culture in which women were respected, but not considered men's physical equals (for the excellent reason that they aren't), appears for the most part to accept the notion that the women with whom he has to do on his travels through time are in fact his equals and treats them that way – until now. When push comes to shove, and it's a matter of a woman taking on physical risk... he can't help it; he has to try to protect her, even though he accepts her as his intellectual and social equal. ("The Doctor's Balls" Kindle Locations 334-349).

Jamie was named in compliment to the *Doctor Who* character. He too struggles with modern women, particularly his World War II nurse Claire, with her own standards of what she can manage. Continuing her story, Gabaldon adds:

So Jamie he was, but with a blank for a last name. Knowing nothing about Scotland when I began, I was reluctant to give him a last name until I knew more about the history of the Highlands and its clans. He remained "Jamie []" for several months, in fact – until I happened in the course of my research to read *The Prince in the Heather,* by Eric Linklater. This book told the story of what happened to the Bonnie Prince and his followers after the disaster at Culloden. Included in the description of those harrowing days was the poignant quote which I later used in *Dragonfly in Amber: After the final battle at Culloden, eighteen Jacobite officers, all wounded, took refuge in the old house and for two days, their wounds untended, lay in pain; then they were taken out to be shot. One of them, a Fraser of the Master of Lovat's regiment escaped the slaughter; the others were buried at the edge of the domestic park.* Now, by this point I had "seen" enough of the story to think that it should end at Culloden – but I had the feeling that there was more to the story than that. So, on the off chance that there might one day be a sequel to this book (cough), I thought it might be advisable for Jamie [] to survive that battle – and if that were the case ... well, plainly his last name should then be Fraser. (*Outlandish Companion,* 135-136)

Coincidentally, Jaime McCrimmon is played by

Frazer Hines. Also coincidentally, as Gabaldon put it, "I came across the legend of the Dun-bonnet – the survivor of Culloden who returned to his estate, and lived seven years in hiding in a cave, protected by his loyal tenants. This struck me as a most romantic and suitable story, so – in the larcenous fashion of novelists – I snatched it and adapted it to my own purposes" Months later, she discovered the man's name was James Fraser (*Outlandish Companion* 136).

Frazer Hines has been cast in the role of a prison warden for a 2015 episode, as a fun salute to his original contribution. In another nod, in the eighth book, Brianna jokes with family friend Joe Abernathy about how much she wishes she had a TARDIS instead of the standing stones (*Written in My Own Heart's Blood*, ch. 97).

Game of Thrones

Ron Moore comments, "Oh, sure. *Game of Thrones* proved that you can do this – that you can take a big literary franchise and convert it into a big television hit. And be faithful to the source material and do it right and do it big, and then an audience will come [for] big serialized ongoing mythology. Absolutely, they opened the door for us" (Prudom, "Ron Moore")

Starz's CEO Chris Albrecht recognizes that many want to classify *Outlander* as Starz's version of *Game of Thrones,* noting, "We should just hope for the kind of success that show has had in popular culture." Nonetheless, he considers the separation between books and show to be a flaw in *Game of Thrones:* "There are a lot of people that watch *Game of Thrones* that never read the books and maybe have still never read the books. What you'd love to see in something like this is for each franchise, the books and the television show, to feed the other" (Prudom, "Strong

Female"). Moore says he's "not particularly worried about attracting new viewers. I think if people try it, they'll get hooked and just keep coming back" (Prudom, "Strong Female").

Of course, there are many superficial similarities: Both are historical-fantasy dramas with lots of sex and violence, filmed in beautiful exotic British locations. Both are adventures on the edge of a cataclysmic war, with stunning period costumes. There are repeat names (Jaime, Ned, Jenny, John, River Run, Brienne/Brianna) and tropes: family loyalty, fate, forbidden love, duty. Both series follow the books closely, with author cameos and involvement. George R.R. Martin and Gabaldon are friends in fact, with her work appearing in several of his anthologies. She notes, "When I told George Martin, who I know quite well, that I had 16 episodes, he said, 'What? *Game of Thrones* only gets 10 a season,' but George's books are not as long and complicated as mine" (Bethune).

Nonetheless, there are fundamental differences: the books *A Song of Ice and Fire* are epic fantasy sagas that emphasize male point of view characters (those who are not male like Brianna and Arya often have masculine behavior patterns). By contrast, *Outlander* begins with Claire's point of view almost exclusively for the first two books. As she time travels and explores a culture and lover so different from anything she's known, she guides readers to see the world through her inherently feminine worldview. *Game of Thrones* with naked women standing about in rooms and long speeches by Littlefinger and Tyrion (contrasted with mystery women like Melisandre) has a noted emphasis on the masculine. Mary McNamara in "HBO, You're Busted," notes that on *Game of Thrones*, "The upper frontals got so gratuitous – two women teaching themselves the tricks of prostitution while a male

VALERIE ESTELLE FRANKEL

character, fully clothed, muses about his personal history and definition of power – that fans took to Twitter to complain."

Albrecht acknowledges an attempt to capitalize on the "lack of female-skewing programs in the premium space," and to attract women with *Outlander*, adding, "When women become attached to something like this, it's pretty hard to pry them away from it. I think they are a much more loyal, less fickle audience than lots of other demographic segments" (Prudom, "Strong Female").

Other Cable Shows

> The "Outlander" books date to 1991, but it seems likely that TV executives looked at them and thought, oh, "Game of Thrones" meets "Downton Abbey." The series ... has some of ye-olde-time grimy violence and sex of "Games" and a little of the plummy accents and cozy Anglophilia of "Downton." (Hale)

Many cable shows, including *The White Queen, Camelot, The Tudors,* and certainly *Game of Thrones* see medieval sex scenes with anachronistic cleanliness and waxing. Indeed, *The New York Times* describes Jaime as "the kindest, buffest and cleanest of the group" (Hale). In most of these, women learn to seduce men, and men, to be the sexual conquerors. On *The Tudors*, King Henry sleeps with every woman he desires, as does the new pope in *The Borgias*. As McNamara notes, these shows are terribly slanted:

> Although there is male nudity – men occasionally, though not always, appear shirtless and/or bottomless when they are having sex with women – there are no male brothels, no scenes of clothed women, or men for that matter, sitting around chatting in a room filled with naked men...For all their many functions, women's bodies are not props and prostitution is not something that should be regularly relegated to atmosphere.

13

A few shows seem to take a women's point of view for a far different story. In the first episode, Claire takes what she wants – including in her marriage. Moore explains that he "wanted to show her as empowered sexually as a person and having her own appetites and desires" (qtd. in Maerz). In the ruins of Castle Leoch, Claire doesn't undress for the audience, and as Frank kneels before her, she pulls his head down. At a preview screening in New York, Mike Hale writes, "the women in the audience loudly expressed their approval." "She's the one who makes the first move, telling Frank what she wants (even removing her own underwear ahead of time!) so she's also the one we get to see enjoying it," critic Melissa Maerz notes in her article "Let's Talk about that 'Outlander' Sex Scene." As she adds:

> Obviously, sex scenes that focus on women getting off are still generally seen as taboo. In the documentary *This Film is Not Yet Rated*, Kimberly Pierce, who directed *Boys Don't Cry*, reveals that the MPAA pressured her to cut a similar sex act from her film to prevent it from earning an NC-17 rating, even though the brutal murder at the film's end was acceptable under an "R" rating. Pierce believes the MPAA was particularly uncomfortable with a shot that featured no nudity at all – it was a close-up that lingered on Brandon Teena's ecstatic expression – because it was such a clear departure from more traditional sex scenes, which have a clear endpoint as their goal, and tend to finish whenever the guys involved do. Maybe that's why it feels somewhat radical that the camera pans upward during the *Outlander* sex scene so that we can see Claire's face.

The Starz show *The White Queen* and HBO shows *Sex and the City* and *True Blood* are all adapted from women's books. Thus all focus on the female protagonists and their emotions and relationships. *Sex and the City* features dating gossip, and the women objectify men far more than the reverse, as they discuss pros and cons in each. In *The White Queen*, the heroine forces the king to submit to her will and marry her rather than "conquering" and discarding her. *True Blood* takes this further, objectifying a fully nude Eric Northman, a handsome vampire happy to walk around in the buff. Sookie's brother is naked as often as Sookie, and he prances around for the camera as well.

This staring at men emphasizes the women as the source of power in the scene and the camera angle through which the viewers experience life. This is the opposite of most shows. As E. Ann Kaplan sums it up: "Within the film text itself, men gaze at women, who become objects of the gaze; the spectator, in turn, is made to identify with this male gaze, and to objectify the women on the screen; and the camera's original 'gaze' comes into play in the very act of filming" (qtd. in Clover 235). However, Claire makes the sexual decisions, eyes Jaime's entire body in a slow walk-around on their wedding night, tells Frank what she wants, and provides the series voiceover. She's directing the action in a way very unusual for women onscreen.

"So far I had been assaulted, threatened, kidnapped, and nearly raped, and somehow, I knew that my journey had only just begun." Claire's words in the first episode emphasize the trauma she's undergone and all she will soon endure, as many women did in this time period. In episode eight, both Claire's consensual encounter with Jaime and her two near-rapes are shown mostly clothed, with a swirling camera to focus on her long-lasting trauma. Like the scene with Jenny's nudity, the emphasis here is on the characters' pain and shock, not the salaciousness.

The *Times* notes, "In keeping with the Starz ethos, though, [*Outlander* is] a lighter show all around – less heavy and also less substantial" (Hale). The gradual speed certainly parallels *Downton Abbey* at times, likely inspiring the comparison. But the genius of both shows is an emphasis on more than battles and beheadings but on daily life in the period dramas, the day-to-day interactions that are more the province of women than men.

Brigadoon

Jaime and Claire note that in Scottish legends, people always travel 200 years. Probably the most famous tale of this sort is *Brigadoon*. Two Americans hunting in Scotland wander into a village, only to discover it's been magically unstuck in time and is in fact filled with people from two hundred years in the past. As Tommy falls in love with a village inhabitant, Fiona, he realizes his bustling city and corporate life lack the romance and charm of the old world. He knows he cannot return to Fiona, as their world only touches his own once per century, but he tries to go back and see her nonetheless, only to find her – true love has made their timelines intersect once more.

This fifties musical with a book and lyrics by Alan Jay Lerner and music by Frederick Loewe, was quite popular, followed by a Gene Kelly movie adaptation. Nonetheless, *Brigadoon* cannot be traced to a particular folktale or novel, except perhaps *Germelshausen*, an 1860 story by Friedrich Gerstäcker that is actually set in Germany. Its cursed village appears for only one day every century. The protagonist, Arnold, comes from the outside and falls for the villager Gertrud, but ends being parted from her forever, with a plot that appears in many German tales by Mueller, Heine, Uhland and others. As such, *Brigadoon* seems an influence on the series, but it would be an exaggeration to say that in the fairy abduction tales it's "always two hundred years, when this modern story, based on another modern tale from Germany, is the only example.

The Wizard of Oz

Claire tells Jaime – with ribbons woven in his hair – that he resembles the Cowardly Lion (*Voyager*, ch. 38), while Brianna compares a time traveler's bewilderment to Dorothy's (*An Echo in the Bone*, ch. 85). There's also Claire's spell in episode four of the show. The chapter title, "Son of a Witch," is a book title from the *Wicked* series. Meanwhile, a World War Two pilot compares himself to Dorothy in *The Wizard of Oz*, adding to himself "maybe it was the resemblance of the Northumbrians to scarecrows and lions" ("All Hallows" 449). All of these emphasize the connection between series, as the hero finds himself in a far-off land.

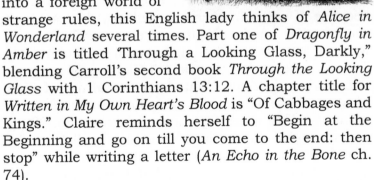

Alice in Wonderland

As Claire enters a magic portal and pops into a foreign world of strange rules, this English lady thinks of *Alice in Wonderland* several times. Part one of *Dragonfly in Amber* is titled 'Through a Looking Glass, Darkly," blending Carroll's second book *Through the Looking Glass* with 1 Corinthians 13:12. A chapter title for *Written in My Own Heart's Blood* is "Of Cabbages and Kings." Claire reminds herself to "Begin at the Beginning and go on till you come to the end: then stop" while writing a letter (*An Echo in the Bone* ch. 74).

Upon discovering Lord John is unexpectedly in Philadelphia, Claire goes to see him "feeling a little like Alice down the rabbit hole" (*An Echo in the Bone*, ch. 85). Likewise, Laoghaire's brother resembles the white rabbit in Brianna's eyes (*The Drums of Autumn*, ch. 33). The prologue of *Voyager* evokes the book as well, as Claire says, "Looking down into reflection, I would see my own round face and frizzled hair against a featureless blue sweep, and think instead that the puddle was the entrance to another sky. If I stepped in there, I would drop at once, and keep on falling, on and on, into blue space." This is a more fitting analogy than the previous, as it's a British story about social mores of previous centuries, all after a magical trip through a portal. Alice's confusion predominates the story, though like Claire, she must discover how to survive.

Anachronisms

The anachronisms delightfully fill the series as time travelers Claire (and later), Roger and Brianna quote from their own heritage whether the references fit or not.

Of course, 1940's Claire is strong – willed enough to be an anachronism herself. In the first book, Frank and his scholar friend are quite shocked when Claire burns herself and yells "bloody fucking hell!" Frank immediately tries to excuse her actions because of her two years exposed to vulgar soldiers. She studies medicine, in an era in which most women had returned to their homes. Much later, Donnor notes that he could tell Claire was a woman out of time, adding, "You don't act afraid of men. Most of the women from now do. You oughta act more afraid" (*A Breath of Snow and Ashes*, ch. 28).

In episode four, Claire creates a spell from *The Wizard of Oz*, in which Laoghaire must chant "there's no place like love" and click her heels three times. Claire, about to do her business over the Waulking kettle in "Rent," cries "Geronimo!" Also in the episode, Claire says "okay," and Ned says it back. Claire calls Jaime a "regular Bob Hope" in the wedding episode. Jaime misunderstands Claire's question about hanging stockings for Yuletide in

"Both Sides Now" and Reverend Wakefield references Sherlock Holmes (while this last is not an anachronism, it may be an homage, as Doyle was Scottish).

The time travelers continue to impact the world around them. In the books, Geillis makes cyanide – unusual but not impossible in the 1740s. After the potato harvest, Claire serves "bangers and mash ... a nice traditional English dish, hitherto unknown in the benighted reaches of Scotland" (*Dragonfly in Amber,* ch. 33). She makes peanut butter in the New World. She also repeats jokes:

> "A hedgehog? And just how does a hedgehog make love?" he demanded.
> No, I thought. I won't. I will not. But I did. "Very carefully," I replied, giggling helplessly. So now we know just how old that one is, I thought." (*Outlander,* ch. 17)

She calls him a sadist when he threatens to beat her. The Marquis de Sade lived 2 June 1740 – 2 December 1814, and thus is a small child, not yet to write the novels that inspired the word "sadism." No wonder literate Jaime hasn't heard of it. He also wants to know what "fuck" means. (Gabaldon notes that while English soldiers were using the word at the time, a Highlander might not know it. He also might be asking simply to break up the tension.)

Claire calls Jaime "frigging John Wayne" for unnecessary heroism in *Outlander* (ch. 36). In book two, When Jaime complains of nearly fighting a duel at the king's ball, Claire snarks, "But aside from that, Mrs. Lincoln, how did you enjoy the play?" to discover if he learned anything useful (ch. 9). Claire also tells Jaime to "Go directly to Hell. Do not pass Go. Do not collect two hundred dollars."

He replies, "When ye start to talk daft, I know you're all right" (ch. 9). Later, Claire quotes, "early to bed and early to rise," only to realize Ben Franklin said it (*Voyager,* ch. 26). As her language rubs off on him, Jaime proudly tells Claire he's been on a "commando raid" (*Dragonfly in Amber,* ch. 36). He uses the expressions "Queer your pitch" and "not for all the tea in China" then realizes he got both from Claire (*The Scottish Prisoner,* ch. 3). After Claire's influence, Jaime washes cutting knives and insists his men and the people at Lallybroch eat vegetables to avoid scurvy. Later, Claire notices that Jaime's been quoting Brianna who's been quoting John Adams, and he's been publishing his letters in the newspaper (*A Breath of Snow and Ashes,* ch. 76).

In the third book, Claire jokes that she doesn't have a scarlet A on her chest and Jaime looks bewildered (*Voyager,* ch. 39). Claire goes sailing and quotes Longfellow's "The Building of the Ship": "She moves! She stirs! She seems to feel/The thrill of life along her keel!" (*Voyager,* ch. 41) and also "Home is the place where, when you have to go there/They have to take you in" from "The Death of the Hired Man," by Robert Frost (1874-1963).

In book four, Claire hears men singing the drinking song "The Anacreontic Song," a tune that was later adapted for "The Star-Spangled Banner." Though the War of 1812 hasn't occurred, she sings the end of "The Star-Spangled Banner" lyrics to it. When the Tuscarora bring gifts of corn, Claire jokes about "the return of Squanto" (*The Drums of Autumn,* ch. 20). On her asking whether her horse led her friends to her like Lassie, Ian tells her the horse is a gelding, not a lassie (*The Drums of Autumn,* ch 23). She tells Jaime about vampires (*Dracula* has not yet been published) and he is revolted. In a similar nod to pop culture, Brianna says, "Nobody expects the Spanish Inquisition!" from *Monty Python,* upon seeing her mother again. Jaime is puzzled (ch. 41). Trapped together in the snow, Claire tells Jaime the story of *A Christmas Carol,* and recalls another occasion when she and Frank were trapped in their car and told the story (ch. 21). "The First Law of Thermodynamics" is a chapter of *The Drums of Autumn,* as is "Bottom of the Ninth."

> "Nothing is lost, Sassenach; only changed."
> "That's the first law of thermodynamics," I said, wiping my nose.
> "No," he said. "That's faith." (*The Drums of Autumn,* ch.16)

In the fifth book, Roger sings "Clementine" to his child on various occasions. Upon hearing of a ghost bear among the Cherokee, Brianna begins humming, "Oh, he'll sleep 'til noon, but before it's dark ... he'll have every picnic basket that's in Jellystone Park ..." Claire can't contain her laughter (*The Fiery Cross,* ch. 81). When they do this again, Jaime calls them "no but loons" suggesting he's accustomed to this behavior (*The Fiery Cross,* ch. 81). Brianna also recites "The Ballad of Paul Revere," realizing that it's happening as she speaks. Claire continues to use modern idioms:

> "What d'ye take me for, Sassenach?"
> "A Scot," I said. "Sex fiends, the lot of you. Or so one would think, listening to all the talk around here." I gave Farquard Campbell a hard look, but he had turned his back, engrossed in conversation.
> Jamie regarded me thoughtfully, scratching the corner of his jaw.
> "Sex fiends?"
> "You know what I mean."
> "Oh, aye, I do. I'm only wondering – is that an insult, would ye say, or a compliment?" (ch. 40)

In the past, Brianna becomes an inventor, inspired by things she's seen or read about. She builds a spinning wheel that mimics something she's seen in a folk-art museum. "Building it had been time-consuming – she'd first had to make a crude lathe, as well as soak and bend the wood for the wheel itself – but not terribly difficult (*A Breath of Snow and Ashes,* ch. 38). She also invents Band-Aids. When she loads them in Jaime's saddlebag, he doubts they or the tin of salve she adds will be of any use, and he doesn't understand the phrase "first aid kit." He dumps out a cake of soap "along with a few more unnecessary fripperies, and carefully hid them under a bucket, lest she be offended" (*A Breath of Snow and Ashes,* ch. 25). Nonetheless, he appreciates the clever compartments for his food, shot, and repair supplies. Briana makes things people of the time had, like paper, and also attempts things they didn't have, like running hot water with clay pipes and matches. She invents a syringe from a rattlesnake fang. She also teaches Jaime a knock from the *Lone Ranger* theme song. Roger joins in and carves wooden cars for the little children.

As the story continues, Ian's dog comes running, and Claire makes a crack that "Bloody Timmy's in the Well" (*A Breath of Snow and Ashes,* ch. 3). Brianna quotes the Girl Scout handbook – people shouldn't eat strange mushrooms (ch. 2). Part ten of *A Breath of Snow and Ashes* is titled "Where's Perry Mason When You Need Him?" and Claire mutters "Very nice, Mr. Ohnat...at least we're already married" when Jaime gets Claire in deeper legal trouble (ch. 96). The time traveler Donner whistles "Yellow Submarine" to identify himself

"James Fraser, Indian Agent," I said, closing one eye as though reading it off a screen. "It sounds like a Wild West television show."

Jamie paused in the act of pulling off his stockings, and eyed me warily.

"It does? Is that good?"

"Insofar as the hero of a television show never dies, yes."

"In that case, I'm in favor of it," he said, examining the stocking he'd just pulled off. He sniffed it suspiciously, rubbed a thumb over a thin patch on the heel, shook his head, and tossed it into the laundry basket. "Must I sing?"

"Si – oh," I said, recollecting that the last time I had tried to explain television to him, my descriptions had focused largely on *The Ed Sullivan Show*. "No, I don't think so. Nor yet swing from a trapeze."
"Well, that's a comfort. I'm none sae young as I was, ken."
(*A Breath of Snow and Ashes* ch. 7)

Chapter titles also play with history. The *Dragonfly in Amber* chapter "The Postman Always Rings Twice" is a novel and several noir films. In *Voyager,* Claire attends the Governor's Ball with Jaime in the chapter "Masque of the Red Death" and indeed the ball turns violent. *The Drums of Autumn* has "O Brave New World" and "Strawberry Fields Forever." "Return of the Native" is a title in *A Breath of Snow and Ashes. The Fiery Cross* offers chapters "A Hard Day's Night" and "A Whiter Shade of Pale." *Written in My Own Heart's Blood* has "The Body Electric" – in which Brianna thinks of Walt Whitman and also electric currents as ley lines.

Particularly Scottish songs and poems also appear, much earlier than they should historically. Claire tells Jamie the line "Freedom and whisky gang tegither" from Robbie Burns's "The Author's Earnest Cry and Prayer" (*Dragonfly in Amber*, ch. 24). Jaime quotes this in a newspaper article he writes, enabling Claire to find him as she and her friends note the paradox – Robbie Burns had barely been born at the time (*Voyager,* ch. 21). Burns' "Auld Lang Syne" is a chapter title in *The Fiery Cross,* though no one sings the song until future decades. On the show, "The Highland Widow's Lament," with lyrics by Burns, plays when Claire sees Highlanders killed by the Black Watch in "Rent." When she and Frank visit Culloden in a flashback, "Ye Jacobites by Name," also with lyrics by Burns, plays.

Later, Roger discusses the first Jacobite rising with Brian Fraser and admires the fact that Brian fought at Sheriffmuir. Roger explains his knowledge by saying, "I heard a song about it. 'Twas two shepherds met on a hillside, talking about the great fight – and arguing who'd won it." At Brian's  insistence, Roger sings him the song, and then writes it down for him, thinking, "Well, what harm could it do to let Robert Burns's poem loose in the world some years in advance of Burns himself?"

> "O cam ye here the fight to shun,
> Or herd the sheep wi' me, man?
> Or were ye at the Sherra-moor,
> Or did the battle see, man?"
> I saw the battle, sair and teugh,
> And reekin-red ran mony a sheugh;
> My heart, for fear, gaed sough for sough,
> To hear the thuds, and see the cluds
> O' clans frae woods, in tartan duds,
> Wha glaum'd at kingdoms three, man.
> (*Written in My Own Heart's Blood,* ch. 31)

In *Outlander*, young Hamish MacKenzie, Colum's son, solemnly recites the classic Selkirk Grace, attributed to Burns: "Some hae meat that canna eat, And some could eat that want it. But we hae meat and we can eat, And so may God be thankit." In a subtler homage, "The best laid plans of mice and men" is the title of chapter 23 of *Dragonfly in Amber*. This comes from "The best laid schemes o' mice an' men gang aft agley" in the poem "To a Mouse."

Claire recites, "Fifteen men on a Dead Man's Chest – Yo-ho-ho, and a bottle of rum!" from Stevenson's *Treasure Island* (*Voyager,* ch. 40). In

Dragonfly in Amber, she quotes his famous "Requiem": "Home is the sailor, home from the sea, And the hunter home from the hill (ch. 31). His "Sing me a Song of a Lad that is Gone" is an anachronism itself, written far after the Jacobite Rebellion.

In *Voyager,* Claire quotes from Sir Walter Scott's "Marmion," with "Oh, what a tangled web we weave/ When first we practice to deceive!" These two phrases are also chapter titles in *Lord John and the Private Matter.* Finally, Jaime tells Claire she should be nice to him, quoting her own "Marmion" phrase back to her: "When pain and anguish wring the brow, A ministering angel thou!"

These many many references emphasize Claire and her friends' connection with present-day readers and provoke thought: if people from our time went back, what would they miss? What would be strangest to the locals? (Young Ian finds the concepts of chocolate with sugar in it and toilet paper indescribably decadent, while Claire struggles with ignorance to teach people about sanitation and nutrition.) As Brianna reinvents things from her own time, from pizza to piping, she tries to puzzle out ways to improve her lifestyle, even while accepting what she's left behind.

Cameos

Writer-producer Ron Moore has a brief cameo at the Gathering, while Diana Gabaldon has a longer one, as she and Mrs. FitzGibbons trade barbs. Moore comments:

> That was our idea. We just said, "We've gotta do this." Why not? It's her world and her story, so she should have a moment of being in it. She's seen a lot of the footage and loved it, and she's been very thrilled. She's been very, very supportive. It's been a remarkably positive relationship with her. Especially after having seen *Saving Mr. Banks,* I was like, "Wow, this could have been much worse!" (Radish)

The episode's writer-producer Matt Roberts adds:

> I wanted to put her up against Annette Badland, who plays Mrs. Fitzgibbons. I thought they would make a good match, and create backstory for their characters. We don't actually say what happens, but you can tell that they have a rivalry that we could tell at another time if we wanted to. There's a sassiness to Diana and I wanted to give that to her character, and I knew she could easily play that – and she did. She did a wonderful job; we gave her a little more to do with the scene of her shushing Murtagh during the speech just to bring her into it a little more. (Ng, "'Outlander' Producer on Brutal Death Scene")

Charlaine Harris cameoed in several episodes of *True Blood* and George RR Martin appeared on his show as well.

Aside from these delightful moments, Gabaldon creates several historical fiction easter eggs in *Dragonfly in Amber*: at Versailles, Claire recognizes the Duchess of Claymore (ch. 9), the heroine's title in Judith McNaught's *Westmoreland Dynasty Saga* series – *Whitney, My Love* and *A Kingdom of Dreams*. In the same chapter, Jamie finds a broadsheet describing the scurrilous affair between the Comte de Sevigny and the wife of the Minister of Agriculture. The former is the main character in Dorothy Dunnett's *Lymond Chronicles*. In turn, Jaime and Claire appear in Sara Donati's *Into the Wilderness* series.

In the later books, Adso the cat gets his name from the main character in Umberto Eco's *The Name of the Rose*, Adso of Melk. Jaime tells Claire:

> "My mother was verra learned – she was educated at Leoch, ye ken, along with Colum and Dougal, and could read Greek and Latin, and a bit of the Hebrew as well as French and German. She didna have so much opportunity for reading at Lallybroch, of course, but my father would take pains to have books fetched for her, from Edinburgh and Paris."

He reached across my body to touch a silky, translucent ear, and the kitten twitched its whiskers, screwing up its face as though about to sneeze, but didn't open its eyes. The purr continued unabated.

"One of the books she liked was written by an Austrian, from the city of Melk, and so she thought it a verra suitable name for the kit."

"Suitable...?"

"Aye," he said, nodding toward the empty dish, without the slightest twitch of lip or eyelid. "Adso of Milk."

A slit of green showed as one eye opened, as though in response to the name. Then it closed again, and the purring resumed.

"Well, if he doesn't mind, I suppose I don't," I said, resigned. "Adso it is." (*The Fiery Cross*, ch. 18)

OUTLANDER COMPANION

Adapting the Books

> I have distinctly mixed feelings about having a movie made
> of the story. It *could* be a perfectly brilliant adaptation, and
> I'd be thrilled and delighted. However, knowing what I do
> about the movie industry, chances are about nine hundred
> to one that it would be horrible, and I'd hate it. For one
> thing, the average movie is two hours long. A s I say to
> people who tell me how much they'd love to see the books
> made into movies: "Fine. Which forty pages would you like
> to see?" Now, if the BBC wants to come along and offer to
> do a twenty-eight- week mini-series, no problem!
> (*Outlandish Companion* 381)

Gabaldon's wish came true when the story was
adapted into seasons of sixteen episodes, with plenty
of time to tell the story. Moore comments of his pitch
to Starz:

> We were on the same page from the very beginning; I
> wanted to do a very faithful adaptation of the book. And
> they said "we want you to do a very faithful adaptation of
> the book," which is kind of remarkable, actually...And [Starz
> CEO] Chris [Albrecht] said to me, "make this show for the
> fans and trust that anyone who's not a fan will be swept up
> in the story the same way all the readers were." And I was
> like, "yes, sir!" It was just great. That's exactly what you
> hope that they're going to do. (Prudom "Ron Moore")

He consulted Gabaldon throughout the experience
and was delighted that she approved. He explains: "I
told her how I wanted to approach it, and some of
the things that I thought I would change from the
book, and she was very open to it. She got it, from

the beginning. She said, 'I get it. It's an adaptation. It cannot be literally the page. I don't do television. I'm an author. You do that'" (Radish).

Gabaldon in turn has urged fans to relax about small differences, such as Claire's eyes being blue not brown. "It's the 18th century," she says. "The lighting is such that 90 percent of the time you can't even tell what color anybody's eyes are" (Loughlin). As the costume designer explains:

> I had always seen clothing in my head as I read the books. It was interesting when I started to design it because I'd realized I'd never paid attention to the clothing descriptions. When I went back and read it again, I went, "Oh wait, that's not what I had in my head." There came a moment when we all had to decide if we were going with the descriptions in the book or going to do the look that we wanted. This dress is not what is written in the books exactly. When we make choices that are not exactly as they are in the book, they are never done casually or dismissively. They're always done with tremendous consideration because we're fans too. (Bell)

The Actors

Four months after Sam Heughan was cast as Jamie, Caitriona Balfe auditioned. "We knew from the second that she came in to test and she left the room that she was the one. She had to play Claire Randall," Heughan notes (Lash). Balfe was a catwalk model in many runaway shows, appearing on the cover of *Vogue*. The actress is actually Irish and her grandmother was a World War II nurse. She's had a few television and film roles, including Breanna Sheehan on the web series *H+*. There, she's a high-powered executive with a troubled marriage and an affair, paralleling her *Outlander* character. She also had small roles in films like *Super 8* and *Now You See Me* with a bigger part in 2013's *Escape Plan*. "I just think it was something that I just always wanted to do. I mean, as a little kid ... my parents [tease] me about it now, but I used to go 'round the house doing Margaret Thatcher impressions," Balfe says (Lash).

Gabaldon thinks fannish adaptations of a photo of model Gabrial Aubrey are a good fit for Jaime, according to her Afterward in the comic. Gabaldon describes him as "a head taller than everyone else (he's 6'4" in a time when the average man stood 5'8")." The Scottish Sam Heughan is about his height, though everyone else is not significantly shorter. The first actor cast on the show, he was known for his role in *Doctors,* though he was in several historical shows as well. In *A Princess for Christmas,* he plays the old-fashioned Ashton, Prince of Castlebury. He's Young Alexander the Great in *Alexander.* His role as Jaime lies between the two, as born war leader and handsome heartthrob from a bygone era.

Tobias Menzies is best known as Brutus in *Rome* and Edmure Tully on *Game of Thrones* – both times the nice guy forced into a brutal situation. He appeared in *A Very Social Secretary,* a satire on Tony Blair and the British government, as well as *The Honourable Woman,* about a strong heroine in conflict who parallels Claire. He began in popular British series such as *Foyle's War, Midsomer Murders,* and *Casualty.*

Graham McTavish (Dougal) is Dwalin in *The Hobbit* movies and Loki on the cartoon *The Avengers: Earth's Mightiest Heroes.* A Scot, he also played the ill-tempered Mercenary Commander Lewis in *Rambo* alongside Sylvester Stallone.

Lotte Verbeek (Geillis) always plays the femme fatale who operates through powerful men. She's Lidewij, secretary for a great writer, in *The Fault in Our Stars.* On *The Borgias,* she's Giulia Farnese, a mistress of Rodrigo Borgia. As she encourages Lucrezia's confidences and protects her from the French army, Giulia parallels Geillis in several ways.

31

Her actress is Dutch, giving her a sense of not-quite-fitting in ancient Scotland.

Scottish actor Bill Paterson was in *The Killing Fields, Comfort and Joy, A Private Function, Richard III, Law and Order: UK, Doctor Who,* and *Little Dorrit.* He told *The Scotsman*: "I play Ned Gowan, an Edinburgh lawyer, who is a bit of an adventurer. He gives up the brass plates on his door and sets off to the Highlands for a bit of late adventure in life. He helps the clan chief to collect rent, but has got a double-dealing thing going on." He describes it as "a lovely wee part," adding, "I thought it was just going to be a cameo, but I've been on the show since February and have got another ten days or so to go on it" (Ferguson).

Duncan Lacroix, Murtagh, has brief parts in *Reign* and *Game of Thrones.* He plays Ealdorman Werferth on the show *Vikings.* Annette Badland, the middle-aged mayor and Slitheen villainess from *Doctor Who,* plays play the charming but dominant Mrs. Fitzgibbons. "Angus Mhor," Stephen Walters from *Layer Cake* (the movie said to have gotten Daniel Craig his role as James Bond) also appeared in Hannibal Rising and Batman Begins. Colum MacKenzie is Gary Lewis from *Billy Elliot, Gangs of New York, Eragon* and *Three and Out.*

The Credits

Discussing the striking song chosen for the credits, series composer Bear McCreary explains:

> We performed "The Skye Boat Song," one of the most famous Scottish folk tunes, one that is known to be about the Jacobite uprising, during which *Outlander* takes place. The lyrics are taken from the lesser-known Robert Louis Stevenson text, with one alteration in the gender of the speaker, which helps the song relate to Claire's character. ("Comic Con 2014 Highlights")

Since Stevenson was born in 1850, this is certainly

an anachronism, but the song is one of the more famous Scottish songs, describing the flight of Prince Charlie. From the first episode, he is thus doomed to fail in his rebellion and flee with Flora MacDonald "over the sea to Skye." Stevenson's version replaces the original Jacobite lyrics of the battle with more lyrical, dreamy ones:

> Sing me a song of a lad that is gone,
> Say, could that lad be I?
> Merry of soul he sailed on a day
> Over the sea to Skye.
>
> Mull was astern, Rum on the port,
> Eigg on the starboard bow;
> Glory of youth glowed in his soul;
> Where is that glory now?
>
> Sing me a song of a lad that is gone,
> Say, could that lad be I?
> Merry of soul he sailed on a day
> Over the sea to Skye.
>
> Give me again all that was there,
> Give me the sun that shone!
> Give me the eyes, give me the soul,
> Give me the lad that's gone!
>
> Sing me a song of a lad that is gone,
> Say, could that lad be I?
> Merry of soul he sailed on a day
> Over the sea to Skye.
>
> Billow and breeze, islands and seas,
> Mountains of rain and sun,
> All that was good, all that was fair,
> All that was me is gone.

The *Outlander* theme tune excerpts a short portion of this, changing the character's gender to indicate Claire:

Sing me a song of a lass that is gone,
Say, could that lass be I?
Merry of soul she sailed on a day
Over the sea to Skye.

Billow and breeze, islands and seas,
Mountains of rain and sun,
All that was good, all that was fair,
All that was me is gone.

Sing me a song of a lass that is gone,
Say, could that lass be I?
Merry of soul she sailed on a day
Over the sea to Skye

McCreary adds, "The Main Title builds energy, until at last it bursts into a rousing march of Great Highland Bagpipes and signature Scottish snare drums" ("Comic Con 2014 Highlights"). The Circle Dancers swirl, juxtaposed with scenes of Claire's adventure (horse riding, wound stitching, romance, Frank, Jaime...). Thus the story unfolds in glimpses in between the stone circle dancers that hurled Claire into the past. The lyrics themselves emphasize the Jacobite storyline but also Claire's connection with the natural world as she abandons a proper English world of cars and electricity for the beautiful green Highlands. Like the poem's speaker, Claire embarks on a magical journey to far off lands, where she must unravel questions of identity and destiny.

First Person

The books recount Claire's story in first person. Later, other points of view are added (Roger in book two, Jaime and Lord John in three, Brianna in four), but they remain third person, leaving Claire's "voice" the audience's most direct line in the books much as in the show. Thus her early twenty century idioms and humor predominate. Gabaldon explains, "I think I may have felt most comfortable with this (aside from the minor fact that Claire Beauchamp Randall

took over and began telling the story herself); because many of my favorite works of literature are first person narratives" (*Outlandish Companion* 372). As she adds, "If you look at the classic novels of the English
language, roughly half of them are written in the first person, from *Moby-Dick* to *David Copperfield, Swiss Family Robinson, Treasure Island* – even large chunks of the Bible are written in the first person!" (*Outlandish Companion* 372).

Caitriona Balfe expounds, "It's kind of unusual, this job, because so much of it is told through Claire's perspective and I think it's unusual to have a show where you have kind of one actor who's predom-inantly in every scene. So there's a responsibility that comes with that." As she concludes, "But I think that's one of the great things about this job is that it's really shown me that I can step up to the plate and do something like this and it's been a really incredible experience" (Lash).

On the show, the narration can feel quite heavy – as a first person book, it's much less noticeable. The prologues, however, like the show, provide the one character a chance to speak directly...sometimes someone who isn't Claire. "To me, the prologue is essentially the voice of the book speaking, if that makes any sense," Gabaldon explains (*Outlandish Companion* 361). As she adds, "Evidently, either the abridger or Ms. James decided (they didn't ask me) that the prologues of the first three books should be read in Claire's voice, while the *Drums of Autumn* prologue was read in Brianna's voice" (*Outlandish Companion* 361).

Oddly, there are no subtitles on the show. Moore wanted to keep the show first person – since Claire can't understand the Gaelic, the audience shouldn't either. "You're very much with Claire," Moore notes. "Stranger in a strange land" (Episode Podcasts 101). In the books, Claire generally summarizes the gist of the speech or expresses confusion over it. Following this point of view, 1940's music follows Claire occasionally through her scenes in the past. Likewise, the blurring filming in "Both Sides Now" emphasizes Claire's disorientation and trauma during the redcoats' near rape. It allows viewers "to be in Claire's reality" with "a skewed sense of time and place," as Moore explains (Podcast, 108).

On the show's wedding night, Jaime gets to tell the flashbacks from his point of view. Moore has mentioned in interviews that the second half of the first season will feature Jaime's voiceovers as well as Claire's, adding a new perspective to the story. While Gabaldon has not precisely written a work like *Midnight Sun* (which was created to retell *Twilight* from the hero's point of view instead of the heroine's), the *Outlander* comic *The Exile* has some parallels.

The comic emphasizes Jaime's story, as he returns from France, horrified by the fact that he killed an innocent young prostitute while trying to defend her (this story is also shown in "Virgins"). Still stunned, Jaime renounces violence and war, only to be dragged into intrigue and conflict. Murtagh meets him at the coast to keep him alive and protected. Meanwhile, Dougal and his men quickly take Jaime and Murtagh into a polite captivity, as the two men try to escape. As they ride together, this time with Claire among then, Dougal thinks, "Damn yon woman! If not for her, I might be rid of my dangerous nephew by now." After the Gathering settles matters, Murtagh tries to save Jaime from marrying Claire – by force if necessary. In the comic, which is from Jaime and Murtagh's point of view, all the Gaelic is translated with footnotes since they speak the language. There's also a subplot with another time traveler named Kenneth who's working with Geillis,

The 1940s

Gabaldon chose to make Claire specifically a World War II nurse because of the conditions and technology of the time. A nurse from this period would be accustomed to the brutality of war and to making do with limited resources. Unlike a modern nurse, she wouldn't bemoan the lack of MRI machines but would understand field medicine. Antibiotics were new and in use, but older remedies were still around.

> While techniques such as bleeding and purging had been abandoned, many older techniques – wound-dressing and surgical practices – were still in common use. Therefore, a nurse who had worked under combat conditions in World War II would not find the conditions of the eighteenth-century Highlands to be nearly as strange or unusual as would a more modern medical practitioner. ... While Claire is appalled at the lack of hygiene, the ignorance of nutrition, the crudity of surgical procedures, and so on – these are all matters of general medical knowledge that the modern reader also shares. Therefore, a person reading of Claire's perceptions and adventures – bone-setting, wound-stitching, curing fevers – would feel herself (or himself) very much in her shoes. (*Outlandish Companion* 196-197)

On the show, the added World War II scenes show Claire's skillset and capability before she must rely on her medical training in the past.

Gabaldon also anticipated sending her character forward in time, and hesitated to date herself by being unaware of new technology twenty years in the future if the books took place in 2010, for instance. Claire's returning after the 1940s would solve the problem. As she adds:

> I didn't realize it consciously at the time, but there was another reason for the choice of World War II as Claire's

OUTLANDER COMPANION

original time – that being the "echo" between the Jacobite Rising and the Second World War, in terms of the effect of these conflicts on society. The '45 put an end to the feudal system of the Highland clans, and – as a side effect – threw a large number of Scottish immigrants out into the New World, where they contributed extensively to the development of what would become America. In a similar way, the disruptions and displacements of World War II resulted in a much larger wave of immigrants, who in their turn altered American society and contributed greatly to its modern form. (*Outlandish Companion* 198)

In Frank's car, he listens to "A radio thing of Patton's death" – around Christmas time in 1945 (Podcast, 108). There's a parallel for Frank and Claire – both have just survived the war, only to encounter disaster just after.

In the forties, book and show do much to set the scene. Claire describes constant power outages and a pay-spout of hot water in the bathroom. Several times, she marvels at the end to rationing. As she notes, "those cottages near the road were nice. The bloom of postwar prosperity had spread as far as a new coat of paint, and even the manse, which must be at least a hundred years old, sported bright yellow trim around its sagging windowframes" (*Outlander*, ch. 3). Caitriona Balfe adds:

I personally love the '40s clothes Claire wears. That blue coat is fantastic! And that nightgown I got to wear in episode one, it's so devastating that I only got to wear it for one scene because it was just fabulous! It was silk chiffon, and sort of 1940s Hollywood glamour. It was the one thing that we had decided that Claire had bought for her trip away. Even at that time, they were still rationing, so a lot of the '40s stuff is still from those patterns, those austerity patterns, but this is the one thing she had kind of splurged on, you know? (Vineyard)

"In Britain, clothes rationing was introduced in June 1941 to control not only the number of garments that might be purchased, but also the type and

38

amount of material used in their manufacture, and restrictions were not lifted until 1949" (Nunn 207). Large numbers of suits bore the "Utility" label, easy to manufacture. Men's suits were made with low wool content in plain navy, brown, or grey, with narrow, single-breasted jackets, no waistcoats, and trousers without pleats or turn-ups (Nunn 218). Women's suits were blocky and simple, with three buttons only and very few pockets. Even more in occupied countries, hats were made of old curtains, plaited straw, or colored paper, while fabric and yarn for new clothes were repurposed from older garments.

Onscreen, Claire dons housedresses and suits, while Terry Dresbach, the show's costume designer, has Frank in a Fedora like Cary Grant or Jimmy Stewart. As she adds: "Ron [Moore] always says these are two periods of war, but Britain after World War II was decimated. You still see and you still feel the ramifications. It was a place without color and a lot of joy and happiness" (Friedlander). Dresbach comments on Claire and Frank's wedding clothes on her blog (July 2014):

> Claire and Frank are getting married just as the war is breaking out, and while there is still optimism in the air, it is a more somber time. Ron [Moore, the show's creator and Dresbach's husband] wanted the clothes to be very faded as in an old photo, so we used tones of grey and brown. But Claire is in love, and it shows up in her jaunty little hat, tipped over one eye. We wanted her suit to carry through some of the deco lines of the 30s, but showing the direction of women's fashions to come during the war years. It is a very tailored, masculine style, nothing frilly or frivolous.
> This suits Claire's character very well, and tells us a lot about who she is. She is a strong and savvy young woman, filled with optimism.

As she adds, "The later scenes with Frank, these are the stolen moments in the midst of war, and the peachy blush color of the peignoir coveys the romance they are trying to hold onto in spite of the war that surrounds them."

The show also uses period music to set the scene. Composer Bear McCreary explains:

> I found the clarinet remarkably effective at signifying our jump in time, every bit as useful as the saturated color scheme and the sounds of cars and telephones. Because we would never otherwise hear a clarinet in the score, its presence announces to our subconscious minds that the narrative is leaping back to where we began. In the first episode, Frank's Theme was wistful, nostalgic and romantic. In "Both Sides Now," I altered the harmonic progression beneath the clarinet to highlight Frank's sullen despair and loneliness; however, the melody remains the same. ("Outlander: The Garrison Commander, The Wedding, Both Sides Now")

Ron Moore wanted forties music "that wasn't instantly recognizable" rather than doing the "best of" hits, and these also serves to set the scene (Episode Podcasts 101). The first episode features "I'm Gonna Get Lit Up (When The Lights Go On In London)" as recorded by Carroll Gibbons & Savoy Hotel Orpheans and "Shuffle Rhythm" as recorded by Jan Savitt & His Top Hatters on the radio as Claire and Frank go driving together. In the Reverend's library, "Beneath The Lights Of Home" plays, recorded by Geraldo & His Orchestra. "Run Rabbit Run," recorded by Harry Roy & His Band emphasizes the time period as Claire reads in her room, then provides a jarring dissonance as she runs from British soldiers in the past. The forties music follows her through her eighteenth century adventure, emphasizing her role as modern point of view character.

The World War II footage is grainy like war footage and desaturated, almost to black and white. The 1740s are filmed with brighter colors. Moore notes, "Some of that is the on-set cinematography. We talk a lot about lighting it differently and shooting it slightly differently. And then, in post-production, we play with color timings and saturation levels, and all of those technical things, to give a separation between the two periods" (Radish).

> "Claire, even in her own time, was not necessarily a normal woman," Balfe admits of her character. "She's quite timeless. She's always been very feisty and modern in a sense. The '40s were a great time for emancipation for women because in the war, they were going to work and [doing] things that they hadn't had the opportunity to do before. So that side of Claire felt quite accessible. And then going back to the 1700s, that clash of ideals, you don't have to look too far to find that in our own time." (Prudom, "Strong Female")

The Episodes

Showrunner Ron Moore set up the first episode so fans would "root for Claire and Frank as a couple" and "hope that they're gonna work it out." This is necessary to show why Claire is so desperate to return (Episode Podcast 101). There's also a Frank and Claire flashbacks thread, meant to make Frank more likeable and show why Claire is so eager to return to him. Moore explains the decision to use flashbacks during a group interview at San Diego Comic-Con:

> "So much of the show is her drive to get back to that life and to get back to Frank and I didn't want to lose touch with that. I thought it was important that the audience keep understanding why she keeps trying to get back to those stones. What's waiting for her? What's that life she led? Otherwise, why wouldn't she just hang around here?
> "You have to understand her relationship with Frank and understand that for her, that's home," he continues. "You have to remind the audience each week and show them more because they're going to get really invested in the show in the 18th century but she's trying to go to this other

place. It's important to keep touching it every once and a while to remind everyone." (Schwartz)

Claire's relationship with Frank is a little bolder on the show – not only are the sex scenes more graphic, but in Castle Leoch, Claire directs the action. Her actress explains:

> What was really important for us, and this was something we talked about with Ron [Moore] from the beginning, is that we want to show that Claire owns her own sexuality. I think that's why we liked that scene, and we liked that she was the one sort of asking for it, and she was the one directing Frank what to do, and I think it shows quite an important side of her character. Like we're so used to seeing women being objectified, and as objects of desire of men, but it is very rare when you see a woman owning her own sexuality, and directing it, or orchestrating the sequence of events! (Vineyard)

The scenes have interesting correspondences with the present, as Claire explores the same Castle Leoch in both times or marries Frank, then Jaime. Frank's saying goodbye to her as she goes off to war in an episode three flashback emphasizes that for the first time she realizes she's stuck in the past.

Other people and scenes subtly changed. Moore left out Roger in episode one, since there were simply "too many elements." When he decided the Reverend Wakefield would be helping in the hunt for Claire in the eighth episode, Roger and Mrs. Graham smoothly worked into the scene. Beltane is changed to Samhain, which serves to make the story creepier and more ghostly.

Filming takes place at Castle Doune, famously used in *Monty Python and the Holy Grail*. Unlike in the books, Frank and Claire visit Castle Leoch in the future, when it's nothing but a crumbled ruin. As she explores the castle in the eighteenth century, she can't help recalling her steamy moments with Frank in the very room that becomes her surgery.

Other touches emphasize the story's roots in a subtle, spiritual magic. The circle dancers are portrayed as beautiful and mystical, in the credits as well as the first episode. On the travel itself, Moore specifically didn't want to do "a scifi light show" instead he preferred the car crash metaphor, brought to life and shown to the audience (Inside the Episode 101).

There are several fake-outs, as episode three has an imaginary sequence in which Claire tells Mrs. Fitz she's a time traveler and is denounced as a witch. In "The Gathering," she appears to be running for her life, but is instead playing tag with the children. Writer-producer Matt Roberts adds:

> From episode three to four, we wanted to show that maybe three weeks or a month have passed. To do that, we had to show that she was comfortable in her surroundings, that the people there were more comfortable with her – in the opening scene when she's playing with the children and they talk about how they played the day before and the day before, and where Angus and Rupert are much more easygoing with her, where they're asking her if they can go somewhere rather than ordering her. Hopefully other people will see that too. (Ng, "'Outlander' Producer on Brutal Death Scene")

New (or expanded) scenes appear as Claire saves a child from poisoning and defies the priest in the third episode. Father Bain's early introduction foreshadows his conflict with Claire, giving him a reason to torment her later and emphasizing the clash between superstition and science. His theme song, a disturbing, organ-like drone, adds menace. This story gives Claire more time with Geillis and a chance to realize how superstitious the Highlanders are.

As Jaime translates for Claire:

> Now this one is about a man out late on a fairy hill on the eve of Samhain who hears the sound of a woman singing sad and plaintive from the very rocks of the hill. "I am a woman of Balnain. The folk have stolen me over again," the stones seemed to say. "I stood upon the hill, and wind did rise, and the sound of thunder rolled across the land. I placed my hands upon the tallest stone and traveled to a far, distant land where I lived for a time among strangers who became lovers and friends. But one day, I saw the moon came out and the wind rose once more. So I touched the stones and traveled back to my own land and took up again with the man I had left behind." (Episode 103)

"The Woman of Balnain" appears in the books, but on the show, the plot has even more of a correspondence, as the woman stolen through the stones grieves for her new lover as well as her old one. McCreary adds:

> Due to the realities of production schedules, "The Woman of Balnain," the song that concludes this episode, was actually the first music I ever composed for *Outlander*. The lyrics are by Diana Gabaldon herself, from her books, and getting to set them for this collaboration was the perfect way to start my experience on this series! ... Gillebride's vocal performance is moving, and the newly recorded harp bridges the performance in the hall with the instrumentation in the score. Even with the layers of source music and score, I think the story is easy to track, and more importantly, the emotional impact is there. We feel Claire's growing elation and surge of adrenaline as she discovers there may yet be a way to get home. ("Outlander: The Way Out, The Gathering and Rent")

"The Gathering" features folksongs "The Haughs o' Cromdale," and "Clean Pease Strae," (the latter during the Shinty game). All the steps of Claire's escape attempt gain immediacy as she makes her plans, and she takes additional time to joke with her two "escorts," helping Angus and Rupert gain more personality as the comic relief. Claire's scenes with Jaime and the Gathering are much the same as in the books.

The rent collecting trip expands many moments, as Claire tries to become one of the men, or at least find some acceptance, and cracks dirty jokes they learn to appreciate. She also tells Ned the truth about the future:

> NED: You sound as though the future has already been decided. Outmanned we may be, but I would match our fighting hearts against the best army in the world."
> CLAIRE: Fighting hearts don't stand a chance against cannons. You are going to lose.
> NED: That's your opinion. And you're entitled to it."
> CLAIRE: It's a fact, Ned. You have to believe me. History will never record the name of another Stuart king, but it will record the names of thousands of highlanders who've died needlessly for a doomed cause.

Meanwhile, traditional music emphasizes the culture as well as the themes when Claire explores the larger world outside Castle Leoch. The folksong "To the Begging I Will Go" plays as Dougal collects funds. Composer Bear McCreary explains: "With the series now tying directly into the politics of the era, I felt compelled to use folk tunes to help establish the narrative" ("Outlander: The Way Out, The Gathering and Rent"). McCreary adds, "Some of the most authentic folk music you will hear this season is in this episode, in the scenes with the wool waulking group, and the traveling songs the Scots sing" ("Outlander: The Way Out, The Gathering and Rent"). The wool waulking song is "Mo Nighean Donn," chosen as a nod to Jaime's nickname for Claire.

By the fire, the men sing "The Maid Gaed to the Mill" (a bawdy song about a woman and a miller who "grinds her corn," along sung in *A Breath of Snow and Ashes*). With a Jacobite flair, "The Skye Boat Song" calls attention and gravity to the moment when Claire finally understands Dougal's true intentions. Scots who have been crucified along the side of the road hang to the tune of "The Highland Widow's Lament," with the most famous lyrics by Robert Burns, though it is certainly conceivable that the melody itself existed during 1743. Later there's a rousing bar brawl underscored with "The High Road to Linton." The last folk tune in "Rent" appears during Claire's flashback of visiting Culloden and the tune "Ye Jacobites by Name" plays, sadly saluting the lost cause.

Throughout the episode, the Black Watch and the British soldiers expand their roles from the books, with more of each seen individually. "Rent" finally ends with a cliffhanger as the redcoats dramatically offer to rescue Claire from the MacKenzies.

"The Garrison Commander" is expanded enormously. "In the book it's a very short section – it's really only a couple of pages" but Moore wanted to "Expand it and make it a big cat and mouse game between Jack and Claire" as the heroine and villain face off for the first time (Inside the World, 106). The whipping flashback appears in great, horrifying detail, completely from Randall's perspective, emphasizing his sadism and need to dominate. The episode also features a large fake out, as Randall apologizes to Claire for the near-rape and has her convinced he's trying to change. She presumably sees much of Frank in him and is comforted by the traces of goodness she thinks she perceives. Suddenly, he punches her in the stomach and tells her he's bad all the way through, shocking the television fans, while reassuring the book fans he hasn't changed. When Claire says there's good in him, Jack Randall responds "it would be pretty to think so," suggesting her belief is only optimistic fantasy. He's quite introspective and self-aware, however, and with his massive monologues, he shares all this with the audience. "It's an opportunity to sort of get deeper into Jack Randall and who he is," Moore adds (Inside the World, 106).

Describing the music for the British officers at dinner (strikingly different from the Scottish instruments normally heard, Bear McCreary explains:

> Arne was a British composer of the time period, best known to modern-day audiences for his patriotic songs "Rule, Britannia!" and "God Save the King," which would eventually become the British National Anthem. Obviously, any of those melodies would have been distracting too 'on the nose' for a scene like this, but Adam sent me an elegant little piece Arne composed for harpsichord and viola da gamba, "Blow, Blow Thou Winter Wind." I made some simple adjustments to the arrangement, and found that it fit the scene perfectly. The harpsichord and viola da gamba evoke upper class parlor music, while music history buffs will chuckle knowing that the tune was composed by a composer arguably more associated with the might of the British empire than any other. ("Outlander: The Garrison Commander, The Wedding, Both Sides Now")

The wedding episode puts events out of sequence, beginning with the wedding night, and following with Jaime's stories of the wedding preparations then the ceremony itself – which a hung over Claire barely remembers. In the book, the wedding scene is all from Claire's point of view, and Jaime is the one to have his wedding clothes suddenly, gloriously revealed when they meet. One reason for the flashback series is likely to break up the long sequence of sex scenes. This also makes the circumstances of the day something Claire and Jaime can discuss, along with stories of their families, as they get acquainted.

The scavenger hunt emphasizes the community's effort at getting the couple wed, emphasized again in the ribbing Jaime takes afterwards. Nonetheless, Ned Gowan negotiating with half-dressed whores for the dress seems unnecessary, as does the humorous sequence with the priest...complete with arguments over Bible verses. Costume designer Terry Dresbach comments on the wedding dress:

> This is a dress that they found at a local whorehouse. When Ron told me that, I screamed at him for about four hours. Like really? You realize that whores wear clothes that advertise they're whores, right? That's the whole point.
> Then he concocted the idea that the dress had been paid for by a wealthy man for services, so they had this dress stashed away in the back. That allowed us the liberty to make something spectacular and amazing. (Friedlander)

The Ned and the Prostitutes scene in the wedding episode features the bawdy tune "Celia Learning on the Spinnet." This plot too comes out as unnecessary. Admittedly, there's some humor in Jaime's delivery. As he recounts all the incidents to Claire and she protests, "Oh come on, now you're just making things up" they add a tinge of the unreliable narrator to the scene – it's actually not certain that television events proceeded as Jaime and Ned recount them.

Meanwhile, Murtagh stands out for the first time, and starts to show himself as Jaime's most trusted companion. As his one relative on the Fraser side and sworn man among the Castle Leoch crowd, Murtagh is meant to be the one man Jaime truly trusts. In the wedding episode, Jamie wants the blessing of his family as he reminiscences about his mother and discusses his father for the first time. Murtagh offers the line, "Your mother had the sweetest smile...Claire's smile is just as sweet." In fact, as book fans already know, Murtagh was in love once and has a romantic side behind the gruffness.

While show Jaime merely seems desperate for sex, book-Jaime is very sensitive about Claire's conflict. His opening line when they're alone isn't a toast to her beauty at all:

"Tell me about your husband," said Jamie, as though he had been reading my mind. I almost jerked my hands away in shock.

...

"Well, I knew ye must be thinking of him. Ye could hardly not, under the circumstances. I do not want ye ever to feel as though ye canna talk of him to me. Even though I'm your husband now – that feels verra strange to say – it isna right that ye should forget him, or even try to. If ye loved him, he must ha' been a good man."

"Yes, he... was." My voice trembled, and Jamie stroked the backs of my hands with his thumbs.

"Then I shall do my best to honor his spirit by serving his wife." He raised my hands and kissed each one formally.

I cleared my throat. "That was a very gallant speech, Jamie."

He grinned suddenly. "Aye. I made it up while Dougal was making toasts downstairs."

I took a deep breath. "I have questions," I said. ... "If you don't mind telling me. Why did you agree to marry me?"

"Ah." He let go of my hands and sat back a bit. He paused for a moment before answering, smoothing the woolen cloth over his thighs. I could see the long line of muscle taut under the drape of the heavy fabric.

"Well, I would ha' missed talking to ye, for one thing," he said, smiling.

"No, I mean it," I insisted. "Why?"

He sobered then. "Before I tell ye, Claire, there's the one thing I'd ask of you," he said slowly.

"What's that?"

"Honesty."

I must have flinched uncomfortably, for he leaned forward earnestly, hands on his knees.

"I know there are things ye'd not wish to tell me, Claire. Perhaps things that ye can't tell me."

You don't know just how right you are, I thought.

"I'll not press you, ever, or insist on knowin' things that are your own concern," he said seriously. He looked down at his hands, now pressed together, palm to palm.

"There are things that I canna tell you, at least not yet. And I'll ask nothing of ye that ye canna give me. But what I would ask of ye – when you do tell me something, let it be the truth. And I'll promise ye the same. We have nothing now between us, save – respect, perhaps. And I think that respect has maybe room for secrets, but not for lies. Do ye

49

agree?" He spread his hands out, palms up, inviting me. I could see the dark line of the blood vow across his wrist. I placed my own hands lightly on his palms.

 "Yes, I agree. I'll give you honesty." His fingers closed lightly about mine.

 "And I shall give ye the same." (*Outlander,* ch. 15)

On the show he's more eager for affection than words. When Claire looks distraught, Jaime gives her pearls or distracts her with compliments, rather than approaching her from a place of straightforward understanding.

In "Both Sides Now," tiny Roger is introduced, to the delight of fans who missed him on Frank's first visit to the Reverend Wakefield – he's the Reverend's adopted son after his parents were killed in the war, and he will be important to the series later on. Mrs. Graham also reappears to tell that she suspects people can travel 200 years as per the folklore. In the books, there's no evidence she's guessed this, but it's certainly possible as she's the leader of the dancers. The episode also shows Frank's plot in the 1940s as he searches hopelessly for Claire. Moore notes that Frank naturally suspects the Highlander ghost of stealing his wife. "In some ways he's right but only in ways he cannot possibly understand" (Podcast, 108). Unlike in the books, Claire gets close enough to touch the standing stones, with Frank rushing towards them on his own side. The drama as Claire is ripped away is thus that much stronger.

Genre

> The surest way to irk Diana Gabaldon, whose latest novel, *A Breath of Snow and Ashes,* debuted atop the *New York Times* best-seller list last week, is to call her a romance writer. If so accused, she'll counter that her books are historical mysteries tinged with science-fiction, and that the love scenes are secondary. (Koerner)

> The *Outlander* series combines romance, historical fiction, science fiction, mystery and the supernatural, to wildly popular effect. But the conventions that once neatly delineated the relationships between genres are not the only ones lying shattered—Gabaldon also cheerfully violates the rules within genres. (Bethune)

At her early signings, Gabaldon tended to match her recommendation to her audience. Depending on the age, gender, and look of passerby, she might label her book as romance, fantasy, science fiction, historical fiction, or even military fiction. Indeed, the book encompasses all these genres and thus is often located in the general fiction section ("An Interview with Diana Gabaldon"). While the love story (and indeed love triangle) is absolutely central, the book is much more adventure than romance. The characters' brushes with death occur every few chapters, and the wars that engulf them are far more important to the plot than fights and makeups.

As Gabaldon describes her experience:

The *Outlander* series has enough historical twists and highbrow touches to attract mainstream readers, which is why Delacorte and Gabaldon have tirelessly pressured bookstores to stock the books in the general-fiction section, rather than the romance aisle; otherwise, the *Outlander* series might have gotten lost amidst thousands of tomes with bare-chested Adonises on the cover. (Koerner)

Historical Fiction

"After considerable thought, it seemed to me that perhaps a historical novel would be the easiest thing to try. I was a research professor, after all; I had a huge university library available, and I knew how to use it," Gabaldon explains (*Outlandish Companion* XX). As she adds about historical fiction:

"Cultural concepts are one of the most fascinating things about historical fiction. There's always a temptation, I think, among some historical writers to shade things toward the modern point of view. You know, they won't show someone doing something that would have been perfectly normal for the time but that is considered reprehensible today. For instance women drinking alcohol while pregnant. I get a lot of people being just appalled that Claire drinks wine while she's pregnant, and I'm saying, 'It was 1743. Everyone drank wine regardless.' And in fact while Claire comes from 1945, there was absolutely no idea in anyone's head that drinking alcohol would cause any problems whatsoever. The thought that you ought not to drink while pregnant came much, much later. In fact, I had my first child in 1982, and I was still told by nurses and so forth, 'Have a glass of wine with dinner. It'll help you relax.'" (Loughlin)

The story follows Jaime and Claire through the Second Jacobite Uprising, which crushed the clan system and all but destroyed the Highlands for a hundred years. As Frank tells Claire on the show, it's not just the death of the men, but of their way of life. After, tartans and Gaelic are forbidden; the clan chiefs are declared traitors.

Jaime and Claire travel from the Highlands to the French Court, exploring the daily lives of those high and low. Historical characters have cameos: Mayer Rothschild, just beginning his coin business; St. Germain, mysterious master of alchemy; King Louis XV of France. Lord John in his own novels attends the coronation of George III and frequents popular London coffeehouses like Boodles and Whites, along with the infamous Hellfire Club. As the second book ends, Claire complains about all the historical fiction that has romanticized Bonnie Prince Charlie: "The fault lies with the artists," Claire says. "The writers, the singers, the tellers of tales. It's them that take the past and re-create it to their liking. Them that could take a fool and give you back a hero, take a sot and make him a king" (*Dragonfly in Amber*, ch. 47).

In the 1730s, many Highland Scots had already immigrated and settled along the banks of the Cape Fear River in present-day North Carolina. After the disaster of Culloden and the following famine, many more emigrated. Thus our heroes finally go as well, only to find the American Revolution looming on the horizon. Reportedly, at the time of the revolution, one in three colonists came from Scotland, and they fought on both sides with great ferocity.

In the course of the series, the Boston Massacre, Paul Revere's ride, and other historical incidents occur, as well as famous encounters like the Battle of Saratoga. George Washington and his generals appear, while Claire frets over Benedict Arnold.

On the other side of the timeline is World War II, through the 1960s and later. Claire deals with rationing and meets George VI as he reviews the troops while Brianna wears Day-Glo and watches the moon landing. Cars, radio programs, and technology all aid in setting the scene.

Much more of the story is spent on adventure and history than time travel. Moore insists:

It's about love and loyalty and trust and obligation. It's more eternal themes than it is really about time travel. It's not about different timelines, or if you change the past, how will it affect the future. Even though those questions do come up, periodically, it's not the central focus of the story. It becomes a more overt science fiction piece, once you really get into intense discussions of timelines and how one event can be like dominoes through history. (Radish)

Fantasy

Gabaldon calls "Lord John and the Succubus" "a supernatural murder mystery, with military flourishes" (42). As she adds, "Lord John began his independent life apart from the *Outlander* books when a British editor and anthologist named Maxim Jukubowski invited me to write a short story for an anthology of historical crime" (xii). Following this came more anthologies, mostly specifically fantasy-themed, and with them came more short stories, following Lord John on adventures in London and occasionally Germany, Quebec, and the Caribbean. In these, Lord John is inducted into the Hellfire Club, and then investigates a succubus, ghosts, and a plague of zombies.

Each time however, the correct solution is a scientific explanation from fraud to drugs, rather than magic. John reflects, "Having encountered German night hags and Indian ghosts, and having spent a year or two in the Scottish Highlands, he had more acquaintance than most with picturesque superstition" ("Lord John and the Plague of Zombies" 321).

Thus the world of *Outlander* is portrayed as mostly historical and realistic. Despite this, there are moments of surprise for the fans. Without explanation, Claire stumbles upon the Loch Ness Monster. Several times, ghosts haunt her. On the show, twentieth-century Claire insists witches, fairies, and demons can't exist. Geillis retorts, "Have you never found yourself in a situation that has no earthly explanation?" (Episode 103). After the standing stones, Claire is speechless.

Jaime has seen the Wild Hunt – fairy riders who stalk animal and human prey. He also tells the story of a *tannagach*, or spirit, that his friend met once (*The Drums of Autumn*, ch. 1). He tells Claire on the show: "I'm an educated man, mistress, if I may be so bold. Maybe not as educated as you, but I had a tutor, a good one. He taught me Latin and Greek and such, not childhood stories of fairies, devils, waterhorses in lochs. But I am also a Highlander, born and bred, and I dinna believe in tempting fate by making light of Old Nick in his very own kirkyard" (Episode 103).

In the Highlands, fairies and ghosts were accepted as the eerie unseen, present in everyday life. Several characters in the books have the gift of Second Sight – a trait that the Scots merely accepted as fact. Lord Simon Fraser, the Old Fox, keeps a seer, Maisri, who knows his ultimate fate. When Claire speaks to her, she bursts out: "Why! Why can I see what will happen, when there's no mortal thing I can be doin' to change it or stop it? What's the good of a gift like that? It's no a gift, come to that – it's a damn curse, though I havena done anything to be cursed like this!" (ch. 41). Claire feels a moment of kinship with her. In the short story "The Space Between," the girl Joan has a more disturbing gift – she can tell when someone is about to die. Other characters with the Sight appear to be Jenny, Brianna, Jem, and even the practical Jaime. To Claire's confusion, he accepts mysterious dreams of the future as an ordinary occurrence:

"I've seen ye there."

The prickling ran straight down the back of my neck and down both arms.

"Seen me where?"

"There." He waved a hand in a vague gesture. "I dreamt of ye there. I dinna ken where it was; I only know it was there – in your proper time."

"How do you know that?" I demanded, my flesh creeping briskly. "What was I doing?"

His brow furrowed in the effort of recollection.

"I dinna recall, exactly," he said slowly. "But I knew it was then, by the light." His brow cleared suddenly. "That's it. Ye were sitting at a desk, with something in your hand, maybe writing. And there was light all round ye, shining on your face, on your hair. But it wasna candlelight, nor yet firelight or sunlight. And I recall thinking to myself as I saw ye, so that's what electric light is like."

I stared at him, open-mouthed.

"How can you recognize something in a dream that you've never seen in real life?"

He seemed to find that funny.

"I dream of things I've not seen all the time, Sassenach – don't you?"

"Well," I said uncertainly. "Yes. Sometimes. Monsters, odd plants, I suppose. Peculiar landscapes. And certainly people that I don't know. But surely that's different? To see something you know about, but haven't seen?"

"Well, what I saw may not be what electric light does look like," he admitted, "but that's what I said to myself when I saw it. And I was quite sure that ye were in your own time."

"And after all," he added logically, "I dream of the past; why would I not dream of the future?"

There was no good answer to a thoroughly Celtic remark of that nature. (*A Breath of Snow and Ashes*, ch. 68)

Science Fiction

When Claire took charge of Gabaldon's "straight historical novel," it soon became a time travel narrative. Gabaldon explains, "She promptly took over the story and began telling it herself, making smart-ass modern remarks about everything. At which point I shrugged and said, 'Fine. Nobody's ever going to see this book, so it doesn't matter what bizarre thing I do – go ahead and be modern, and I'll figure out how you got there later.' So the time-travel was all her fault. {g}" (FAQ).

Thus Gabaldon needed to formulate rules and theories of time travel. She comments, "The most successful stories of this type most often involve either a resolution or a process in which the main character ends up as his or her own ancestor and/or descendant. The two best-known classics of this type are Robert Heinlein's *By His Bootstraps*, and David Gerrold's *The Man Who Folded Himself*" (*Outlandish Companion* 335). Her article "The Gabaldon theory of time travel," actually appeared in the Journal of Transfigural Mathematics in 2010,

Time travel fiction works in different ways, each time with a set of strict rules to avoid paradoxes. One typical convention, appearing several times in the early books, is that one's actions cause everything to take place just as history says, even while attempting to prevent it. In book and show, there's a terrible sense the characters are heading inexorably toward Culloden. When Claire visits the battlefield in the future, it's clear that events have literally been set in stone as she gazes at her friends' tombs. Nonetheless, she continues to act, always to save those around her with medicine and advice. Later she notes:

> "I do wonder – there are lots I can't save, but some I do. If someone lives because of me, and later has children, and they have children, and so on . . . well, by the time you reach my time, say, there are probably thirty or forty people in the world who wouldn't otherwise have been there, hm? And they've all been doing things meanwhile, living their lives – don't you think that's changing the future?" For the first time, it occurred to me to wonder just how much I was single-handedly contributing to the population explosion of the twentieth century. (*The Fiery Cross*, ch. 85)

Though each time the characters think destiny is set, it is not. Gabaldon explains:

> For me, stories that involve free choice on the part of the protagonists are more interesting to write, and, I think, much more likely to be attractive to readers. In this particular time and culture, the idea that we do have individual power over our own destinies is not only widely accepted, but highly desirable (the fiction of other times and cultures naturally may – and does – reflect different notions of individual power). How to deal with these opposing choices, then? That's a decision for an individual writer; for myself, I decided to have it both ways – to allow free choice, but not to change major historical events (ah, what it is to be a godlike Writer!). The Gabaldon Theory of Time Travel therefore depends on this central postulate:
>
> A time-traveler has free choice and individual power of action; however, he or she has *no more* power of action than is allowed by the traveler's personal circumstances.
>
> A necessary corollary to this postulate does not deal with time travel at all, but only with the observed nature of historical events:
>
> Most notable historical events (those affecting large numbers of people and thus likely to be recorded) are the result of the collective actions of many people (*Outlandish Companion* 334-335)

This means that one stranger to a new time, such as Claire, can affect events, but only to the extent a single human can manage. She can try to persuade leaders who may or may not listen to cancel a war ... but one more advisor often won't make a difference. Further, she's unlikely to succeed if she stands on the battlefield and screams for everyone to stop. Counseling one foot soldier to avoid the battlefield (advice he might or might not take) will work better.

This obviously operates inside the historical record – readers are aware that Bonnie Prince Charlie failed and England did not turn Catholic in the 1740s. George III inherited, leading to the Revolutionary War in the US. Not writing alt-universe stories, Gabaldon prefers to leave this in place. But whether the people at fictional Lallybroch went hungry or planted potatoes and survived, or how many MacKenzies fought at Culloden, those have less historical weight and Gabaldon can play if she chooses.

As Roger and Jaime argue predestination, Jaime points out that one way to stop Culloden and its force of history was assassinating Prince Charles. Roger retorts, "You don't know. If Claire had tried to poison him, I'm betting something would have happened; the dish would have spilled, a dog would have eaten it, someone else would have died – it wouldn't have made a difference!"

> Fraser's eyes opened slowly.
> "So ye think it's all destined, do ye? A man has no free choice at all? ... If there is nay free ...then there is neither sin nor redemption, aye?"...
> "It's only...well, if something's already happened one way, how can it happen another way?"
> "It's only you that thinks it's happened," Fraser pointed out.
> "I don't think it, I know!"
> "Mmphm. Aye, because ye've come from the other side of it; it's behind you. So perhaps you couldna change something – but I could, because it's still ahead of me?"
> Roger rubbed a hand hard over his face.
> "That makes – " he began, and then stopped. How could he say it made no sense? Sometimes he thought nothing in the world made sense anymore. "Maybe," he said wearily. "God knows; I don't." (*The Fiery Cross*, ch. 90)

Thus far, it's unclear whether Jaime and Claire (or only Jaime) might have saved the Highlands by killing Prince Charlie, though the story suggests it's possible.

Repeatedly, it appears that Jack Randall is dead or incapable of fathering children. Historically, his child, Frank's heir, is meant to be born after Culloden – after his death. Claire worries what this will mean for Frank: "If he's dead, Jaime – if he won't exist, because Jonathan is dead – then why do I still have the ring he gave me?" (*Dragonfly in Amber*, ch. 22). Claire is terrified that Jack Randall's death would kill Frank (quite logically) and she has a similar conflict over the descendants of Geillis. It's unclear whether she actually could snuff out future lives, or whether the people she cherishes might be born some other way.

Jaime insists that he has no particular obligation to preserve Frank's life.

> As for Frank," he said, "well, it's true enough that I've taken his wife, and I do pity him for it – more sometimes than others," he added, with an impudent quirk of one eyebrow. "Still, is it any different than if he were my rival here? You had free choice between us, and you chose me – even with such luxuries as hot baths thrown in on his side."
>
> ...
>
> "As for owing him his life, on general principles," he continued, ignoring my attempts to escape, "that's an argument Brother Anselm at the Abbey could answer better than I. Certainly I wouldna kill an innocent man in cold blood. But there again, I've killed men in battle, and is this different?...No, there are a good many arguments ye might make about that, but in the end, such choices come down to one: You kill when ye must, and ye live with it after. I remember the face of every man I've killed, and always will. But the fact remains, I am alive and they are not, and that is my only justification, whether it be right or no" (*Dragonfly in Amber*, ch. 22).

However, this thought process seems short-sighted. If Frank had never lived, then why would Claire be traveling in Scotland in 1946 and travel through the stones to meet Jaime? (Of course, if this is unraveled further to its logical conclusion, then Claire would not travel back and would not save Jaime's life multiple times and thus he would die before killing Jack Randall, and the paradoxes would continue to unspiral).

In other moments, both Jack Randall and Jaime

insist that if their death times or places are known, then they are immortal until then. This also seems highly unlikely – while they may be charmed against accidents, surely they are not literally proof against suicide. Or more to the point, murder. As soon as they are told they're immortal, history has been changed, leading them possibly to be more foolhardy and thus cause their own deaths.

In the future, Brianna and Roger see a newspaper article's date change, then a letter from Roger spontaneously appears in Brianna's desk. The future is literally being changed, opening up many possibilities about tampering with history.

Romance

> *Outlander* actually won 1991's "Best Romance of the Year" award from the Romance Writers of America, an honor that Gabaldon claims was probably undeserved. For new authors, there are few richer markets to target than romance readers, who have a great hunger for new material: According to the RWA, 52 percent of all paperbacks published in the United States are romances, and the industry rakes in $1 billion per year. (Koerner)

One-quarter to one-third of the 400 paperbacks published each month are original romances of one kind or another, as Janice A. Radway notes in her seminal *Reading the Romance: Women, Patriarchy, and Popular Literature* (44). In today's world of self-publishing, it's probably a similar percentage. Middle-class women with children in school appear to be one of the largest groups of readers; Harlequin and Silhouette have noted that the majority of their readers are between 25 and 45 (Radway 45).

Gabaldon believes that for female readers, "the social aspect" of being a fan provides "a great deal of their enjoyment of the book." As she adds:

They want to share it with their friends, and talk about it at length, and do activities that are connected with it. They put together trips to go to Scotland. Men don't do that sort of social activity. Consequently, the women fans tend to be much more visible, but the male fans definitely exist. (Prudom, "Strong Female")

Gabaldon plays with romantic conventions in self-aware fashion. Claire notes that "Black Jack" is "A common name for rogues and scoundrels in the eighteenth century. A staple of romantic fiction, the name  conjured up charming highwaymen, dashing blades in plumed hats." In chapter 35 of *Outlander*, she adds to herself, "One never stops to think what underlies romance. Tragedy and terror, transmuted by time. Add a little art in the telling, and voila! a stirring romance, to make the blood run fast and maidens sigh. My blood was running fast, all right, and never maiden sighed like Jamie."

She adds in the second book:

> Lying on the floor, with the carved panels of the ceiling flickering dimly above, I found myself thinking that I had always heretofore assumed that the tendency of eighteenth-century ladies to swoon was due to tight stays; now I rather thought it might be due to the idiocy of eighteenth-century men. (*Dragonfly in Amber*, ch. 24)

In *A Breath of Snow and Ashes*, Brianna imagines herself in a romance novel, waiting for her true love to ride up on a stallion to rescue her. Then, defying the convention, she knocks a hole in the ceiling and escapes. Trying to write about a sexual experience in her dream journal, Brianna finally crosses it out and writes, "Well, none of the books I've ever read could describe it, either!" emphasizing the plight of the erotic writer (ch. 38).

The book celebrates conventional marriage (though between a battle-scarred older World War II nurse and a virginal young hero from another time). Nonetheless, in a flip of conventions, there are several quite unconventional relationships, mixing gender, race, and even threesomes.

The most popular romantic heroines as "extremely intelligent," "spunky," independent," and "unique" (Radway 101). Meanwhile, many readers like a romantic hero "who is strong and masculine but equally capable of unusual tenderness, gentleness, and concern for her pleasure" (Radway 81). Romantic heroes are leaders of the community, so morally strong other men will follow them (Radway 130). As such, Claire and Jaime are perfect models – the one a modern everywoman in an ill-fitting marriage in search of romance, and the other a perfect gentleman, humorous, self-deprecating, handsome, and heroic.

When considering essential ingredients, the happy ending was rated most important. (Though the end hasn't been published yet, Gabaldon has promised it will be reasonably happy). Second most important is a "a slowly but consistently developing love between hero and heroine" (Radway 66). Romances are known for raising readers' spirits by guiding the reader through a gradual buildup of feelings between the couple. Details about the couple after they've gotten together are also valued (in contrast with Disney, which frequently ends at the wedding). Jaime and Claire have the slow buildup (resulting in no sex scenes on the show for several episodes and a large chunk of the book). At last they wed, but there are still many stages of love and trust yet to conquer, as both are keeping secrets.

The first two books are especially romantic, as the young couple risk their lives to be together and take desperate chances. There's also jealousy, first over Laoghaire and Frank, then in France as Jaime plays politics at brothels and Claire flirts in low-cut court gowns. At last comes the second book's climax and its poignant separation: "I stood still, vision blurring, and in that moment, I heard my heart break. It was a small, clean sound, like the snapping of a flower's stem" (*Dragonfly in Amber* ch. 46).

> "I will find you," he whispered in my ear. "I promise. If I must endure two hundred years of purgatory, two hundred years without you - then that is my punishment, which I have earned for my crimes. For I have lied, and killed, and stolen; betrayed and broken trust. But there is the one thing that shall lie in the balance. When I shall stand before God, I shall have one thing to say, to weigh against the rest." His voice dropped, nearly to a whisper, and his arms tightened around me. "Lord, ye gave me a rare woman, and God! I loved her well." (*Dragonfly in Amber* ch. 46)

In the fourth through eighth books, the couple is more settled. Their relationship comes from a place of trust and long familiarity – each knows what the other will do, and many truths of their life go without saying. It's the next generation who have romantic drama as they choose partners and wed. Nonetheless, there are many delightful moments, and touching words as well:

> "You are beautiful," he whispered to me.
> "If you say so."
> "Do ye not believe me? Have I ever lied to you?"
> "That's not what I mean. I mean – if you say it, then it's true. You make it true." (*The Fiery Cross*, ch. 85)

> "When the day shall come, that we do part," he said softly, and turned to look at me, "if my last words are not 'I love you' – ye'll ken it was because I didna have time." (*The Fiery Cross*, ch. 111)

Characters

Claire

Gabaldon explains the creation of her character: Claire in fact appeared fully formed in a cottage full of Scotsmen.

> The leader got to his feet and introduced himself courteously as Dougal MacKenzie. "Dougal," because at that point I knew very few appropriate Scottish names, but did know that my husband's name – Douglas – was Scottish in origin, meaning "dweller by the dark water." I got "MacKenzie" off a tartan patterned cooler I'd seen in the grocery store (well, look, I'd only been writing for two or three days; I hadn't had a lot of time to do research yet). So, Dougal MacKenzie stood up and introduced himself, asking – with furrowed brow – who this visitor might be? To which she replied, speaking quite clearly, "Claire Elizabeth Beauchamp – and who the hell are you?" (*Outlandish Companion* XX)

"Whereupon Claire Elizabeth Beauchamp promptly took over the story and began telling it herself" (*Outlandish Companion* XI). Claire's modern, opinionated viewpoint very much forms the story as her indignation and sense of justice drive her interactions with the characters.

Caitriona Balfe describes the character's care in finding her way: "I think all of that [deciding what to reveal] is her finding confidence within herself – 'I know things about this time. I know certain things these people don't know.' That's what allows her to believe she can survive and perhaps maneuver her way or figure out a way to be useful. She could use her information to get by" (Ng, "Caitriona Balfe on Claire").

> "Her defining characteristic is that she's intelligent," executive producer Ron Moore says of Claire. "She's smart and everything flows from there. Her strength comes from there. I think her sex appeal comes from there. Her wit, her resourcefulness, her skill set, it's all because this is a very smart woman. ... That defines what I found appealing to the character in the book pages and we had to find an actress who conveyed that idea as well." (Prudom, "Strong Female")

Claire has a lively curiosity about the past, presumably similar to that of readers. As such, she enjoys exploring the environment and trying the lovely period costumes. Balfe adds:

> In the beginning – I wouldn't say she's enjoying learning and experiencing this – there's a moment of fascination like, "Wow, this is what life was actually like at this point." We get asked a lot, "If you could go back, what time would you go back to?" There is that sense of that for certain moments in history: "I wonder what life was really like. I wonder what people were like. Were they the same as us? Did they experience the same trials and tribulations that we did?" (Ng, "Caitriona Balfe on Claire")

Upon seeing Claire's intelligence and willpower, Gabaldon decided to make her a no-nonsense nurse: "Given the state of things in the Scottish Highlands at the times – i.e., barbaric, violent, and lacking in hygiene – it struck me that doctoring might be a very useful talent indeed. Of all the assorted skills that might aid survival in the eighteenth century, a minimal knowledge of the healing arts certainly seemed one of the most desirable – and the most feasible" (*Outlandish Companion* 191). Piece by piece, everything fell into place.

Of course, she's best known for her independent outspokenness. In episode six, Claire's mouth runs away with her for the hundredth time. After spending a dinner party charming the British officers (and possibly drinking too much of the special claret, admittedly), she bursts out with her opinions about how the British are the aggressors in Scottish lands and committing as many brutalities or more as the Scottish. "The Scots just want the same freedoms we enjoy, freedoms we take for granted. They are not the aggressors, Captain, we are. It is their land and we are occupying it!" The officers, who had been enjoying being gallant to an English lady, instantly decide she's a spy or has Stockholm Syndrome and has become a traitor to her country. As such, they refuse to escort her back to Inverness and the standing stones nearby. Balfe reveals:

> It's a very hopeful moment [when she meets Lord Thomas] and then Black Jack Randall comes in to thwart it all. But it's great because it's a real tete a tete. They really just go at each other and she can't help it," she laughed. "That's the great thing about Claire, she just can't help fighting back. Sometimes that's not always the smartest thing but it makes it very interesting. And also a lot of the guys who are playing the redcoats, they are kind of new to the cast. And so it's a whole different dynamic to what I'm usually used to. I'm usually with all the hairy highlanders – that's what we call them – so it's quite cool because it's [now] well-spoken British people. And it's a great thing because she thinks she's on her way out and then everything's dashed. (Prudom, "Post-Mortem")

Jaime
Ron Moore notes:

> Jamie, he has a certain twinkle in his eye. There's an easy charm, a charismatic quality to him. And you see the humanity in him. We had to believe that this is a guy who was nearly flogged to death and has endured enormous tragedy in his life – I mean there are really some horrible things in this guy's backstory – and yet he can still get up

every day with a smile and still feel like it's rolling off his back. But also understand that the tragedy and the pain is there at the same time. And Sam has that... it's a certain ineffable quality. You see it in him. There's an easy charm and yet there is something darker back there that he can touch on periodically. So he just embodies the idea of Jamie. (Prudom, "Ron Moore")

The character is heartbreakingly kind as he saves Claire from Jack Randall by agreeing to marry her, making her heir to Lallybroch and vowing to protect her with his life (as he does, repeatedly). Caitriona Balfe says of him:

I think there was an immediate recognition of a kindred soul there. For whatever reason there is a chemistry between them, and he doesn't seem like the rest of the men there. There's something different about him. He becomes a friend and an ally at this time. Dougal and Angus are very suspicious of her. They're weary of her, and they don't treat her very well. Jamie has this gentleness and kindness. He's just got that wit and that humor. Very quickly, what you see is the developing of their friendship.

Jaime is decidedly unworldly through the series: He gives away Lallybroch and refuses a plantation. He only works for his uncle's wine business for a short time. Each time, he risks his own life in battle or lives rough in the wilderness, rather than accepting a life of safety and luxury. He regrets that he can't give Claire the world, but she tells him it doesn't matter to her. When she finds him in *Voyager*, he lives austerely, with a plain attic room, spare change of clothes, and small cot. In *The Drums of Autumn*, he says he has "all that man could want ... A place, and honorable work. My wife at my side ... and a good friend" (ch. 26).

Self-Sacrifice

> "But why you?" I asked. He looked as though he thought this an odd question.
> "Why not me?" he said.
> Why not? I wanted to say. Because you didn't know her, she was nothing to you. Because you were already hurt. Because it takes something rather special in the way of guts to stand up in front of a crowd and let someone hit you in the face, no matter what your motive.
> (*Outlander*, ch. 6)

Jaime insists on taking whippings instead of or along with those being punished – Laoghaire is only the first seen. In the second book, he punishes those who failed to keep watch when John Grey finds the camp. Then he adds, "It was my unshielded fire drew the lad to us," and orders a beating for himself (ch. 66). When Claire asks why he did it, he replies, "Could be I thought I owed it to you. Or maybe to myself." One of his men is accused of hoarding a square of forbidden tartan, so Jaime claims it and takes the punishment on himself in a chapter titled "Sacrifice" (*Voyager*, ch. 12). When he's forced to beat Young Ian after tempting him to run away, he then insists Ian beat him in return. As they walk back to the house after, he tells Ian, "If it's all the same to you, Ian, I dinna want to have to that again, aye?" knowing Ian will never run from his parents again (ch. 32).

In *Lord John and the Brotherhood of the Blade*, he tells John, "Whatever my own feelings in the matter, my family would not prefer my death to my dishonor. While there is anyone alive with a claim upon my protection, my life is not my own" (ch. 20). As a youth, he offers his life to save Jenny from rape. For years, he sends money to Jenny and her family and to Laoghaire and her daughters, even when he has little himself. This way he lives for others, taking full responsibility for their welfare, is his defining characteristic, even before he has any dependents. Occasionally, his selflessness grows to be too much:

> "Aye," he whispered, as though to himself, "I'm a big chap. Big and strong. I can stand a lot. Yes, I can stand it." He whirled on me, shouting. "I can stand a lot! But just because I can, does that mean I must? Do I have to bear everyone's weakness? Can I not have my own?"
> (*Dragonfly in Amber,* ch. 21)

Despite the hardship, Jaime protects his men with all he has – the thirty at Culloden, the ones in the prison, the crofters of Fraser's Ridge. In book two, he tells Claire, "I was born laird. I'm the steward of that land and the people on it, and I must make the best of my own bargain wi' them" (ch. 7). On parole in England, he still feels pain for the men in prison whom he can no longer protect, and he looks them up individually as soon as he can. He keeps Fergus as his man from the age of ten on and insists on giving him a decent tract of land later in life. When Fergus proves unsuitable for farming, Jaime finds him a job as printer.

In book five, he decides to fight off death not for love but because with a war coming, his people still need him.

> There was a huge lump in my throat; I couldn't speak, but squeezed his hand very tight.
> "Why?" I asked at last. "Why did you . . . choose to stay?" My throat was still tight, and my voice was hoarse. He heard it, and his hand tightened on mine; a ghost of his usual firm grip, and yet with the memory of strength within it.
> "Because ye need me," he said, very softly.
> ...
> "I didna mean only you, Sassenach. I have work still to do. I thought – for a bit – that perhaps it wasna so; that ye all might manage, with Roger Mac and auld Arch, Joseph and the Beardsleys. But there is war coming, and – for my sins – " he grimaced slightly, "I am a chief."
> He shook his head slightly, in resignation.
> "God has made me what I am. He has given me the duty – and I must do it, whatever the cost." (*The Fiery Cross,* ch. 93)

Gender Roles

Jaime faints a great deal for such a heroic warrior and constantly needs his injuries tended. Presumably his weaknesses emphasize his vulnerability in the heavy romance of the novel. He calls himself "a maiden still – that way at least," to mean the Duke of Sandringham didn't seduce him (*Outlander,* ch 24). He's also the least vulgar of all the men in the series. As he tells Claire, the nuns convinced him to stop swearing at the Abbey of St. Anne de Beaupré – he had to do penance for taking the Lord's name in vain "by lying for three hours at midnight on the stone floor of the chapel in February (*Outlander,* ch. 3).

> Claire, in many ways, has the traditional male role: She's the one who's older and more experienced (including sexually), the one with two spouses (a husband per century), the one with advanced knowledge (particularly medical—Claire upgrades from 20th-century nurse to 18th-century doctor) and the one who can move through time (Jamie lacks the "gift"). (Bethune)

Claire has far more scientific, medical, and mechanical knowledge, while Jaime is better in literature, languages and more liberal arts. As Balfe describes Jaime:

> His emotional intelligence is what, for me, stands out. In this very rough and barbaric world, here's a young guy who's, emotionally, so much more modern. And he's willing to learn and he's looking for that guidance. And I think that's the beautiful thing that they find in each other. I truly believe that she was very much in love with Frank, but I think that this is something that she has never experienced before... (Prudom, "Strong Female")

Jaime's first kiss was from an aggressive cousin who trapped him behind the barn door at age fifteen, rather than the reverse (while Claire's first kiss occurred at age eight!). As Claire discovers, Jaime remained a virgin through worry over getting the woman pregnant, something the man traditionally worries about less than the woman. As Jaime tells Claire:

> Once I got old enough for such a thing to be a possibility, he told me that a man must be responsible for any seed he sows, for it's his duty to take care of a woman and protect her. And if I wasna prepared to do that, then I'd no right to burden a woman with the consequences of my own actions ... He said the greatest thing in a man's life is to lie wi' a woman he loves. (*Outlander*, ch. 28)

Claire appears to have had more romance, though it's unclear how many men she actually slept with. She tells readers, "I had kissed my share of men, particularly during the war years, when flirtation and instant romance were the light-minded companions of death and uncertainty" (ch. 16), though even by the later books, she hasn't clearly confirmed whether she slept with men before her first husband.

Love Triangle

Frank and Jaime are positioned as rivals, though they can never meet. Claire compares her two husbands repeatedly on her wedding day and night. They are different in every possible way:

> The form of the Catholic marriage service has not changed appreciably in several hundred years, and the words linking me with the red-headed young stranger at my side were much the same as those that had consecrated my wedding to Frank. I felt like a cold, hollow shell. The young priest's stammering words echoed somewhere in the empty pit of my stomach. (ch. 14)

> Somewhat tentatively, he reached out and took my hands between his own. They were large, blunt fingered, and very warm, the backs lightly furred with reddish hairs. I felt a slight shock at the touch, and thought of an Old Testament passage – "For Jacob's skin was smooth, while his brother Esau was a hairy man." Frank's hands were long and slender, nearly hairless and aristocratic-looking. I had always loved watching them as he lectured. (ch. 15)

> In fact, it would be difficult to imagine a greater contrast. Frank was slender, lithe and dark, where Jamie was large, powerful and fair as a ruddy sunbeam. While both men had the compact grace of athletes, Frank's was the build of a tennis player, Jamie's the body of a warrior, shaped – and battered – by the abrasion of sheer physical adversity. (ch. 16)

> Nor was the physical the only dimension where the two men varied. There was nearly fifteen years' difference in their ages, for one thing, which likely accounted for some of the difference between Frank's urbane reserve and Jamie's frank openness. As a lover, Frank was polished, sophisticated, considerate, and skilled. Lacking experience or the pretense of it, Jamie simply gave me all of himself, without reservation. And the depth of my response to that unsettled me completely. (ch. 16)

Jaime notes, "I wish I could have fought him for you...If I'd fought him man to man and won, ye'd not need to feel any regret over it" (ch. 25). Caught between these very different husbands, with their opposing rings pulling her in diverging directions, she must choose, over and over, whom she wishes for her husband.

Frank

"Sex was our bridge back to one another. The one place where we always met. Whatever obstacles presented themselves during the day or night, we could seek out and find each other again in bed. As long as we had that, I had faith that everything would work out" (Episode 101). Claire and Frank begin the story estranged – a love fading rather than growing. Nonetheless, the story spends a great deal of time following their life together, in episode one and in many flashbacks.

> Showrunner Ron Moore explains the decision to use flashbacks during a group interview at San Diego Comic-Con, explaining to Zap2it, "So much of the show is her drive to get back to that life and to get back to Frank and I didn't want to lose touch with that. I thought it was important that the audience keep understanding why she keeps trying to get back to those stones. What's waiting for her? What's that life she led? Otherwise, why wouldn't she just hang around here?
>
> "You have to understand her relationship with Frank and understand that for her, that's home," he continues. "You have to remind the audience each week and show them more because they're going to get really invested in the show in the 18th century but she's trying to go to this other place. It's important to keep touching it every once and a while to remind everyone." (Schwartz)

Frank is Claire's past but also her anchor in the 1940s (literally, as it's eventually revealed that time travel works better when one focuses on reaching a particular loved one). She notes, "The war had taught me to cherish the present because tomorrow might not ever come to pass. What I didn't know at the time was that tomorrow would prove less important than yesterday" (Episode 101).

Moore set up the first episode so fans would "root for Claire and Frank as a couple" and be "hope that they're gonna work it out." This is necessary to show why Claire is so desperate to return (Episode Podcast 101).

The show follows Frank's quest for Claire in "Both Sides Now" (1.8). In the episode, Frank is understandably having a meltdown from losing his wife. But as he makes snide English comments to the Scottish police and finally beats on the robbers awaiting him, he proves himself an arrogant Sassenach with more than a touch of darkness...a proper relative of Black Jack.

Gabaldon comments, "There's more to Frank than you see in the books. He was a spy during World War II. He's a man who keeps secrets. And I said I know some of his secrets but not all of them" (*Outlander Podcast*). Frank is seen recruiting Roger's father for a dangerous spy mission in "A Leaf on the Wind of All Hallows." Considering this aspect pushed Gabaldon to include the spy plot in book eight.

The same actor plays Frank and Black Jack on the show, emphasizing their link. Nonetheless, Moore notes that "He physically holds himself differently." In the red coat he stands taller, while in the suit and fedora "he was much more academic and more approachable" (Inside the World, 101). Symbolically, good-natured Frank is revealed as a threat, since his ancestor and lookalike is a monster. During the rape scene in "Both Sides Now" and in the book, Claire is struck several times by the similarity, so much so "that I was seized by a horrible impulse to open my legs and respond to him" (ch. 21). Moore describes looking for moments of similarity between Frank and Jack – he creates one in the ferocity in Frank's attack on Sally (Podcast, 108).

Black Jack

"I dwell in darkness and darkness is where I belong," Black Jack says. The first thing he does is try to rape Claire, making her flee from a possible English ally straight to the foreboding-looking but far kinder Highlanders. In episode six, "The Garrison Commander," they meet again. "In the book it's a very short section – it's really only a couple of pages" but Moore wanted to "Expand it and make it a big cat and mouse game between Jack and Claire" as the heroine and villain face off for the first time (Inside the World, 106). "It's an opportunity to sort of get deeper into Jack Randall and who he is," Moore adds (Inside the World, 106).

"Sadly, just when Claire thinks she's found a spark of humanity in her husband's ancestor, he delivers a literal punch to the gut, stunning both Claire and the audience" (Prudom, "Post-Mortem").

"It's a great twist, I think," Menzies said at Comic-Con. "Watching it, I'd completely forgotten that I beam at her just at that moment – there's that big broad smile and I hadn't remembered doing that, and it's a great moment. You go, 'oh wow, she's gotten through to him,' and to understand that it's all deception is heartbreaking" (Prudom, "Post-Mortem").

When she mouths off to Randall about his abuse of Jaime, it's another poorly-chosen impulse, as she reveals she's spoken to Jaime or people that know him and reminded Randall of his existence. This also gives Randall the excuse to give her all the details in creepy fashion.

> CLAIRE: Yes, I'm told that you once administered a hundred lashes upon a hundred lashes to a poor highlander boy.
> RANDALL: A poor highlander boy? If I take your meaning, that boy is a wanted thief and murderer.
> CLAIRE: I was told he'd merely stolen a loaf of bread.

RANDALL: Did Dougal Mackenzie tell you that? Hmm? He was there. He witnessed it. The thief had been flogged before for trying to escape. 100 lashes administered by the corporal, a man not without skill in using the cat-o'-nine-tails, but the thief didn't break. No, he took his punishment without making a single sound. It set a bad example for the assembled onlookers, both soldier and civilians, and I could not allow that insult to the crown to pass unchecked.

Menzies adds, "it had to be a very visceral, guttural [display] of malevolence, really. It's important because it's a driver throughout the story, it's something that Jack refers back to, something that Jamie is scarred for the rest of his life from. Both of their lives are not the same after, so it felt like an important thing to get, the weirdness and mania of whatever that event was. But it's definitely a day where you have to commit massively to what you're doing." (Prudom, "Post-Mortem").

At the same time, he displays likely honest hints of his misery at what he's become, what Scotland has made him. "I came to Scotland to fulfill a soldier's responsibility, to serve my king, and protect my country. Instead I find myself the watchman of a squalid, ignorant people prone to the basest superstition and violence. The darkness has grown within me. A hatred for the very world itself." When he says his reflection fills him with loathing, it's likely he speaks the truth.

Episode eight has her meet Randall again and has her spouting off at him again, both making flippant comments about his flogging people for amusement, and constructing a weak bluff about the Duke that falls apart in less than five minutes. In a scene likely more violent than the book's, he prepares to maim her as well as raping her. Only Jaime's timely rescue prevents him. Following this is book one's climax and the indescribable horrors he commits. Claire says later, "Jack Randall was a bloody sociopathic, grade-A pervert" (*A Breath of*

Snow and Ashes, ch. 29)

Despite his terrible acts, an odd reversal appears later on, when he's revealed to honestly love his brother Alex. Alex in turn loves him despite his darkness and entrusts him with his family, clearly believing Jack will protect them in kindness and honor ... though he's a sadist who tortures and rapes prisoners. This emphasizes the different faces one presents to different people – possibly the saintly Alex really does bring out the best in Jack, or possibly Jack is desperate to win his beloved brother's approval. During Jack's savage attack on Jamie, he cries, 'Tell me you love me! Tell me, Alex!" While this might mean the prisoner Jack abuses to death, Alex MacGregor, his total love for his brother makes him a more likely target. Certainly, a British gentleman and officer of the time was supposed to bury any homosexual feelings, and incestuous feelings would be even worse. While Alex Randall says he understands his brother and accepts him, it's possible Jack never confessed his feelings. Either way, Jack Randall expresses his feelings of rejection from the world as savagery, rape, and torture – on the helpless of both genders.

Laoghaire

Foils and love triangles create an arena of mistrust and suspicion that the romantic pair must battle through to be more united. Claire and Jaime each have a rival, or so they fear, in Laoghaire and Frank.

Each is the polar opposite of his or her foil – while Claire is mature and worldly, Laoghaire MacKenzie "will always be a girl." Laoghaire is just sixteen, with a basic education, contrasted with Claire's frightening occult powers and knowledge (as the villagers see her, at least). Laoghaire has an extensive family and has likely never left the area surrounding Castle Leoch, while Claire is much more independent and worldly. When older, Laoghaire's prone to shrieking and suspicion. She doesn't enjoy sex. "Laoghaire – she doesna seem to know how to fight properly, like my Mam and Uncle Jamie. She just weeps and wails a lot. Mam says she snivels," Young Ian says in *Voyager* (ch. 35). While Claire is likely to explode in anger (with angry speeches and swearing that can get her in all kinds of trouble, sweet, lovely Laoghaire is capable of plotting murder and carrying it out.

At the story's start, Laoghaire is accused by her father of "loose behavior; consorting improperly wi' young men against his orders." When Jaime rescues her, she imagines there's much more between them and throws herself at him, while Claire is playing matchmaker for them, failing to realize all Jaime wants is her. At the same time, Claire feels an unreasonable, seething jealousy of the girl – she has a beauty and likely a protection tough Claire truly envies: "I found that the thought of Jamie sharing Laoghaire's bed upset me as much as the thought of leaving him. I cursed myself for idiocy, but I couldn't help imagining her sweet round face, flushed with ardent longing, and his big hands burying themselves in that moonbeam hair..." (*Outlander,* ch. 38).

Geillis

Geillis makes a strong foil for Claire, as she shares her skill with herbs but challenges her to think. Claire, like the audience, is busy dismissing all possibility of witchcraft and demonic possession, only to be startled when Geillis asks, "Have you never found yourself in a situation that has no earthly explanation?" Claire stops dead, realizing that the standing stones have cast a spell on her if nothing else has.

She tells another truth as well, though Claire

ignores her. Geillis insists, "People believe the boy is possessed, Claire. You challenge that at your peril. I'll not go near him, and neither should you" (Episode 103). Geillis understands the superstition of the time and the threat of witchcraft, while Claire is far from cautious. She explodes with passion and directly challenges the men of the community, while Geillis marries for power and tactfully manipulates her husband. Lotte Verbeek (Geillis) notes:

> I feel like she plays a different role in every scene she has, which is intriguing because when do you see her real self? With all the different colors that she has, maybe she's a rainbow, you know? I like the fact that even though you might describe her as being dark, she's driven by something which you'll get to see later on. From the get-go, you feel like she's on to something and it takes a little while for that be revealed but that was cool to discover that and what her passion actually is.

Geillis shows her art of seduction before episode end. Claire's logical pleas to show mercy for a young thief don't sway the fiscal, but Geillis's sweet wheedling succeeds. "Arthur ... Imagine if our own union had been blessed, then how would you feel if your son were taken so? Oh. Surely it was but hunger that made the lad take to thievery. ... Can you not find it in your heart to be merciful, and you the soul of justice?" (Episode 103). Following this lesson, Claire tries a bit of her own guile and faints as a distraction so Jaime can free the boy.

The "monkey jacket," as the costume designer calls the hand-felted piece, makes Geillis seem an exotic animal. Her red shoes subtly cast her as a prostitute. When Geillis invites Claire into her workroom, it seems an Aladdin's cave of sparkling treasures, from the endless jars stacked along one wall to the collection of necklaces dangling over a cushioned bench (possibly kept for their jewel magic). Geillis is a source of port, herbs, and recipes

Claire can't get, along with enormous knowledge the perplexed heroine must learn. Verbeek adds of Geillis, "She needs a friend and obviously Claire is a good candidate. They're both probably the same age and ahead of their time in different ways so there's a lot of stuff that makes them become BFFs."

In the next episode, Geillis wonders aloud if Claire is barren – something Claire must have wondered herself. She also cautions Claire that as a woman alone, she's at risk, and indeed, the drunken man of the clan soon try to assault her. She tells Claire of her own life, this time demonstrating how different the two women are: "When I first came to Cranesmuir, all I had was my wits, ye ken? I had a fairish knowledge of the plants and their good uses. I found a man with a respectable position. Decent house. Some money put away. I know he's not much to look at, as ye well ken. But that doesn't trouble me much. I'm free" (Episode 104).

Claire specifically does not marry a rich man like Dougal or the fiscal but instead the outlaw Jaime with only "a soldier's pay." However, there is a fondness between them that quickly turns to love. She does however find herself taking the advice Geillis tags on the end: "Sometimes ye find yerself on a path you never expected. Doesn't mean it can't lead you to a bonny place." It certainly does.

Murtagh

Murtagh as Jaime's godfather and protector has a subtle, growing presence in the story. He's the one to save Claire from Jack Randall when they meet, but at this point, she hasn't really differentiated him from all the other Scots in Dougal's band. The comic book shows him as far different from them – the one person guarding Jaime's back from the schemes of Clan MacKenzie. As such, he's prepared to do battle at the Gathering, and only Jaime's quick wit saves them both.

Murtagh had one great love in his life – Jaime's mother, for whose sake he swore to always guard her son. In the comic, he's seen remembering her and finally accepting Jaime's love for Claire (a possible fairy woman or witch!) because he remembers how his own young love felt. On the show, he speaks to Jaime about his mother on his wedding day and gives advice. He also pushes Claire toward Jaime much earlier, telling her Jaime needs a mature woman. "He needs a woman, not a lassie. And Laoghaire will be a girl until she's 50. I've been around long enough to ken the difference very well, and so do you, mistress," he says (Episode 103).

The later half of season one sees Jaime and Claire leave the MacKenzies and go on independent adventures, Murtagh ever at their side. He follows them after to France, to Fraser lands, and to Culloden itself, always Jaime's most loyal body-guard.

Angus and Rupert

This pair make the comic relief on the show. Moore notes that Angus has become an original character, while Rupert is closer to his book counterpart (Podcast, 108).

Angus is the first character whose television role deviates significantly from that in the books. In the latter, he's Colum's enforcer, who provides Jaime's beating as he did on another occasion when Jaime was much younger. He's "Angus Mhor," "Big Angus," for his immense height and strength.

> I stared at this giant with some awe. Coarse black hair grew far down on his forehead, barely meeting the beetling eyebrows. Similar mats covered the immense forearms, exposed by the rolled-up sleeves of his shirt. Unlike most of the men I had seen the giant did not seem to be armed... A broad leather belt circled what must be a forty-inch waist... In spite of his size, the man had an amiable expression,

and seemed to be joking with the thin-faced man, who looked like a marionette in comparison with his huge conversant. (*Outlander*, ch. 6)

On the show, he's much smaller, hardly Colum's terrifying enforcer. He's ordered to watch Claire, and he does so, complaining and pranking all the while (even trying to give Claire a look up his kilt!). His partner in this is Rupert.

In the books, Rupert is Dougal's "closest friend, the kinsman who rode and fought on his right-hand side, as Ian did for Jaime" (*Dragonfly in Amber* ch. 43). On the show, he stands out long before this as the comic relief. Both men squabble over girls and want to abandon their Claire-watching duties for fun, or at least convince her to sag along with them. As such, they bring a fun presence to the seriousness of the show.

> RUPERT: So there I am in bed, harelip Chrissie on my left and sweaty Netty, the butcher's daughter, on my right.
> They get jealous of each other, start arguin' about who I'm goin' to swive first. Can you believe it?
> CLAIRE: I believe your left hand gets jealous of your right. That's about all I believe.
> JAIME (to Claire): You're a witty one.
> RUPERT: I never heard a woman make a joke.
> CLAIRE: There's a first time for everything. ("Rent")

Ned

As Ned Gowan is described in the books, "He's a lowlander from Edinburgh, wi' no kin of his own, but he's taken the MacKenzies for his clan" (*The Drums of Autumn,* ch. 33). He's a force for good, as he and Claire take to each other on the rent-collecting trip and (on the show) even quote John Donne together. During the witch trial, he defends Claire with every contrivance he can manage and arguably saves her life. While he isn't seen riding down the enemy, pistol in hand, he shows that law can be a weapon as much as a sword ... when in the right hands.

Jenny

> "She was ten when our mother died, Jenny was," [Jaime] said at last. "It was the day after the funeral when I came into the kitchen and found her kneeling on a stool, to be tall enough to stir the bowl on the table.
>
> "She was wearing my mother's apron," he said softly, "folded up under the arms, and the strings wrapped twice about her waist. I could see she'd been weepin', like I had, for her face was all stained and her eyes red. But she just went on stirring, staring down into the bowl, and she said to me, 'Go and wash, Jamie; I'll have supper for you and Da directly.' "
>
> His eyes closed altogether, and he swallowed once. Then he opened them, and looked down at her again.
>
> "Aye, I ken fine how strong women are," he said quietly. (*The Drums of Autumn,* ch. 48).

Jenny first appears when Jaime describes Jack Randall's savage attack on her. He and Claire finally meet her on their arrival at Lallybroch. There, Jaime and Jenny get in a spitting fight, demonstrating the Fraser temper and their desperate love for each other. "If your life is a suitable exchange for my honor, tell me why my honor is not a suitable exchange for your life?" she finally demands. "Or are you telling me that I may not love you as much as you love me? Because if ye are, Jamie Fraser, I'll tell ye right now, it's not true!" (ch. 26).

For years, Jaime has been gone, and for that time, Jenny took over the complete management of Lallybroch and the surrounding sixty crofter families, all never knowing when her brother would return. Jaime says in the books that he sends money sometimes, but cannot bear to write, knowing he failed to protect her from Jack Randall. Nonetheless, she does the family duty, waiting for her brother to return and reclaim his home. Though she's cautious on Jaime's behalf, she accepts Claire as a fast friend...though if anything happened to Jaime, Lallybroch would be Claire's.

Days after giving birth, with Jaime in danger, Jenny adroitly manages both loved ones, setting out to save Jaime, then racing back to her newborn when she's no longer needed on the quest. "You see as far as the end o' your nose, duine, and that's short enough," Jenny tells Murtagh. "And if ye've lived so long without knowing better than to stand between a nursing mother and a hungry child, ye've not sense enough to hunt hogs, let alone find a man in the heather" (*Outlander*, ch. 33). Her sharp tongue and strong presence emphasize her formidable character, even compared to the war nurse Claire.

Ian

As Jaime describes him, "Ian... he's the part of me that belongs here, that never left," he said, struggling to explain. "I thought... I must tell him; I didna want to feel... apart. From Ian. From here." He gestured toward the window, then turned toward me, eyes dark in the dim light. "D'ye see why?" (*Dragonfly in Amber*, ch. 33). Like Jenny, Jaime's best friend Ian Murray remained at Lallybroch and helped to manage both the estate and Jenny herself. Like Murtagh, he spends his life knowing his duty is to protect Jaime, "guarding his weaker side." In this case, that weak side is his family and estate, while Jaime has adventures. As such, Ian represents the quieter part of Jaime that would be happiest farming and caring for tenants...a part disrupted by the war.

Colum

Colum MacKenzie has a great Machiavellian streak. He is the brains of the MacKenzie brothers, calculating enough when he views Claire or Jaime as threats, cold enough to arrange a son when he cannot sire one. His illness inspires sympathy, but he rejects all trace of friendliness, as he offers Claire an escort to Inverness on the show, then shockingly rescinds it. Caitriona Balfe adds, "The [medical condition] with Colum is great because, knowing what she knows about his medical condition, she gains empathy toward him and it makes him more human to her, so he's not this completely intimidating figure. Being able to figure out the balance of power between Dougal and Colum, that comes into play as well" (Ng, "Caitriona Balfe on Claire").

Dougal

On the show and in the book, Dougal firmly says, "I don't hold wi' rape," and adds "and we've not the time for it, anyway" (ch. 4), giving Claire a worrying moment.

Dougal has his disturbing violent side, as he rescues her from drunken rapists at the Gathering, then forces a kiss on her himself (book and show have identical scenes). Even more disturbingly, he makes a pass at Claire on her wedding night, revolting her. In the book, Dougal can't marry her himself because he's married (while in the show, he simply appears to prefer his options open). In the comic, he eyes her and thinks. "Ah well, if Jaime's gone, we'll see. A widow twice-over ... she'll need a bit of comforting, nay doubt." His actor, Graham

McTavish, adds, "It doesn't matter that he might arrange the marriage between Claire and Jamie. Hey, that's just a piece of paper. She says, that doesn't stop you from 'sampling other pleasures.' He's quite bold. That line sums up the character quite nicely" (Ng, "Graham McTavish").

Writer-producer Matt Roberts adds: "Like Jamie, Dougal has never seen a woman like Claire before in his life. He's physically attracted to her and he's also intellectually attracted to her. This could be the woman who could put him on the path to being the ultimate power next to the king in Scotland if the whole Jacobite rising would work. He sees that in Claire – if he could only convince her of it" (Ng, "'Outlander'" Producer on Brutal Death Scene).

In the book, Dougal's serious attempt comes later. Claire is disgusted when, with Jaime out of the picture as Dougal thinks, he woos her for himself (clearly with designs on Lallybroch as much as her)

> "Claire. My sweet Claire." The voice was soft now, and he ran an insinuating hand lightly down my arm. So he had decided to try seduction rather than compulsion.
>
> "I know why ye talk so cold to me, and why ye think ill of me. You know that I burn for ye, Claire. And it's true – I've wanted ye since the night of the Gathering, when I kissed your sweet lips." He had two fingers resting lightly on my shoulder, inching toward my neck. "If I'd been a free man when Randall threatened ye, I'd ha' wed ye myself on the spot, and sent the man to the devil for ye." He was moving his body gradually closer, crowding me against the stone wall of the cavern. His fingertips moved to my throat, tracing the line of my cloak fastening.
>
> He must have seen my face then, for he stopped his advance, though he left his hand where it was, resting lightly above the rapid pulse that beat in my throat. "Even so," he said, "even feeling as I do – for I'll hide it from ye no longer – even so, ye couldna imagine I'd abandon Jamie if there were any hope of saving him? Jamie Fraser is the closest thing I've got to a son!" (ch. 32)

His affection for Jaime (his foster son when

Jaime was fifteen as well as his actual nephew) blends with his lust for Claire in a disturbingly incestuous blend. McTavish notes, "With Claire, one moment he's literally saving her from the hands of Black Jack Randall and the next moment he's preparing to cut her throat [both in "The Garrison Commander"]. It's the same as his relationship with Jamie, his nephew. He has a genuine love for him, but again, wouldn't hesitate to kill him" (Ng, "Graham McTavish").

Nonetheless, Claire cannot regard him as completely evil, and she demands his help on several occasions, which he always gives. His morality makes sense to him at least. Writer-producer Matt Roberts says, "That relationship is one of our most complex in the series," and it's easy to see why. (Ng, "'Outlander' Producer on Brutal Death Scene").

At the same time, they connect when helping Geordie through his fatal boar wound just after the Gathering. As Claire tells it, "Dougal and I leaned close together over the struggling body, murmuring and comforting, sharing the messy, heartrending, and necessary task of helping a man to die" (ch. 10). Writer-producer Matt Roberts explains, "the scene isn't about Dougal and Geordie, it's really about Dougal and Claire, and her seeing him let his guard down and Dougal seeing that she's hiding the fact that she's seen much more death than she's let on. They have a moment when Dougal realizes Claire is doing a good thing for Geordie in putting his mind at peace. They bond over it, but only briefly, because he turns the tables on her in the last scene" (Ng, "'Outlander'" Producer on Brutal Death Scene).

Of course, in his own mind, the Stuart cause is paramount for Dougal. Graham McTavish explains, "While there's a part of him that finds her attractive, there's also a part that is mindful of his duty toward the clan, and over and above, to his duty toward the restoration of the Stuart monarchy" (Ng, "Graham McTavish"). In the books, he harasses the noncommittal Colum to send money and arms, and also plots with Geillis. He is a fanatic, and he finally finds his destiny at Culloden.

Eighteenth Century Scottish Culture

Bagpipes

> There was a piper walking next to me; I could hear the creak of the bag under his arm and see the outline of the drones, poking out behind. They moved as he walked, so that he seemed to be carrying a small, feebly struggling animal.
>
> I knew him, a man named Labhriunn MacIan. The pipers of the clans took it in turns to call the dawn at Stirling, walking to and fro in the encampment with the piper's measured stride, so that the wail of the drones bounced from the flimsy tents, calling all within to the battle of the new day.
>
> …
>
> There are the small Irish pipes, used indoors for making music, and the Great Northern pipes, used outdoors for reveille, and for calling of clans to order, and the spurring of men to battle. It was the Northern pipes that MacIan played, walking to and fro. (*Dragonfly in Amber,* ch. 43)

It's hardly a shock to see bagpipes at the Gathering, tied to the Highlands as they are. Yet they've been seen in other places as well. As folklorist J.F. Campbell comments, "those who are curious in such matters may hear *bagpipes* in nearly all the European countries where Celts have been. I have heard the pipes

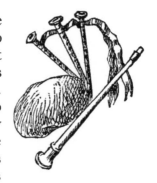

in Ireland, Scotland, Spain, Portugal, and Italy, I believe they are in Albania, and I have heard tell of something of the kind in the Himalayan mountains" (IV 369).

In 1627, Alexander MacNaughton was commissioned to raise a body of Highland bowmen, and on January 15, 1628, he wrote to the Earl of Morton and reported "newis frome our selfis [and] our bagg pypperis" (Campbell IV 370). The instrument appeared among the Trojans, Greeks, and Romans, though the history of its introduction into Scotland is unknown. Like the bodhran, or war drum, it is considered an instrument of battle.

> The effects of this national instrument in arousing the feelings of those who have from infancy been accustomed to its wild and war-like tunes are truly astonishing. In halls of joy and in scenes of mourning it has prevailed; it has animated Scotland's warriors in battle, and welcomed them back after their toils to the homes of their love and the hills of their nativity....When every other instrument has been hushed by the confusion and carnage of the scene, it has been borne into the thick of battle, and, far in the advance, its bleeding but devoted bearer, sinking on the earth, has sounded at once encouragement to his countrymen and his own coronach. ("Gaelic Music")

Beggars

At one point, Jamie jabbed a thumb at the rectangular bits of lead that adorned Munro's strap.

"Gone official, have ye?" he asked. "Or is that just for when the game is scarce?" Munro bobbed his head and nodded like a jack-in-the-box.

"What are they?" I asked curiously.

"Gaberlunzies."

"Oh, to be sure," I said. "Pardon my asking."

"A gaberlunzie is a license to beg, Sassenach," Jamie explained. "It's good within the borders of the parish, and only on the one day a week when begging's allowed. Each parish has its own, so the beggars from one parish canna take overmuch advantage of the charity of the next." (*Outlander*, ch. 17)

Hugh Monro represents the disenfranchised of his world – sold as a slave and literally deprived of a voice with his tongue cut out. When Claire meets him, he is a poacher and beggar, but nonetheless has useful intelligence for Jaime. He also tries to save Claire in the second book. In this and every other case, Gabaldon has done her research. As one history book records:

The Poor Law has removed many ancient usages, but at no very remote period the magistrates and church session of Montrose met at a particular time of the year, and gave out badges to such as they knew to be under the necessity of begging. These licensed beggars went through the towns on the first of every month, but were not allowed to beg at any other time, nor could they go beyond the bounds of the parish. Fortunately, however, the good people of Montrose were so liberal in their donations to the applicants for aid that these did not require assistance from any public funds except when incapacitated from begging by sickness. There formerly existed other mendicants, known as the "Gaberlunzia" or travelling beggar, and the King's Bedesmen or Blue Gowns. The number of this latter and higher class of privileged beggars corresponded with the years of the king's life. They received annually a cloak of coarse blue cloth, a pewter badge, and a leathern purse containing some "Pennies Sterling," the amount of which varied with the age of the sovereign. Sir Walter Scott, in his beautiful novel of the Antiquary, introduces the reader to one of this venerable confraternity in the person of Edie Ochiltree. (Guthrie vi)

Black Watch

I had heard of the famous Black Watch, that informal police force that kept order in the Highlands, and heard also that there were other Watches, each patrolling its own area, collecting "subscriptions" from clients for the safeguarding of cattle and property. Clients in arrears might well wake one morning to find their livestock vanished in the night, and none to tell where they had gone – certainly not the men of the Watch. (*Outlander*, ch. 17)

Claire and the MacKenzies avoid them on the rent-collecting trip, while debating the morality of the Watch on one side, the Redcoats on the other, and the impoverished crofters caught in the middle. As a paper said to have been written in 1747 describes the remedy for cattle-theft:

As the government neglect the country, and don't protect the subjects in the possession of their property, they have been forced into this method for their own security, though at a charge little less than the land-tax. The person chosen to command this *watch,* as it is called, is commonly one deeply concerned in the theifts himself, or at least that have been in correspondence with the thieves, and frequently who have occasioned thefts, in order to make this watch, by which he gains considerably, necessary.

Black Watch Officer, 1743

The people employed travell through the country armed, night and day, under pretence of enquiring after stolen cattle, and by this means know the situation and circumstances of the whole country. And as the people thus employed are the very rogues that do these mischiefs, so one-half of them are continued in their former bussiness of stealing that the busieness of the other half may be necessary in recovering. (qtd. in Keltie)

Claire describes the Watch as

One of those organized bands of armed men that rode the country, charging fees from the Highland chiefs to protect tenants, land, and cattle – and if the black rent they charged was not paid, promptly seizing goods and cattle themselves. I had. And in all truth, I'd heard of them burning and killing now and then, too – though generally only to create an example and improve cooperation. (*A Breath of Snow and Ashes,* ch. 33)

Cattle Raiding

Since the wealth of the Highlanders consisted chiefly of sheep and cattle, the usual methods of continuing clan feuds or making reprisals was carrying off the cattle of the hostile clan. Claire meets Jaime and his band just after they're finishing a cattle raid themselves, and another raid occurs in the eighth episode and the equivalent scene of the book.

"These Creachs, as such depredations were termed, were carried on with systematic order, and were considered as perfectly justifiable. If lives were lost in these forays, revenge full and ample was taken, but in general personal hostilities were avoided in these incursions either against the Lowlanders or rival tribes" ("A Social History," ch. 15). Lowlanders, the Highlanders' natural enemy, were often the victims of these raids. As commentary of the time describes the matter:

> It is not easy to determine the number of persons employed in this way; but it may be safely affirmed that the horses, cows, sheep, and goats yearly stoln in that country are in value equall to £5,000; that the expences lost in the fruitless endeavours to recover them will not be less than £2,000 that the extraordinary expences of keeping herds and servants to look more narrowly after cattle on account of stealling, otherways not necessary, is £10,000. There is paid in *blackmail* or *watch-money,* openly and privately, £5,000; and there is a yearly loss by understocking the grounds, by reason of theifts, of at least £15,000; which is, altogether, a loss to landlords and farmers in the Highlands of £37,000 sterling a year. (qtd. in Keltie)

Charms

Gabaldon takes her charms from real Highlands history. As she explains:

During the late part of the nineteenth century, an exciseman and scholar named Alexander Carmichael performed a great service to future generations by collecting a massive amount of traditional Gaelic oral lore: poems, prayers, songs, incantations, charms, and hymns, which were published early in the twentieth century as the *Carmina Gadelica*....I used small bits of several of the invocations and prayers from this huge collection, as seemed appropriate to the occasion. (*Outlandish Companion* 526)

Several of them follow, said by Jaime, Jenny, and their companions in times of celebration or trouble.

THE BATTLE TO COME
JESUS, Thou Son of Mary, I call on Thy name,
And on the name of John the apostle beloved,
And on the names of all the saints in the red domain,
To shield me in the battle to come,
    To shield me in the battle to come.
When the mouth shall be closed,
When the eye shall be shut,
When the breath shall cease to rattle,
When the heart shall cease to throb,
    When the heart shall cease to throb.
When the Judge shall take the throne,
And when the cause is fully pleaded,
O Jesu, Son of Mary, shield Thou my soul,
O Michael fair, acknowledge my departure.
    O Jesu, Son of Mary, shield Thou my soul!
    O Michael fair, receive my departure! (Vol. I 113)

SOUL PEACE
SINCE Thou Christ it was who didst buy the soul – -
At the time of yielding the life,
At the time of pouring the sweat,
At the time of offering the clay,
At the time of shedding the blood,
At the time of balancing the beam,
At the time of severing the breath,
At the time of delivering the judgment,
Be its peace upon Thine own ingathering;
Jesus Christ Son of gentle Mary,
Be its peace upon Thine own ingathering,
    O Jesus! upon Thine own ingathering.

And may Michael white kindly,
High king of the holy angels,
Take possession of the beloved soul,
And shield it home to the Three of surpassing love,
    Oh! to the Three of surpassing love. (Vol. I 121)

Gabaldon adds: "This is the prayer that Jamie recommends to Young Ian, for use when one has been compelled to kill in battle or in self defense. Or, if time is too short to allow for this, he recommends the shorter version, 'Soul Leading'" (*Outlandish Companion* 528).

THE SOUL LEADING
    By this soul on Thine arm, O Christ, Thou King of the City of Heaven. Amen.
    Since Thou, O Christ, it was who brought'st this soul, Be its peace on Thine own keeping. Amen.
    And may the strong Michael, high king of the angels, Be preparing the path before this soul, O God. Amen.
    Oh! the strong Michael in peace with thee, soul, And preparing for thee the way to the kingdom of the Son of God. Amen. (Vol. I 117)

Jaime also says a very short traditional Celtic invocation, called "The Death Blessing" from *Carmina Gadelica*: "God, omit not this woman from Thy covenant, and the many evils that she in the body committed" (Vol. I 119).

On another occasion, he presides over a funeral: "Jamie took a deep breath and a step to the head of the grave. He spoke the Gaelic prayer called the Death Dirge, but in English, for the sake of Fanny and Lord John."

Thou goest home this night to thy home of winter,
To thy home of autumn, of spring, and of summer;
Thou goest home this night to thy perpetual home,
To thine eternal bed, to thine eternal slumber.
Sleep thou, sleep, and away with thy sorrow,
Sleep thou, sleep, and away with thy sorrow,
Sleep thou, sleep, and away with thy sorrow,

Sleep, thou beloved, in the Rock of the fold.
The shade of death lies upon thy face, beloved,
But the Jesus of grace has His hand round about thee;
In nearness to the Trinity farewell to thy pains,
Christ stands before thee and peace is in His mind.

Jenny, Ian, Fergus, and Marsali joined in, murmuring the
final verse with him.

Sleep, O sleep in the calm of all calm,
Sleep, O sleep in the guidance of guidance,
Sleep, O sleep in the love of all loves,
Sleep, O beloved, in the Lord of life,
Sleep, O beloved, in the God of life!
(*Written in My Own Heart's Blood,* ch. 134)

Other charms celebrate the good times and
summon God's blessing. In book four, Jaime and his
friends dedicate a new house. Jaime prays on the
cross of his dagger, then buries iron under the new
hearthstone to ensure prosperity. The men circle the
house with a torch, chanting words from "House
Protecting" (Volume I, 103) and "The Driving" (Vol. I,
43):

The safeguard of Fionn MacCumhall be yours,
The safeguard of Cormac the Shapely be yours,
The safeguard of Conn and Cumhall be yours,
From wolf and from birdflock
From wolf and from birdflock.
The Shield of the King of Fiann be yours
The shield of the king of the sun be yours
The shield of the king of the stars be yours
In jeopardy and distress
In jeopardy and distress
The sheltering of the King of Kings be yours
The sheltering of Jesus Christ be yours
The sheltering of the spirit of Healing be yours
From evil deed and quarrel
From evil dog and reddog (*The Drums of Autumn* 304)

Circle Dancers
Frank tells Claire, there's "a local group that still

observes rituals on the old sun-feast days." When they sneak off to see it, the book describes the beautiful solemnity of the dance:

> They assembled outside the ring of stones, in a line from eldest to youngest, and stood in silence, waiting. The light in the east grew stronger.
>
> As the sun edged its way above the horizon, the line of women began to move, walking slowly between two of the stones. The leader took them directly to the center of the circle, and led them round and round, still moving slowly, stately as swans in a circular procession.
>
> The leader suddenly stopped, raised her arms, and stepped into the center of the circle. Raising her face toward the pair of easternmost stones, she called out in a high voice. Not loud, but clear enough to be heard throughout the circle. The still mist caught the words and made them echo, as though they came from all around, from the stones themselves.
>
> Whatever the call was, it was echoed again by the dancers. For dancers they now became. Not touching, but with arms outstretched toward each other, they bobbed and weaved, still moving in a circle. Suddenly the circle split in half. Seven of the dancers moved clockwise, still in a circular motion. The others moved in the opposite direction. The two semicircles passed each other at increasing speeds, sometimes forming a complete circle, sometimes a double line. And in the center, the leader stood stock-still, giving again and again that mournful high-pitched call, in a language long since dead.
>
> They should have been ridiculous, and perhaps they were. A collection of women in bedsheets, many of them stout and far from agile, parading in circles on top of a hill. But the hair prickled on the back of my neck at the sound of their call.
>
> They stopped as one, and turned to face the rising sun, standing in the form of two semicircles, with a path lying clear between the halves of the circle thus formed. As the sun rose above the horizon, its light flooded between the eastern stones, knifed between the halves of the circle, and struck the great split stone on the opposite side of the henge.
>
> The dancers stood for a moment, frozen in the shadows to either side of the beam of light. Then Mrs. Graham said something, in the same strange language, but

this time in a speaking voice. She pivoted and walked, back straight, iron-grey waves glinting in the sun, along the path of light. Without a word, the dancers fell in step behind her. They passed one by one through the cleft in the main stone and disappeared in silence. (*Outlander,* ch. 2)

In the book, Frank notes that the words are ancient Norse but the dance is "very much older," perhaps from the Beaker Folk. Moore calls the scene "tribal, paganistic, primitive" (Episode Podcasts 101). This precise ritual is invented by the author. However, there are strong traces of pagan and druid rites mixed into Scottish daily life and festivals. Corn dollies of the goddess Bride appear for the Catholic St. Brigit's Day, and young people collect flowers and jump through bonfires at Beltane still. The sacrificing of black cockerels is not much of an exaggeration.

Clans

The clan system was very tribal. It was composed of extensive family units, and as it grew larger, the clans became political entities. And you didn't have to be born to a clan, you could come in and swear allegiance to your clan chief, and you'd become a MacKenzie or a Grant or whatever, and then you'd change your surname. People usually did this as a trade of armed service or farm service in return for food or land…The level of the clan chieftain was different than the system in England – it wasn't hereditary. The son of a chief might have the inside track, but the next chieftain was elected by consent of the senior clansmen present. So they sometimes got better leaders than the British did on a hereditary system. (DeLuca)

The famous clans and their descendants play a major part in the story, emphasizing the larger community around Claire and Jaime.

"Let's see," I said counting on my fingers. "According to you, Frasers are stubborn, Campbells are sneaky, MacKenzies are charming but sly, and Grahams are stupid.

What's the Murrays' distinguishing characteristics?"
    "Ye can count on them in a fight," said Jamie and Ian
together, then laughed.
    "Ye can too," said Jamie recovering. "You just hope
they're on your side." And both men went off into fits again.
(*Outlander,* ch. 29)

Back in the 1940s, Claire mentions she saw a lot of
Camerons and Gordons in the field hospital at
Amiens (*Outlander,* ch. 1). Exploring Culloden Field
in the 1960s, Brianna and Roger see clan stones for
Chisholm, Grant, MacGillivray, MacDonald,
MacKenzie, and Fraser (*Dragonfly in Amber,* ch. 4).

    The great Celtic Earls became extinct, early in
the 13th century, It was then the clans began to take
over, each a mighty family with newcomers sworn in
as part of it. They dwelt in the inaccessible areas of
the Highlands, with little more than a token
allegiance to the Scottish king. "To the denizens of
each glen, all within the visible horizon was 'a
country'" (Grant). These clans were always at war
among themselves, or more often with the
Lowlanders, their constant enemies.

Early in the 14th century clanship seemed to have become
pretty well defined over all the Highlands, and by 1587 a
distinct and formidable roll of the clans is given in the Acts
of the Scottish Parliament under that date; and, despite the
oppressive act of the British Parliament in 1747 clanship
existed in Scotland till the middle of the 18th century, in as
much strength and purity as it ever did in ancient times.
...
An affront or an injury to the most humble individual, from
one of another clan was held as an insult to the whole, and
too often one never to be forgotten or forgiven. Blood alone
could atone for it, and, if not avenged by one generation,
the feud was bequeathed as a precious legacy to the next;
and there have been occasions, as we shall show, when
the extermination of an entire community was not deemed a
sacrifice too great for vengeance. Thus, in such a state of
society, when men never went unarmed, either to field,

church, or market, human life was held exceedingly cheap. (Grant)

Clan life was a vital part of Highland culture. Jaime notes in *Lord John and the Brotherhood of the Blade*. "Our honor *is* our family. I could not see a close kinsman condemned, no matter his crime" (ch. 32). As he adds, it was the clan chief who would deal with "infamous crime." However, this was the man's kin, not the law.

The Clan Chief was the ultimate authority of this system. "A chief's personal and family talent played its role in securing him that dignity in the first place, but once inaugurated, a new chief took on a new aspect. As chief, he symbolized the manifestation of the spirit of the tribe, ritualistically reincarnated in each succeeding chief, presumably since the beginning of time" (Cairney 7). Colum is sly and manipulative, while Fraser of Lovat is selfish. They symbolize the corrupt old way of life, a signal that the lost Highland culture was far from perfect. Samuel Johnson wrote: "Wherever we roved, we were pleased to see the reverence with which his subjects regarded him. He did not endeavour to dazzle them by any magnificence of dress; his only distinction was a feather in his bonnet; but as soon as he appeared, they forsook their work, and clustered about him: he took them by the hand, and they seemed mutually delighted" (Morison).

The inherent power of the chief, even Dr. [Samuel] Johnson admits, was strengthened by the kindness of consanguinity and reverence of patriarchal authority. "The laird was the father of the clan," he adds, "his tenants commonly bore his name, and to the principles or original command was added, for many ages, an exclusive right of legal jurisdiction. This multifarious and extensive obligation operated with a force scarcely credible; every duty, moral and political, was absorbed in affection for, and adherence to the chief."

To his chief, the clansman bore all the blind devotion of a child to his parent; his obedience sprang from the same law of nature. The clansman, who scrupled to save his chief's life at the expense of his own, was regarded as a coward who abandoned his parent in the hour of peril. His duty was indelible and no feudal grant or human engagement, marriage or death, could be preferred to the service of his chief. Limited to its own glen, each clan increased in numbers far beyond the means of subsistence there; but each little mountain farm was divided and subdivided by the clansman among his children, grandchildren, and so on; but a high military spirit was unfortunately combined with a profound contempt for labour. (Grant)

Of course, the clan system helped to cement the failure of the Jacobite Rebellion:

Twenty years before the '45, Burt noticed that, "were it not for their fond: attachment to their chiefs, and the advantages these gentlemen take ... I verily believe there are but few among them that would engage in an enterprise so dangerous to them as rebellion." More than half the gallant failures, on which the Highland name for desperate fighting powers is based, were schemes of the Highland leaders supported by the natural obedience of their liegemen. (Morison)

After defeat in 1746, many of the clan leaders who had rebelled were executed, their property seized, their families driven from their homes. The lifestyle thus vanished forever. Jaime notes that his crew of smugglers in *Voyager* are not really his men – he is not their laird or chief "only the man who pays them." As he tells Claire, "More died at Culloden than the Stuart cause" (ch. 43).

Drinks

The streams in wild country appear to be perfectly safe, and Jaime notes he's drunk water every day of his life (in contrast with people in medieval cities, whose water supply was notably tainted).

102

Nonetheless, the characters spend an enormous amount of time drinking alcohol by today's standards. Most of the men travel with flasks of whiskey. Through the series, Claire develops a taste for it, especially the older vintages.

In addition, she insists on sterilizing everything with alcohol, fire, or boiling water, thus adding to the amount of liquor onscreen. Jaime's uncle Jared is in the wine business in Paris, and shipping wine and other spirits is an important part of the second book. The third book features alcohol smuggling, and the revelation that no Scottish tavern will ever open a cask of Crème de menthe, as beer and whiskey are all the Highlanders drink. An inventory of bottles in the home of the Dunbars of Thunderton, in the parish of Duffus, May 25, 1708 reveals a significant variety:

"An Account of Bottles in the Salt Cellar.

"June the first 1708.

Of Sack, five dozen and one, ...	5	1
Of Brandie, three dozen and three, ...	3	3
Of Vinegar and Aquavitie, seven, ...	0	7
Of Strong Ale, four dozen and four, . . .	4	4
Of other Ale, nine dozen, ...	9	0
In the ale cellar, fifteen dozen and ten, . .	15	10
In the hamper, five dozen empty, ...	5	0
In the wine cellar, nine with Inglish Ale, . .	0	9
White Wine, ten, ...	0	10
Of Brandy, three, ...	0	3
With Brandy and Surop, two, ...	0	2
With Claret, fifteen, ...	1	3
With Mum, fifteen, ...	1	3
Throw the house, nineteen, ...	1	7
There is in all, forty-nine dozen and two, . .	49	2
And of mutchkin bottles twenty-five, . . .	2	1

An accounting note describes: "Received ten dozen and one of chapen bottles full of claret. More received – eleven dozen and one of pynt bottles, whereof there was six broke in the home-coming. 1709, June the 4th, received from Elgin forty-three chopen bottles of claret." (qtd. in Keltie)

The Fair Folk

"There's no place on earth with more of the old superstitions and magic mixed into its daily life than the Scottish Highlands. Church or no church, Mrs. Baird believes in the Old Folk, and so do all the neighbors," Frank notes in *Outlander,* (ch. 1). Indeed, even in recent times, scholars gathering folktales discovered a reluctance to discuss the fair folk and especially to describe them by name. These were not the tiny Tinkerbells of children's stories, but creatures unnaturally *other* who might help or cause vicious harm. As Young Ian tells Brianna:

> "Ye call them *sidhe* in the Gaelic. The Cherokee call them the Nunnahee. And the Mohawk have names for them, too – more than one. But when I heard Eats Turtles tell of them, I kent at once what they were. It's the same – the Old Folk."
> "Fairies?" she said, and her incredulity must have been clear in her voice, for he glanced up sharply at her, a glint of irritation in his eyes.
> "No, I ken what *you* mean by that – Roger Mac showed me the wee picture ye drew for Jem, all tiny things like dragonflies, prinking in the flowers. . . ." He made an uncouth noise in the back of his throat.
> "Nay. These things are . . ." He made a helpless gesture with one big hand, frowning at the grass.
> "Vitamins," he said suddenly, looking up.
> "Vitamins," she said, and rubbed a hand between her brows. It had been a long day; they had likely walked fifteen or twenty miles and fatigue had settled like water in her legs and back. The bruises from her battle with the beavers were beginning to throb.
> "I see. Ian...are you sure that your head isn't still a bit cracked?" She said it lightly, but her real anxiety lest it be true must have shown in her voice, for he gave a low, rueful chuckle.
> "No. Or at least – I dinna think so. I was only – well, d'ye see, it's like that. Ye canna see the vitamins, but you and Auntie Claire ken weel that they're there, and Uncle Jamie and I must take it on faith that ye're right about it. I ken as much about the – the Old Ones. Can ye no believe me about *that*?"

> "Well, I – " She had begun to agree, for the sake of peace between them – but a feeling swept over her, sudden and cold as a cloud-shadow, that she wished to say nothing to acknowledge the notion. Not out loud. And not here.
> "Oh," he said, catching sight of her face. "So ye *do* know." (*A Breath of Snow and Ashes*, ch. 69)

This is how Highlanders have always seen them, as an otherworldly presence, the power and force of nature and old things. These included helpful house brownies or *bwca*. The *Slaugh*, Host of the Unseelie Court (evil fairies), rode through the skies. *Fuath*, or water spirits, included mermaids, selkies and the *kelpies, nucklavee,* or *each uisge,* all waterhorses. "Hill spirits, kirk spirits, and water spirits, were held responsible for sickness and divers other misfortunes. 'Trows'' inhabited Trolhouland – the hill of demons or Trows and within its recesses had their abodes, whose walls were dazzling with gold and silver" (Guthrie, ch. 1). At one point, Lizzie notes, "her gentle, kindly mistress had vanished like smoke, taken over by a *deamhan,* a she-devil" (*The Drums of Autumn,* ch. 40). She worries that next her mistress will become an *ursiq,* a werewolf. Reverend Kirk explains in his study:

> The Siths, or Fairies, they call *Sluagh Maith*, or the Goodpeople, it would seem, to prevent the dint of their ill attempts (for the Irish used to bless all they fear harm of), and are said to be of a middle nature betwixt man and angel, as were demons thought to be of old, of intelligent studious spirits, and light changeable bodies (like those called astral), somewhat of the nature of a condensed cloud, and best seen in twilight.

As Roger notes, most of the history of the Highlands is oral, up to the mid-nineteenth century or so. "That means there wasn't a great distinction made between stories about real people, stories of historical figures, and the stories about mythical things like water horses and ghosts and the doings of the Auld Folk" (*Voyager,* ch. 3). It's easy for the doings of men and women, especially travelers from other times, to merge with these supernatural tales.

In a more specific link with Claire's situation, Gwyllyn the bard tells the story of the Wee Folk who tried to steal Ewan MacDonald's wife to be a wetnurse to their own fairy children when she's staying at Castle Leoch (*Outlander,* ch. 8). This story, repeated on the show, emphasizes how Claire has tumbled into Scottish folklore.

> "It was a time, two hundred years ago…" He spoke in English, and I felt a sudden sense of déja vu. It was exactly the way our guide on Loch Ness had spoken, telling legends of the Great Glen.
>
> It was not a story of ghosts or heroes, though, but a tale of the Wee Folk he told.
>
> "There was a clan of the Wee Folk as lived near Dundreggan," he began. "And the hill there is named for the dragon that dwelt there, that Fionn slew and buried where he fell, so the dun is named as it is. And after the passing of Fionn and the Feinn, the Wee Folk that came to dwell in the dun came to want mothers of men to be wet nurses to their own fairy bairns, for a man has something that a fairy has not, and the Wee Folk thought that it might pass through the mother's milk to their own small ones.
>
> "Now, Ewan MacDonald of Dundreggan was out in the dark, tending his beasts, on the night when his wife bore her firstborn son. A gust of the night wind passed by him, and in the breath of the wind he heard his wife's sighing. She sighed as she sighed before the child was born, and hearing her there, Ewan MacDonald turned and flung his knife into the wind in the name of the Trinity. And his wife dropped safe to the ground beside him."
>
> The story was received with a sort of collective "ah" at the conclusion, and was quickly followed by tales of the cleverness and ingenuity of the Wee Folk, and others about their interactions with the world of men. Some were in Gaelic and some in English, used apparently according to which language best fitted the rhythm of the words, for all of them had a beauty to the speaking, beyond the content of the tale itself. True to his promise, Jamie translated the Gaelic for me in an undertone, so quickly and easily that I

thought he must have heard these stories many times before.

There was one I noticed particularly, about the man out late at night upon a fairy hill, who heard the sound of a woman singing "sad and plaintive" from the very rocks of the hill. He listened more closely and heard the words:

"I am the wife of the Laird of Balnain
The Folk have stolen me over again."

So the listener hurried to the house of Balnain and found there the owner gone and his wife and baby son missing. The man hastily sought out a priest and brought him back to the fairy knoll. The priest blessed the rocks of the dun and sprinkled them with holy water. Suddenly the night grew darker and there was a loud noise as of thunder. Then the moon came out from behind a cloud and shone upon the woman, the wife of Balnain, who lay exhausted on the grass with her child in her arms. The woman was tired, as though she had traveled far, but could not tell where she had been, nor how she had come there.

In book and show, the story is meant to parallel Claire's own situation and also provide her with hope – after their travels, the women usually return home. As Claire thinks after hearing the tale:

"It was a time, two hundred years ago..."

It's always two hundred years in Highland stories, said the Reverend Wakefield's voice in memory. The same thing as "Once upon a time," you know.

And women trapped in the rocks of fairy duns, traveling far and arriving exhausted, who knew not where they had been, nor how they had come there.

I could feel the hair rising on my forearms, as though with cold, and rubbed them uneasily. Two hundred years. From 1945 to 1743; yes, near enough. And women who traveled through the rocks.

On returning to Castle Leoch, Claire discovers a changeling child. This is a sickly baby abandoned on a hill with a bouquet and bowl of milk for the fairies. Geillis defines a changeling, saying, "When the fairies steal a human child away, they leave one of their own in its place...you know it's a changeling because

it cries and fusses all the time and doesn't thrive"
(ch. 24). Geillis adds that if the fairy babe is left on
their hill the fairies must take it back and return the
proper human child. Jaime reminds Claire that the
parents are comforted believing their child is well in
fairyland, even if their own never returns. These tales
are staple of fairy kidnappings:

> About 1730, it is said, a man of the name of Munro had a
> sickly attenuated child, which he and his neighbours
> considered to be a changeling, substituted by the sportive
> elves, at an unguarded moment, In place of his own. There
> is a conical knoll in the carse called Tom Earnais, or
> Henry's Knoll, which was famed as the scene of the
> moonlight revels of Titania and her court; and it was
> believed, that if the changeling were left overnight on the
> hillock, the real child would be found in its stead in the
> morning. The infatuated father actually subjected his ailing
> offspring to this ordeal, and in the morning found it a
> corpse. (Guthrie, ch. 9)

Fairies live are said to live under the manmade
cairns or burial chambers from the ancient peoples,
suggesting they may in fact be a memory of those
pre-Iron Age folk. Tomnahurich Hill near Inverness is
famed as a fairy hill. Reverend Kirk made a special
study of the fairies and their homes, explaining:

> There be many places called fairy-hills, which the mountain
> people think impious and dangerous to peel or discover, by
> taking earth or wood from them, superstitiously believing
> the souls of their predecessors to dwell there. And for that
> end (say they) a mole or mound was dedicate beside every
> churchyard to receive the souls till their adjacent bodies
> arise, and so became as a fairy-hill; they using bodies of air
> when called abroad.

Food

Jaime and Claire eat turnips, kale, onions, bannocks
with molasses or honey, cheese, butter, berries,
cherries, bacon, stew, roast mutton, beef, and lots of
parritch (oat porridge) and herring. There's pastries,

sweets, and fruitcake on special occasions. On one memorable occasion, they pick the first potato crop and try to convince the villagers to eat it.

> As a rule, the only crops attempted to be raised were oats and barley, and sometimes a little flax; green crops were almost totally unknown or despised, till many years after 1745; even potatoes do not seem to have been at all common till after 1750, although latterly they became the staple food of the Highlanders. (Keltie)

Thus oat porridge was a major staple as were oat bread and barley bread. Drammach – a handful of oats and water – was another (*Outlander*, ch. 6). Jaime warns Claire as they wander the hills after their wedding, "I should have warned ye before that we'd likely end up sleeping in haystacks, wi' naught but heather ale and drammach for food" (chapter 16).

Brose is an uncooked form of porridge – oats with boiling water added to them. Geillis makes this for Arthur and other characters serve it on occasion. Brose can also be made into a pudding with cream, whiskey, nuts, honey, etc. This is eaten at Lallybroch (*Outlander,* ch. 32). Claire notes:

> If Scotsmen were stubborn about anything-and, in fact, they tended to be stubborn about quite a number of things, truth be known- it was the virtues of oatmeal parritch for breakfast. Through eons of living in a land so poor there was little to eat but oats, they had as usual converted necessity into a virtue, and insisted that they liked the stuff. (*Dragonfly in Amber*, ch. 7)

In the New World, Claire is somewhat revolted by barley crowdie – more boiled grain and water. She comments, "Living in a country normally barren of much that was edible, they were capable of relishing glutinous masses of cereal, untouched by any redeeming hint of spice or flavor. From a feebler race myself, I didn't feel quite up to it," and pours it back into the pot (*The Drums of Autumn,* ch. 23).

For more formal occasions, Mrs. Fitz serves roast pheasant stuffed with honeyed chestnuts and suckling pig when the Duke of Sandringham visits Castle Leoch (*Outlander,* ch. 24). For the Oathtaking, there's pheasant, roasts, chicken, eel, and haggis.

Living with the outlaws, Jaime would snare rabbits and hunt deer. He's quite skilled at stream fishing and making snares. Jamie tells Claire he was looking for big orange fungus that grow on trees as something to eat when he was an outlaw and that he had to eat grass once when he was starving, though he should have boiled it (*Outlander,* ch. 6).

Fish was another staple, so close to the coast. In the 1940s, Claire notes, "Dinner the night before had been herring, fried. Lunch had been herring, pickled. And the pungent scent now wafting up the stairwell strongly intimated that breakfast was to be herring, kippered" (ch. 1). In Castle Leoch, she's served the same. Geillis makes Arthur Cullen skink – a thick soup of haddock, root vegetables and onions (*Outlander,* ch. 25).

By contrast in Paris, Claire and Jaime serve hot chocolate, spiced bacon and bean cassoulet, chestnut tarts, trout with almonds, and salmon mousse in their townhouse. The Palace at Versailles offers shrimp served in aspic, toast with salmon, roast venison, tarlets, sorbet, three varieties of spiced pickles, and honey-glazed nightingales stuffed with almond paste There's also a scene when Jaime fights off assailants with a Dunedin sausage "made of spiced duck, ham and venison, boiled, stuffed and sun-dried, a Dunedin sausage measured eighteen inches from end to end and was hard as seasoned oakwood" (*Dragonfly in Amber,* ch. 12). He jokes that it was especially strange to carry it into a brothel as he fled pursuit, but thriftily serves it for supper after.

Freemasons

"Free and accepted masons from the world's oldest association of men. Its members belong to a lodge presided over by a master and wardens. Its principals, or craft, as freemasonry is called, is to 'build' good men" (Bruce-Mitford 109). The secret and complex initiation rites and passwords include the tools of masons – builders, such as a compass and square, as well as myth and ritual from the Temple of Solomon.

Jaime is made a Freemason in prison ... ironically so the snobby officers will have someone to complete their lodge. He then makes all the prisoners join, so they can form a community without being divided by religion or politics – things the lodge forbids being discussed. They form the second lodge in the prison, called Ardsmuir Lodge Number 2.

After prison, he seeks safe passage to the New World from his cousin Jared in France. Jared tests him by saying "We meet upon the level." To which Jamie replies "and we part upon the square" (*Voyager,* ch. 40).

In *The Fiery Cross,* a man from Ardsmuir offers Roger a handshake with the distinctive pressure against his knuckle of a masonic greeting. Roger thus realizes the Ardsmuir men and Jaime are all Freemasons as he is, and he finally hears the details of the story. Jaime notes after reading a doctor's journal that a drawing of a compass is significant: "'Rawlings must have been one as well,' he said, clearly reluctant to talk about Freemasonry, but unable to keep from making logical connections. 'Else he'd not have kent what that is.'" (*The Fiery Cross,* ch. 96).

Aitchison's Haven, a masonic lodge in Musselburgh, Scotland, has the oldest written records, dating back to January 9, 1599. It ceased to exist in 1856.

The Grand Lodge of Scotland (GLOS) Museum and Library contains a most unusual archive with records from 1598. The names of Freemasons from that date are recorded from that time although not in a comprehensive way until 1736 when membership records for all of Scotland's Lodges exist from then to the present day. The first Freemason in America was a guy from Aberdeen in 1680. Paul Revere was a member (in fact Secretary and Master) of a Scottish Lodge in Boston Mass. John Paul Jones was a Mason in a Lodge in Kirkcudbright, George Washington brought stonemasons (who were members of Masonic Lodge) to the USA to build the White House. At least two Scottish Freemasons married native Americans and became head of their adopted tribe (the clan - tribe similarities together with the oral tradition on which Scottish Freemasonry is based has not been explored). One of them negotiated a treaty directly with George Washington because they were both Freemasons! The list of such stuff is pretty lengthy. There is heaps more of a similar kind. Scottish Freemasonry is mentioned in the Guinness Book of Records and on their Website as having the oldest Masonic Lodges in the world. That means that Freemasonry originated in Scotland and of course we, and all Scots should be, very proud of that fact. (Cooper)

Gaelic Language

I wasn't offended by the lewdness of their jokes or squeamish over the fact that my dinner looked like a shriveled Easter rabbit, nor was I too dainty to sleep on a pillow made of stone. What troubled me was that they were clearly using Gaelic to exclude me. I just had to remember my time with them would be over soon. (Episode 105)

Huddled by the campfire, Claire resents the men's Gaelic jokes. In fact, the show features long conversations in Gaelic without translation (in the book, Claire summarizes these, adding her own thoughts on the exchanges).

Describing filming the Gaelic scenes on the rent collecting trip, Dougal's actor Graham McTavish comments, "It was a joy to do those. It was a great challenge doing those speeches in what is for me, I'm ashamed to say, is a foreign language even though my great grandparents spoke the dialect. It was fantastic to be able to play that out without subtitles and get across the meaning of those speeches without being able to understand the words" (Ng, "Graham McTavish").

One article interviews the show's Gaelic coach. Adhamh Obroinn remained on set to help the cast with pronunciation and delivery. He said that helping the cast learn the subtleties of Gaelic was something he relished and that he hoped the high-profile series would promote the language throughout Scotland and across the world. As he added, "I'm hoping that the exposure of Gaelic will hit home to people in Scotland that we have something absolutely priceless here. We will see what happens but it's all very positive so far" ("Big Budget").

Of course, Claire's and the audience's incomprehension of Gaelic is a shared link between them that strengthens Claire's position as the lens through which the audience interacts with the world. In the comic, which is from Jaime and Murtagh's point of view, all the Gaelic is translated with footnotes since they speak the language.

In a delightful cut scene from the fifth book, Gabaldon shows the characters' relationship with Gaelic, as Jaime teaches Brianna and chats with Roger. Claire notes:

> In fact, I understood Jamie much better than I did Roger, when it came to Gaelic. The language appeared to have evolved somewhat over the two hundred years between them, and while the overall effect seemed quite the same to the naked ear, Jamie spoke something Roger referred to — with an academic fascination that Jamie bore fairly patiently – as "Erse." I had been exposed to the dialect Jamie and other Highlanders spoke for some time, now, whereas I had never heard much modern Gaelic at all.

When asked why Jaime teaches Brianna but not Claire, Gabaldon responds on the blog to her official website: "Well, he didn't teach her in the beginning, because he had no reason to suppose that she'd necessarily stay with him. And he does value her 'otherness' – her *being* a Sassenach; he probably subconsciously wants to keep that aspect of her. And he may also worry about what kind of trouble she might get into if she was able to join Gaelic conversations. [g]" (*Voyages of the Artemis*). Gabaldon had her own adventure using Gaelic expressions in the series. She explains:

> Now, with reference to my own novels, I did know that Gaelic was the native tongue of the Scottish Highlands, when I began writing *Outlander*. Finding someone in Phoenix, Arizona (in 1988), who *spoke* Gaelic was something else. I finally found a bookseller (Steinhof's Foreign Books, in Boston) who could provide me with an English/Gaelic dictionary, and that's what I used as a source when writing *Outlander*.
>
> ...
>
> And then I met Iain. I got a wonderful letter from Iain MacKinnon Taylor, who said all kinds of delightful things regarding my books, and then said, "There is just this one small thing, which I hesitate to mention. I was born on the Isle of Harris and am a native Gaelic-speaker – and I think you must be getting your Gaelic from a dictionary." He then generously volunteered his time and talent to provide translations for the Gaelic in subsequent books, and the Gaelic in *Voyager, Drums of Autumn, The Fiery Cross, The Outlandish Companion*, and *A Breath of Snow and Ashes* is due to Iain's efforts, and those of his twin brother Hamish and other members of his family still residing on Harris.
>
> At this point, Iain was no longer able to continue doing the translations, but I was extremely fortunate in that a friend, Catherine MacGregor, was not only a student of Gaelic herself but was also a friend of Catherine-Ann MacPhee, world-famous Gaelic singer, and a native speaker from Barra. The two Cathys very generously did the Gaelic for *The Exile* and *An Echo in the Bone*. (Author's Notes, *The Scottish Prisoner*)

The language can be difficult – even Sir Walter Scott, who wrote amongst a Gaelic population, made the strangest of mistakes when he used Gaelic words (Campbell IV 371). Gabaldon lists several specific ones, including the phrase "Lag Cruime" (page 316 in book one) which she admits to making up. She adds that over and over in the first two books, "mo duinne" should be "mo nighean donn." As she adds: "This was an attempt on my part to render 'my brown one,' using a Gaelic dictionary. My Gaelic expert, Iain Taylor ... informs me that the correct form should really be "mo nighean donn" (my brown haired girl), and so I used that form in the later books" (*Outlandish Companion* 503). On the show, "mo nighean donn" is used.

Historically, Scots Gaelic and Irish Gaelic were quite similar (as shown in *The Scottish Prisoner* when Jaime communicates with an Irishman). As S.E. Gunn explains in *Scottish History and Celtic Studies*:

Anyone who speaks Scottish Gaelic and has some knowledge of Irish Gaelic will recognize the similarity of the languages. ... The repertoire of Scots and Irish Gaelic storytellers is startlingly similar: stories of Fionn, Gràinne, Cuchallain, Deirdre, the Speckled Bull, the Battle of the Birds etc. Belief in the supernatural much the same: the Banshee, Banbha (Banff), the ways of making prophecies and of cursing and blessing. ... Most historians agree that a considerable migration took place in the 5th-6th centuries AD; however, there have been migrations between Ireland and Scotland (and the other bits of Britain) for millenia. The society of Gaelic Ireland and Scotland, whose basic unit was the clan (Gaelic: fine) is similar as is the Gaelic terminology to describe it. The laws were shared, although differentiated by contact with feudal law, introduced by French and English-speaking peoples.

After Culloden, when Clan life was taken apart piece by piece, Gaelic went with it. In the 1980s, Roger and Jem's school principal discuss Gaelic's decline, a nod to the real life speakers and vanishing culture of the

Highlands today:

Menzies smiled briefly, but didn't look up.

"No. You won't find much of the Gaelic there these days. Spanish, Polish, Estonian... quite a bit of those, but not the Gaelic. Your wife said ye'd spent a number of years in America, so you'll maybe not have noticed, but it's not much spoken in public anymore."

"To be honest, I hadn't paid it much mind – not 'til now."

Menzies nodded again, as though to himself, then took off his spectacles and rubbed at the marks they'd left on the bridge of his nose. His eyes were pale blue and seemed suddenly vulnerable, without the protection of his glasses.

"It's been on the decline for a number of years. Much more so for the last ten, fifteen years. The Highlands are suddenly part of the UK – or at least the rest of the UK says so – in a way they've never been before, and keeping a separate language is seen as not only old-fashioned but outright destructive.

"It's not what you'd call a written policy, to stamp it out, but the use of Gaelic is strongly... discouraged... in schools. Mind" – he raised a hand to forestall Roger's response – "they couldn't get away with that if the parents protested, but they don't. Most of them are eager for their kids to be part of the modern world, speak good English, get good jobs, fit in elsewhere, be able to leave the Highlands... Not so much for them here, is there, save the North Sea?"

"The parents..."

"If they've learnt the Gaelic from their own parents, they deliberately don't teach it to their kids. And if they haven't got it, they certainly make no effort to learn. It's seen as backward, ignorant. Very much a mark of the lower classes."

"Barbarous, in fact," Roger said, with an edge. "The barbarous Erse?"

Menzies recognized Samuel Johnson's dismissive description of the tongue spoken by his eighteenth-century Highland hosts, and the brief, rueful smile lit his face again. "Exactly. There's a great deal of prejudice – much of it outspoken – against..."

"Teuchters?" "Teuchter" was a Lowland Scots term for someone in the Gaeltacht, the Gaelic-speaking Highlands, and in cultural terms the general equivalent of "hillbilly" or "trailer trash." (*An Echo in the Bone,* ch. 29)

The principal asks Roger to teach a Gaelic class for the children and he speedily agrees.

> He'd brought one volume of the *Gadelica* [Gabaldon's real-life source for spells, songs, and charms] with him, and while he passed the ancient hymnal round the room, along with a booklet of waulking songs he'd put together, he read them one of the charms of the new moon, the Cud Chewing Charm, the Indigestion Spell, the Poem of the Beetle, and some bits from "The Speech of Birds." (*Echo in the Bone,* ch. 46)

All these can be read in the collection today.

A Gentleman's Education

> There was a small, three-shelf bookcase in Jamie's study, which held the entire library of Fraser's Ridge. The serious works occupied the top shelf: a volume of Latin poetry, *Caesar's Commentaries, the Meditations of Marcus Aurelius,* a few other classic works, Dr. Brickell's *Natural History of North Carolina*, lent by the Governor and never returned, and a schoolbook on mathematics, much abused, with Ian Murray the Younger written on the flyleaf in a staggering hand.
>   The middle shelf was given over to more light-minded reading: a small selection of romances, slightly ragged with much reading, featuring *Robinson Crusoe; Tom Jones,* in a set of seven small, leather-covered volumes; *Roderick Random*, in four volumes; and Sir Henry Richardson's monstrous *Pamela,* done in two gigantic octavo bindings – the first of these decorated with multiple bookmarks, ranging from a ragged dried maple leaf to a folded penwiper, these indicating the points which various readers had reached before giving up, either temporarily or permanently. A copy of *Don Quixote* in Spanish, ratty, but much less worn, since only Jamie could read it. (*The Fiery Cross,* ch. 38)

The books relate, "he had been schooled in the Classics at the Université in Paris, and – while disagreeing now and then with some of the Roman

117

philosophers – regarded both Homer and Virgil as personal friends" (*The Drums of Autumn,* ch. 8). As Claire adds, "Jamie was a natural polygogue; he acquired languages and dialects with no visible effort, picking up idioms as a dog picks up foxtails in a romp through the fields" (*The Drums of Autumn,* ch. 8). He knows Gaelic and English from childhood of course. He speaks good Greek and Latin, and excellent French, as well as German, Spanish, and Biblical Hebrew. He picks up some words of Chinese, West Indies slave pidgin, Cherokee and Iroquois, and Hugh Monroe's sign language. Gabaldon comments:

> A working knowledge of Latin and Greek and an appreciation for the major works of the ancient philosophers were hallmarks of a "man of worth" – a gentleman – in the eighteenth century. Jamie, grandson of a noble (even if illegitimate), and nephew of a clan chieftain, has certainly been well educated, and thus well versed in ancient languages and writings. Small wonder that he turns to these both as expressions of his love for Claire, and as tutoring for his beloved nephew Ian. (*Outlandish Companion* 523)

VALERIE ESTELLE FRANKEL

As she adds:

> One of the aspects of eighteenth-century literature and letters that I particularly enjoy is the frequent and easy use of quotes and classical allusion. In the eighteenth century, an educated man (or woman; there were not a few) would have been familiar with the best-known of the classical writers, and it was common to employ both specific references and less direct allusion, both as a means of establishing one's social credentials, and – I suspect – for fun. (*Outlandish Companion* 523)

Jaime has Voltaire to dinner in Paris and reads Tacitus at the Abbey of Ste. Anne de Beaupre. When he returns to Lallybroch and his dog recognizes him, he and Claire joke about the *Odyssey* – Jaime quoting from it in Greek and adding the Celtic epic of Fingal and his Hounds for good measure. While chopping wood, Jaime recites from the "Meditations" of Marcus Aurelius Antonius on "body, soul, and mind" (*The Drums of Autumn,* ch. 20). He trains Young Ian in "the rudiments of Greek and Latin grammar, and to improve his mathematics and conversational French" (*The Drums of Autumn,* ch. 8). Claire must confess, "All I remember is Arma virumque cano...My arm got bit off by a dog" (*The Drums of Autumn,* ch. 8) though she can read simple Latin like the clan mottos.

The Highlanders had close ties to France and its philosophers and writers. Moreover, they placed a great value on education, though the families of gentlemen also learned to farm. Highland epics were mostly passed along orally, but children learned the great works of other languages. One history recounts:

> The children of chiefs and gentlemen seem to have been allowed to run about in much the same apparently uncared for condition as those of the tenants, it having been a common saying, according to Captain Burt, who was an English soldier surveyring Scotland   "that a gentleman's

119

bairns are to be distinguished by their speaking English." To illustrate this he tells us that once when dining with a laird not very far from Inverness – possibly Lord Lovat – he met an English soldier at the house who was catching birds for the laird to exercise his hawks on. This soldier told Burt that for three or four days after his first coming, he had observed In the kitchen ("an out-house hovel") a parcel of dirty children half naked, whom he took to belong to some poor tenant, but at last discovered they were part of the family. "But," says the fastidious English Captain, "although these were so little regarded, the young laird, about the age of fourteen, was going to the university; and the eldest daughter, about sixteen, sat with us at table, clean and genteelly dressed." (Keltie)

Claire's wedding ring of the books is inscribed with a Latin quote Hugh Monro passes along:

"Then let amourous kisses dwell
On our lips, begin and tell
A Thousand and a Hundred score
A Hundred and a Thousand more"

"Da mi basia mille," he whispered, smiling. Give me a thousand kisses. It was the inscription inside my ring, a brief quotation from a love song by Catullus. I bent and gave him one back. "Dien mille altera," I said. Then a thousand more. (*The Drums of Autumn,* ch. 10)

Gabaldon offers some background on her choice:

The Catullus poem referred to in *Outlander* is titled "Lesbia," and was translated in the seventeenth century by Richard Crashaw...Both versions were sent to me originally by Janet McConnaughey, an online friend from the CompuServe Literary Forum, whose knowledge of poetry and lyrics is simply staggering. Having read the scene in which Jamie gives Claire the silver ring, Janet suggested that perhaps da mi basia mille would be appropriate as an inscription. I liked the notion, but wanted to use somewhat more of the poem than would fit inside the average ring. I therefore used small quotations from the poem in the course of the dialogue in *Outlander,* referring to the inscription only later, in *Dragonfly in Amber*. (*Outlandish Companion* 524)

LESBIA
– Catullus (84? – 54 B.C.)
Come and let us live my Deare,
Let us love and never feare,
What the sow rest Fathers say:
Brightest Sol that dyes today
Lives againe as blith tomorrow,
But if we darke sons of sorrow
Set; o then, how long a Night
Shuts the eye of our short light!
Then let amorous kisses dwell
On our lips, begin and tell
A Thousand, and a Hundred, score
An Hundred, and a Thousand more,
Till another Thousand smother
That, and that wipe of another.
Thus at last when we have numbred
Many a Thousand, many a Hundred;
Wee'l confound the reckoning quite,
And lose our selves in wild delight:
While our joyes so multiply,
As shall mocke the envious eye.
– translation by Richard Crashaw

Kelpies and the Loch Ness Monster

At Loch Ness, Frank and Claire's guide tells them, "Weel, the loch's queer, and no mistake. There's stories, to be sure, of something old and evil that once lived in the depths. Sacrifices were made to it – kine, and sometimes even wee bairns, flung into the water in withy baskets" (*Outlander,* ch. 2).

Claire actually sees the monster while returning to Castle Leoch. She comments, "Oddly enough, I was not really afraid. I felt some kinship with it, a creature farther from its own time than I" (ch. 19). Gabaldon suggests there may be a time portal *inside* Loch Ness, accounting for the vanishing monster.

Now, if you believe that time-travel is possible–and both
Stephen Hawking and I think it is – then you don't have to
have either a set quantity of biomass or a breeding
population of monsters. All you need is a time-portal under
Loch Ness, which would occasionally allow a prehistoric
creature to pass through it.

OK, if this is the case, then the monster could quite
easily be a plesiosaur, elasmosaur, or any other aquatic
prehistoric reptile. Going just on the basis of the most
popular published photo of the supposed monster, my
guess would be plesiosaur. (FAQ)

The tale of the waterhorse in episode eight is meant
as a nod to the appearance of the Loch Ness
Monster. On the show, Moore considers the creature
a step too far into the world of fantasy – he doesn't
want to suggest monsters and magic will appear
(Podcast, 108). There are several tales through the
books of a kelpie who dwells in the sea and may be
the same as the famous monster. (A kelpie was a
fairy or demon horse known for drowning its rider.)

If anyone suggested to a Lochaber or Rannoch Highlander
that the cleverest horse-tamer could "clap a saddle on one
of the demon-steeds of Loch Treig, as he issues in the grey
dawn, snorting, from his crystal-paved sub-lacustral stalls,
he would answer, with a look of mingled horror and awe,
'Impossible!' The water-horse would tear him into a
thousand pieces with his teeth and trample and pound him
into pulp with his jet-black, iron-hard, though unshod hoofs!"
(Mackinlay, ch. 11)

Rupert's tale in the books (identical on the show)
proceeds in a traditional fashion:

The waterhorse of Loch Garve, like so many of his kind,
had stolen a young girl who came to the loch to draw water,
and carried her away to live in the depths of the loch and be
his wife. Woe betide any maiden, or any man, for that
matter, who met a fine horse by the water's side and
thought to ride upon him, for a rider once mounted could
not dismount, and the horse would step into the water, turn

into a fish, and swim to his home with the hapless rider still stuck fast to his back.

"Now, a waterhorse beneath the waves has but fish's teeth," said Rupert, wiggling his palm like an undulating fish, "and feeds on snails and waterweeds and cold, wet things. His blood runs cold as the water, and he's no need of fire, d'ye ken, but a human woman's a wee bit warmer than that." Here he winked at me and leered outrageously, to the enjoyment of the listeners.

"So the waterhorse's wife was sad and cold and hungry in her new home beneath the waves, not caring owermuch for snails and waterweed for her supper. So, the waterhorse being a kindly sort, takes himself to the bank of the loch near the house of a man with the reputation of a builder. And when the man came down to the river, and saw the fine golden horse with his silver bridle, shining in the sun, he couldna resist seizing the bridle and mounting.

"Sure enough, the waterhorse carries him straight into the water, and down through the depths to his own cold, fishy home. And there he tells the builder if he would be free, he must build a fine hearth, and a chimney as well, that the waterhorse's wife might have a fire to warm her hands and fry her fish."

...

"So the builder, havin' little choice, did as he was bid. And so the waterhorse kept his word, and returned the man to the bank near his home. And the waterhorse's wife was warm, then, and happy, and full of the fish she fried for her supper. And the water never freezes over the east end of Loch Garve because the heat from the waterhorse's chimney melts the ice." (*Outlander,* ch. 18)

This has several correspondences with the series, beyond the monster: Claire has, in a sense, been stolen away, and she finds herself missing ordinary human comforts like hot baths, much like the woman in the tale. Jaime must endeavor to please his bride from another place and time. Also, the story is told against a scene of horse theft and violence, emphasizing the treacherous and implacable nature of the world.

Kilts

Claire tells Jaime, "Actually, it's your kilt that makes me want to fling you to the floor and commit ravishment ... But you don't look at all bad in your breeks" (*The Drums of Autumn*, ch. 13). When asked a man in a kilt is such a romantic figure, Gabaldon notes that while "really tired" she said, "Well, I suppose it's the idea that you could be up against a wall with him in a minute" ("The Doctor's Balls," Kindle Locations 376-379). The interview was immediately reprinted everywhere. As she adds:

> A man who you know is running around with his dangly bits so immediately accessible is plainly a bold spirit, up for anything at the drop of a hat (or some more appropriate garment) and entirely willing to risk himself, body and soul. The English Government understood this very well; hence the DisKilting Act, passed after Culloden, which – as part of a program of cultural punishment and ethnic cleansing – forbade Highland men to wear the kilt or possess tartan. ("The Doctor's Balls" 382-385)

What's under the kilt? Claire reveals after traveling on the rent-collecting trip that she's observed many times that usually there's *nothing* under the kilt. In episode six, the British officers joke about what's under Dougal's kilt until Dougal points out they're embarrassing Claire. "The question of the kilt will remain an enigma," Brigadier General Thomas announces nastily. In a later book, Roger says at a Scottish gathering, "As my auld grand-da used to say, when ye put on yer kilt, laddie, ye ken for sure yer a man!" (*The Drums of Autumn*, ch. 4).

In the 16th century a simple length of cloth, belted round the waist, came into use. The "feileadh breacan" or "feileadh mor" (the big kilt) was several yards long and the Highlander had to lay it on the ground, gathering the cloth into pleats from the waist and hang a length over his shoulder and pin it there. "This was a particularly convenient style of dress, as the plaid hung loosely behind, and did not encumber the arms, and in wet weather could be drawn over the shoulders, and formed a sufficient covering for a Highlander, while, in the event of a camping out at night, it could be thrown loose, and covered the whole body" ("The Highland Garb"). After borrowing one of these, Jaime explains:

> "It's a bit undignified to get into, but it's verra easy to take off"
> "How do you get into it?" I asked curiously.
> "Well, ye lay it out on the ground, like this" – he knelt, spreading the cloth so that it lined the leaf-strewn hollow – "and then ye pleat it every few inches, lie down on it, and roll."
> I burst out laughing, and sank to my knees, helping to smooth the thick tartan wool. (*Dragonfly in Amber*, ch. 36)

In the books and on the show, Jaime generally wears the little kilt with a separate plaid, which functions as sleeping bag, cloak, and ground cover. Six yards by two, the plaid was a voluminous garment wrapped in several different ways. He wears his kilt with a long shirt and optional plaid, and a jacket and waistcoat for more formal occasions. At night he sleeps in the same shirt or in nothing.

One historian recounts, "The basic dress for men into the seventeenth century included Celtic brogues (black leather shoes not unlike ballerina slippers: a kind of moccasin), knee-length tartan hose of an argyle pattern, a long, saffron dyed linen shirt of ample folds and yardage, and a mantle of wool, which in Scotland evolved into the kilt of today" (Cairney 10). As another critic describes the plaid:

> The Breacanfeile, literally, the variegated or chequered covering, is the original garb of the Highlanders, and forms the chief part of the costume; but it is now almost laid aside in its simple form. It consisted of a plain piece of tartan from four to six yards in length, and two yards broad. The plaid was adjusted with much nicety, and made to surround the

waist in great plaits or folds, and was firmly bound round the loins with a leathern belt in such a manner that the lower side fell down to the middle of the knee joint, and then, while there were the foldings behind, the cloth was double before. The upper part was then fastened on the left shoulder with a large brooch or pin, so as to display to the most advantage the tastefulness of the arrangement, the two ends being sometimes suffered to hang down; but that on the right side, which was necessarily the longest, was more usually tucked under the belt. In battle, in travelling, and on other occasions, this added much to the commodiousness and grace of the costume. By this arrangement, the right arm of the wearer was left uncovered and at full liberty; but in wet or very cold weather the plaid was thrown loose, by which both body and shoulders were covered. To give free exercise for both arms in case of need, the plaid was fastened across the breast by a large silver bodkin, or circular brooch, often enriched with precious stones, or imitations of them, having mottos engraved, consisting of allegorical and figurative sentences. ("A Social History," ch. 2)

"The Regent Murray" with gun, pistol, powder horn, dirk, and sword. 1560

VALERIE ESTELLE FRANKEL

Medicine

> Aside from the fact that it would be helpful to know how to
> dress wounds and treat minor problems like scurvy, I'd
> noticed in the course of research that there were in fact
> almost no "official" physicians at all in the Highlands. ... In
> most times and places, there has been no medical
> assistance save for the wisdom and experience of family
> and neighbors – and among family and neighbors, those
> who are most likely to have any knowledge or skill in
> medical matters are the women because (owing to the
> undeniable fact that women bear and nourish children) they
> are the members of the community who are stuck at home,
> growing plants, feeding all and sundry, and generally
> keeping things going while the menfolk are out killing
> mammoths or each other (*Outlandish Companion* 191-192)

The novels are poised on the edge of the scientific
revolution, as the Europeans slowly discarded
superstition and charms in favor of study,
experimentation, and drugs. Cleanliness was not
practiced by all physicians and bleeding was
common, with a special surgeon's tool called a fleam.
Doctors were scares, and most had not trained in
university – their education and abilities thus varied
widely. At the same time, Claire identifies some of
the popular herbs and medicines as cures she
approves, and discovers leeches and maggots are
quite effective for reduction of bruises and removing
dead tissue.

> "Still bleedin' under the skin. Leeches will help, then." She
> lifted the cover from the bowl, revealing several small dark
> sluglike objects, an inch or two long, covered with a
> disagreeable-looking liquid. Scooping out two of them, she
> pressed one to the flesh just under the brow-bone and the
> other just below the eye.
> "See," she explained to me," once a bruise is set, like,
> leeches do ye no good. But where ye ha' a swellin' like this,
> as is still comin' up, that means the blood is flowin' under
> the skin, and leeches can pull it out." (*Outlander*, ch. 6)

Apparently, this scene was planned for the show, but the artificial leeches wouldn't stay in place.

The painkiller of choice was laudanum – an alcoholic tincture of opium. Surgery existed (with laudanum or alcohol the only available painkillers) but the risk of infection afterwards was high and blood transfusions were not possible. When Claire does surgery, she discovers trouble getting enough light for procedures, along with the lack of ether or other anesthetic.

With doctors rare, books of household cures were popular ... eventually Claire writes one herself.

> In Scotland several books were in use, designed for those who knew a little medicine, such as the clergymen, lairds or great ladies who took an interest in their retainers. Of these books, one of the best known was "The Poor Man's Physician, or the Receits of the Famous John Moncrief of Tippermalloch." This, as its title-page records, is " a choice collection of simple and easy remedies for most distempers, very useful for all persons, especially those of a poorer condition." The first edition was published in 1712, and the third edition in 1731.
>
> ....
>
> Some of these appear to be quite natural and salutary, and some can only be described as extremely disgusting. The following is a fair average sample of [one] book:
>
> 38. For the Colick.
> The Hoofs of living Creatures are singularly good, being drunk. Rhasis. Or dry Oxdung drunk in Broth, or the Juice pressed from the Ox-dung drunk, is better. Gesnerus. 2. The Heart of a Lark bound to the Thigh, is excellent against the Colick, and some have eaten it raw with very good Success. A Spaniard. 3. This is certain, that a Wolf's Dung, Guts, or Skin eaten, will cure the Colick, or if yo11 do but carry them about you; for they strengthen the Choler.
> (Comrie 113-114)

"Towards the end of the 18th century, as regular medicine became more easily available, these ancient recipes passed out of use, and excited a great deal of ridicule" (Comrie 114). For instance, Geillis tells Claire bloodwort or roseroot will make warts grow on someone's nose and that wood betony can turns toads into pigeons (*Outlander,* ch. 9), comments Claire views with skepticism.

She disinfects with several herbs:

> I threw several cloves of peeled garlic into the boiling water with some of the witch hazel, then added the cloth strips to the mixture. The boneset, comfrey, and cherry bark were steeping in a small pan of hot water set by the fire. The preparations had steadied me a bit. If I didn't know for certain where I was, or why I was there, at least I knew what to do for the next quarter of an hour. (*Outlander,* ch. 4)

On the show, Moore insists on the correct herbs for Claire's picking expeditions and in her surgery to add a "sense of authenticity" and stay true to the spirit of the book (Inside the World, 103). In the poison scene, Claire identifies lily of the valley as a toxic herb that could have been mistaken for wood garlic. When Geillis visits Claire in her surgery in "The Gathering," she notices that Claire has been working with valerian, and cautions her to boil it first...she probably uses this to knock out the guards. In "Rent," Claire treats Ned Gowan's asthma with thornapple or jimson weed. In other moments, Claire uses gallberries to treat malaria when she can't find imported cinchona bark – both contain quinine. The Native Americans in North Carolina teach her about dauco seeds for birth control. There's willowbark tea, ginseng, and sometimes laudanum. Claire also makes marigold lotion, a burn salve of sarsaparilla and bittersweet, and a lavender salve for rashes.

When she finds a stable home at last, she begins experimenting with penicillin. Gabaldon notes:

> I occasionally get letters inquiring why Claire is not slapping moldy bread on wounds throughout the books, since surely she knows about penicillin? Well, actually, she does –

which is why she *isn't* slapping moldy bread on people. What she knows is that a) while there are quite a number of different molds in the genus Penicillium, this is far from being the only kind of mold that grows on bread; and b) there's no telling whether a particular piece of moldy bread contains any active penicillin (which is not the mold itself, by the way, but rather a substance secreted *by* the mold); and c) a piece of moldy bread is, in all likelihood, harboring all kinds of other bacterial and chemical contaminants, which it is quite possibly not a good idea to go stuffing into an open wound. Besides... rather difficult, I should think, to arrange always to have moldy bread on hand, just in case someone should cut themselves? (*Outlandish Companion* 288)

Money

The pound Scots was the unit of currency in Scotland before unification with England in 1707. It lost value after its twelfth century introduction, and, by the time of James III, the English pound sterling was valued at four pounds Scots. When James VI became King James I of England in 1603, the coinage was reformed to closely match that of England, with a value of 12 pounds Scots equal to the pound sterling. In 1707, the pound Scots was replaced by the pound sterling at a rate of 12 to 1, although the pound Scots continued to be used in Scotland as a unit of account for most of the 18th century. The 1707 currency continued until decimalization in 1971. Before decimalization, there were 20 shillings per pound and 12 pence per shilling, and thus there were 240 pence in a pound.

Thus, Jaime differentiates between pounds Scots and pounds sterling, adding to the confusion of pricing. The price on his head is ten pounds sterling, as much as a crofter makes in a year. By the terms of his mother's dowry agreement, Jaime is entitled to about twenty pounds per quarter from the MacKenzies but "Scots not sterling. About the price of half a cow" (*Outlander,* ch. 23). The magnificent wedding dress on the show oddly only costs six shillings ... though perhaps English shillings are meant or the gown is being rented. Pounds are mentioned more than coins, but Jaime and Claire occasionally make purchases with small change: pennies, shillings, and groats (four pence). A history book gives Scottish prices of the time:

> A pound of beef or mutton, or a fowl could be obtained for about a penny, a cow cost about 30 shillings, and a boll of barley or oatmeal less than 10 shillings; butter was about two pence a pound, a stone (21 lbs.) of cheese was to be got for about two shillings. The following extract, from the Old Statistical Account of Caputh, will give the reader an idea of the rate of wages, where servants were employed, of the price of provisions, and how really little need there was for actual cash: "... Salt was a shilling the bushel: little soap was used: they had no candles, instead of which they split the roots of fir trees, which, though brought 50 or 60 miles from the Highlands, were purchased for a trifle. Their clothes were of their own manufacturing. The average price of weaving ten yards of such cloth was a shilling, which was paid partly in meal and partly in money. The tailor worked for a quantity of meal, suppose 3 pecks or a firlot a-year, according to the number of the farmer's family. In the year 1735, the best ploughman was to be had for L.8 Scots (13s. 4d.) a year, and what was termed a bounty, which consisted of some articles of clothing, and might be estimated at 11s. 6d. ; in all L.1, 4s. 10d. sterling. Four years after, his wages rose to L.24 Scots, (L.2) and the bounty. Female servants received L.2 Scots, (3s. 4d.) and a bounty of a similar kind; the whole not exceeding 6s. or 7s. Some years after their wages rose to 15s. Men received for harvest work L.6 Scots, (10s.); women, L.5 Scots, (8s. 4d.). Poultry was sold at 40 pennies Scots, (3½d.) Oat-meal, bear and oats, at L.4 or L.5 Scots the boll. A horse that then cost 100 merks Scots, (L.5 : 11 : 1¾) would now cost L.25. An ox that cost L.20 Scots, (L.1 : 13 : 4) would now be worth L.8 or L.9. Beef and mutton were sold, not by weight, but by the piece; about 3s. 4d. for a leg of beef of 3½ stones; and so in proportion." (qtd. in Keltie)

Music

Folksongs and Jacobite songs appear on the show, underscoring the link with Scottish culture. Claire cleans out the surgery to "Coming through the Rye." In "Rent," she follows the waulking song to discover the hidden women's community among the villages. At episode end, Claire understands Dougal's true intentions, and the Jacobite anthem "To the Begging I Will Go" plays as he begs for funds in each village. Claire is surrounded by Scottish instruments in the score: Scottish fiddle, penny whistle, bodhrán, accordion, viola da gamba, Uilleann pipes, and of course bagpipes. Jaime and Claire's theme plays quite often, sometimes poignantly on a single penny whistle. With different end credits music each time, the final mood of the ending lingers.

In the Highlands, there were many types of working songs. "At harvest the reapers kept time by singing; at sea the boatmen did the same; and while the women were graddaning, performing the *luadhadh*, or waulking of cloth, or at any rural labour, they enlivened their work by certain airs called luinneags."

"No songs could be more happily consructed for singing during labour than those of the Highlanders, every person being able to join in them, sufficient intervals being allowed for breathing time. In a certain part of the song, the leader stops to take breath, when all the others strike in and complete the air with a chorus of words and syllables, generally without signification, but admirably adapted to give effect to the time." (Logan, qtd. in "Gaelic Music")

Peat

Almost the only fuel used by the Highlanders, not only in the early part but during the whole of last century, was peat, still used in many Highland districts, and the only fuel used in a great part of Orkney and Shetland. The cutting and preparing of the fuel, composed mainly of decayed roots of various plants, consumed a serious part of the Highlander's

> time, as it was often to be found only at a great distance from his habitation; and he had to cut not only for himself but for his land, the process itself being long and troublesome, extending from the time the sods were first cut till they were formed in a stack at the side of the farmer's or cottar's door, over five or six months; and after all, they frequently turned out but a wretched substitute for either wood or coal; often they were little else than a mass of red earth. It generally took five people to cut peats out of one spot. One cut the peats, which were placed by another on the edge of the trench from which they were cut; a third spread them on the field, while a fourth trimmed them, a fifth resting in the meantime ready to relieve the man that was cutting. (Keltie)

Jaime must cut peat in *Voyager,* while he and his men live close to freezing. Yet he insists on a modicum of civility: the storyteller who entertains them each evening must have the prime spot by the fire. Jaime always excuses himself, however, on account of his long legs. Peat digging is more of a plot point in *The Scottish Prisoner,* in which an ancient cup and its owner are unearthed from a bog.

Redcoats

> For the first time since I passed through the standing stones at Craigh na Dun, I found myself surrounded by my own people. They might be called Redcoats instead of Tommies, but they were still the British Army I had been a part of for six long years. And somehow it felt liberating to be looked upon with sympathy and respect instead of hostility and suspicion. (Episode 106)

Fighting with the Scots, then in the American Revolution, Claire finds it disconcerting to always battle the English – a vision of home to her from their accents to their flag. The Recoats fought in a bygone era, but they are still her culture.

As a soldier, Jack Randall wears a dragoon's coat, described in the books as a long-tailed deep scarlet coat with buff cuffs, gold braid, and frogging down the front (*Outlander,* ch. 3). The classic "redcoats" look was employed by the British from 1645 to 1885, and thus has become quite iconic. Adapting for the show, Ron Moore described wanting a more somber red and less of a clichéd pattern to the classic dress, so new uniforms were fashioned.

Gentlemen of the time wore large cuffs, embroidered waistcoats, full-bottomed wigs, and ruffled shirts. For the middle class, the breeches and waistcoat would be plainer brown wool, something like Lowlander Ned Gowan's. Gowan wears a neat queue and tricorn, though many middle class British men also wore the powdered wig (Nunn 80-81).

The Redcoats have a society dinner in "The Garrison Commander," as they serve fine wines with background music supplied by the composer of "Rule Britannia." They also refuse Dougal a seat at their table. His actor notes:

> It's a wonderful scene where Dougal suddenly is a fish out of water, he's not the guy in charge, he has to watch his step and he's surrounded by the enemy. And one of those enemies might be Claire. It's an interesting episode — all the shifting sands and where it leads. (Ng, "Graham McTavish")

Rent Collecting

> "In some rentals you. may see seven or eight columns of various species of rent, or more, viz., money, barley, oatmeal, sheep, lambs, butter, cheese, capons, &c. ; but every tenant does not pay all these kinds, though many of them the greatest part. What follows is a specimen taken out of a Highland rent-roll, and I do assure you it is genuine, and not the least by many." (Keltie)

These actual tallies suggest the types of goods people used to pay their tithe to the clan chief. As Ned Gowan insists, "That bag is for the laird's rents. It comes in turners and bawbees, small coins. But we also get bags of grain and cabbages. And fowl suitably trussed, I've got no argument with, even goats, although one of them ate my handkerchief last year. But I have given explicit instructions – this year that – [coughing] that we will not accept live pigs" (Episode 105).

	Scots Money.	English.	Butter. Stones. Lb. Oz.			Oatmeal. Bolls. B. P. Lip.				Muttons.
Donald mac Oil vic ille Challum ...	£3 10 4	£0 5 10½	0	3	2	0	2	1	3	⅛ and 1/16
Murdoch mac ille Christ.	5 17 6	0 9 9½	0	6	4	0	3	3	3	¼ and 1/16
Duncan mac ille Phadrick......	7 0 6	0 12 3½	0	7	8	1	0	3	0¼	¼ and ⅛

The money..£0 5 10½ Sterling.
The butter, three pounds two ounces, at 4d. per lb. 0 1 1½
Oatmeal, 2 bushels, 1 peck, 3 lippys and ¼, at 6d. per peck... 0 4 9½ and ½
Sheep, one-eighth and one-sixteenth, at 2s....................... 0 0 4¼

The yearly rent of the farm is.........................£0 12 1½ and 1/16."

There was a barter system in place – goods might travel in either direction as needed. Labor, too, was a necessary commodity.

Even in some parishes, so late as 1790, the tenant for his laird (or *master,* as he was often called) had to plough, harrow, and manure his land in spring; cut corn, cut, winnow, lead, and stack his hay in summer, as well as thatch office-houses with his own (the tenant's) turf and straw; in harvest assist to cut down the master's crop whenever called upon, to the latter's neglect of his own, and help to store it in the cornyard; in winter frequently a tenant had to thrash his master's crop, winter his cattle, and find ropes for the ploughs and for binding the cattle. Moreover, a tenant had to take his master's grain from him, see that it was properly put through all the processes necessary to convert it into meal, and return it ready for use; place his time and his horses at the laird's disposal, to buy in fuel for the latter, run a message whenever summoned to do so; in short, the condition of a tenant in the Highlands during the early part of last century, and even down to the end of it in some places, was little better than a slave. (Keltie)

When a Highlander needed anything he could not produce or make, there were few towns where he might buy provisions – The only one worthy of mention was Inverness. However, some of the landowners would stock goods the tenants might need – iron, corn, sugar, wine, brandy, tobacco, and so on. These goods the tacksman would supply to his tenants as they needed them, charging nothing at the time, but he would expect their value in cattle later on. "As the people would seldom have any idea of the real value of the goods, of course there was ample room for a dishonest tacksman to realize an enormous profit, which, we fear, was too often done" (Keltie).

A Cottage in Islay. From Pennant's *Voyage to the Hebrides*, 1774.

Silkies

"A silkie is a creature who is a man upon the land, but becomes a seal within the sea," Jaime explains (*A Breath of Snow and Ashes*, ch. 49). These ancient legends are found throughout Scotland, and also in the American Northwest. With their big, limpid eyes and playfulness, seals resemble humans enough that legends see one changing into the other. The tales all follow the same pattern:

> A story is told of an inhabitant of Unst, who, in walking on the sandy margin of a voe, saw a number of mermen and mermaids dancing by moonlight, and several seal-skins

strewed beside them on the ground. At his approach they immediately fled to secure their garbs, and, taking upon themselves the form of seals, plunged immediately into the sea. But as the Shetlander perceived that one skin lay close to his feet, he snatched it up, bore it swiftly away, and placed it in concealment. On returning to the shore he met the fairest damsel that was ever gazed upon by mortal eyes, lamenting the robbery, by which she had become an exile from her submarine friends, and a tenant of the upper world.

In love with her, he weds her, but after, she gazes unhappily out to sea, searching for her lost seal-husband. One day, their child discovers the cloak hidden away.

The husband immediately returned, learned the discovery that had taken place, ran to overtake his wife, but only arrived in time to see her transformation of shape completed – to see her, in the form of a seal, bound from the ledge of a rock into the sea. The large animal of the same kind with whom she had held a secret converse soon appeared, and evidently congratulated her, in the most tender manner, on her escape. But before she dived to unknown depths, she cast a parting glance at the wretched Shetlander, whose despairing looks excited in her breast a few transient feelings of commiseration. "Farewell!" said she to him, "and may all good attend you. I loved you very well when I resided upon earth, but I always loved my first husband much better." (*Folk-Lore and Legends of Scotland*)

There are symbolic echoes with Claire's story – she too comes from a magical place but is stolen away and married to an ordinary Scot, kept far from her home and any chance of returning. In the tales, the seal-wife always returns to the sea. Jaime appears to understand this, as he takes Claire to the stones and gives her the chance to return.

As Old Alec tells Claire at Castle Leoch, Jaime's father Brian was black-haired and "folk in the village would tell the tale to each other that Ellen MacKenzie was taken to the sea to live among the seals...Brian

Fraser was said to have hair like a silkie" (*Outlander*, ch. 24). In the comic, Murtagh spies seals as he stands on the coast awaiting Jaime's arrival from France. "Is that you, Brian? Come to welcome back your son?" he wonders.

Much later, little Germain explains that some people, upon seeing Jaime's scarred back, speculate that he was a silkie and someone cut his skin away (*A Breath of Snow and Ashes*, ch. 49). Jaime confirms this.

Tartan

1749 painting by William Mosman

Onscreen, the costume designer created unique plaids for the show – a blue and brown MacKenzie tartan and a Fraser blue-green one with a little red, with similarities indicating the family link (Podcast 107). In fact, neither is the authentic clan pattern.

The MacKenzie tartan is described in *Outlander* as a "plaid of dark green and black with a faint red and white over-check" (ch. 6), while in *Cross Stitch*, it's green and blue below. In the Scottish Tartans World Register, it is actually green and blue with a black background and a faint red and white over-check. In the books, the Fraser dress tartan is a brilliant crimson, blue and black in *Cross Stitch*, crimson and black in *Outlander* (ch. 14). Jamie's has a faint white stripe to distinguish Lallybroch from other areas (*Dragonfly in Amber*, ch. 7). The Fraser hunting tartan in the book is green

138

and brown, with a faint blue stripe (*Outlander,* ch. 6). The actual Fraser of Lovat Clan Tartan (WR391) is mostly red, with green and blue behind, or for the hunting tartan, green and blue with a thin red stripe.

Ancient dyes produced many bright colors, both for earth-toned "hunting tartans" and more dramatically colored ones for formal occasions.

> When the great improvements in the process of dyeing by means of chemistry are considered, it will appear surprising, that without any knowledge of this art, and without the substances now employed, the Highlanders should have been able, from the scanty materials which their country afforded, to produce the beautiful and lasting colours which distinguish the old Highland tartan, some specimens of which are understood still to exist, and which retain much of their original brilliancy of colouring. ("A Social History," ch. 2)

When Jaime arrives for his wedding in book and show, he's remarkably changed. Claire tells readers, "A Highlander in full regalia is an impressive sight – any Highlander, no matter how old, ill-favored, or crabbed in appearance. A tall, straight-bodied, and by no means ill-favored young Highlander at close range is breath-taking."

> His tartan was a brilliant crimson and black that blazed among the more sedate MacKenzies in their green and white. The flaming wool, fastened by a circular silver brooch, fell from his right shoulder in a graceful drape, caught by a silver-studded sword belt before continuing its sweep past neat calves clothed in woolen hose and stopping just short of the silver-buckled black leather boots. Sword, dirk, and badger-skin sporran completed the ensemble.
>
> Well over six feet tall, broad in proportion, and striking of feature, he was a far cry from the grubby horse-handler I was accustomed to – and he knew it. Making a leg in courtly fashion, he swept me a bow of impeccable grace, murmuring "Your servant, Ma'am," eyes glinting with mischief.
>
> "Oh," I said faintly. (ch. 14)

The book leaves it unclear where Jaime got a Fraser tartan, though the show sees Murtagh borrowing one from a local widow. In the comic, Murtagh had brought it originally for Jaime to wear back to Lallybroch "so ye'd not look a beggar." Dougal and Murtagh complain through the various stories that Jaime is risking being caught by the British soldiers by wearing it (though it's unclear how much the redcoats known about tartan). History records many colors and styles through accounts of clan tartan as a legitimate historical fact vary widely:

> "In dyeing and arranging the various colours of their tartans, they displayed no small art and taste, preserving at the same time the distinctive patterns (or sets, as they were called) of the different clans, tribes, families, and districts. Thus a Macdonald, a Campbell, a Mackenzie, &c., was known by his plaid; and in like manner, the Athole, Glenorchy, and other colours of different districts were easily distinguishable. Besides those general divisions, industrious housewives had patterns, distinguished by the set, superior quality, and fineness of cloth, or brightness and variety of the colours. In those times, when mutual attachment and confidence subsisted between the proprietors and occupiers of land in the Highlands, the removal of tenants, except in remarkable cases, rarely occurred; and, consequently, it was easy to preserve and perpetuate any particular set or pattern, even among the lower orders." ("A Social History," ch. 2)

> In Scotland, the circumscribing geography of mountain and glen encouraged the association of certain district setts with the dominant local clan. However, the modern idea of the Scottish tartan as a kind of "clan uniform" seems to have developed by analogy to the regimental tartans of the 1780s, after the repeal of the ban on Highland dress. Before that time, a poor Highlander wore any wool he could get his hands on, while a rich one traded with other districts or else had a sett of his own made to suit his individual taste. In any case, mixing and matching was the rule, and with the addition of the tartan waistcoat and jacket in the

> eighteenth century, the Highland squire cut a variegated
> figure indeed. (Cairney 10)

Gabaldon mentions in her notes at the end of the comic book that one plaid representing each clan is not historically accurate. As she adds, "You would see groups of related men wearing similar colors and patterns, just because they were all getting their cloth from the same local weaver." After the Rising, tartan of any sort was outlawed from 1746 to 1786. Much later, as Victoria and Albert visited, an interest in traditional clothing and clan patterns grew. "Whereupon the Lowland woolen merchants... recognized a Good Thing and swung into gear, producing 'traditional' clan tartans," Gabaldon adds. While some were reconstructed from portraits or scraps of old clothing, "traditional" tartans appear to be made up far after the fact by the Lowlanders. As Gabaldon adds, this invented tradition is far more well-known that the truth so she "had to sort of walk the line between what I knew to be historically accurate, and this very popular misconception." Costume designer Terry Dresbach adds:

> There's a huge debate – I talk to fans all the time who are still having a debate with me about the weaving of the 18th century. There's a school of thought that the really bright-colored tartans that we see today were invented by the Victorians and there were those who say no, they were always there. That's often the case where you have a lot of conflicting opinions on what was worn historically, so we made it a creative choice based on talking with Ron about the look of the show. (Friedlander)

Tea Leaves and Palmistry

Reading tea leaves is an English tradition – the drinker would leave about a teaspoon in the cup, swirl it around three times, then dump it into the saucer to judge the pattern that remained. For the Scots, tea was more expensive, and thus tea leaf reading was an occasion of great ceremony. In tea reading, a chain of small leaves indicates a journey, three small leaves close to one leaf indicate a man. A heart or broken heart suggest love or a divorce a triangle can suggest a love triangle. A dagger is danger, a circle represents a marriage or close partnership (Rakoczi, "Tea-Leaf Reading" 2586). Perhaps Mrs. Graham saw some of these images.

> CLAIRE: Well? Am I going to meet a tall, dark stranger - and take a trip across the sea?
> MRS. GRAHAM: Could be. Or could not. Everything in it's contradictory. There's a curved leaf, which indicates a journey, but it's crossed by a broken one, - which means staying put. And there are strangers there, to be sure. Several of them. And one of them's your husband, if I read the leaves aright. Show me your hand, Dear. Odd. Most hands have a likeness to them. There are patterns, you know? But this is a pattern I've not seen before.
> CLAIRE: Oh.
> MRS. GRAHAM: The large thumb, now, means that you're strong-minded and you've a will not easily crossed. And this is your mount of Venus. In a man, it means he likes the Lasses. But it is a bit different for a woman. To be polite about it, your husband isna likely to stray far from your bed. [Laughs] The lifeline's interrupted, all bits and pieces. The marriage line's divided. Means two marriages. But most divided lines are broken. Yours is forked. (Episode 101)

This of course tells Claire's future with perfect accuracy, setting the scene before she embarks on her adventure.

In Western Europe, the three most important lines in the palm are the heart line, life line, and head line. Meanwhile, the Mount of Venus represents "love, instincts, vitality, sensuality, fecundity, and bounty" (Rakoczi, "Palmistry" 1969), while there are other mounts – Jupiter is ambition, Mars is violence, and so on. "A highly developed subject in India, which was perhaps its birthplace, palmistry was known in China, Tibet, Persia, Mesopotamia, and Egypt, and flowered, more or less in its present form, in Greece" (Rakoczi, "Palmistry" 1967). It was popular throughout the world, as ancient minds found the variation of hands fascinating.

Thistles

The thistle has been a national symbol of Scotland for centuries, available on all manner of keepsakes and souvenirs. It first appeared on Scottish coins in 1470, during the reign of King James III. The Order of the Thistle, founded in 1687, was said to be a recreation of an older order. Their motto is "Nemo me impune lacessit," which translates as "No one assails me with impunity."

According to legend, during the invasion of Scotland by the Norse in 1263, the Norsemen crept up on the sleeping Scottish Clansmen under cover of darkness. To move stealthily, the Norsemen removed their footwear. However, as they crept barefoot, one stepped on a thistle and let out a shriek that alerted the Clansmen to the attack.

In the book, Jaime's wedding ring for Claire is "a wide silver band, decorated in the Highland interlace style, a small and delicate Jacobean thistle bloom carved in the center of each  link" (ch. 23). On the show, it's made from the iron key to Lallybroch. The first has a sinuous continuing pattern beautiful and everlasting, around the hardy thistles of Scottish defensiveness and survival. The other is Jaime's home, a gift he offers to Claire. These both contrast with Frank's more expensive and traditional gold band. As shown at the end of the wedding episode, Claire's contrasting rings suggest obligation to these opposite husbands and the worlds they represent. Through the books, she wears them one on each hand, as shown in that final scene. As she describes a scene with Jaime after he gives her the ring:

> He held me, arms outstretched, wrists pinioned. One hand brushed the wall, and I felt the tiny scrape of one wedding ring chiming against the stone. One ring for each hand, one silver, one gold. And the thin metal suddenly heavy as the bonds of matrimony, as though the rings were tiny shackles, fastening me spread-eagled to the bed, stretched forever between two poles, held in bondage like Prometheus on his lonely rock, divided love the vulture that tore at my heart. (ch. 23)

Tourism

> I wondered just how many tiny tea shops there were in Inverness. The High Street is lined on both sides with small cafes and tourist shops, as far as the eye can see. Once Queen Victoria had made the Highlands safe for travelers by giving her Royal approval of the place, tourists had flocked north in ever-increasing numbers. The Scots, unaccustomed to receiving anything from the South but armed invasions and political interference, had risen to the challenge magnificently.
>
> You couldn't walk more than a few feet on the main street of any Highland town without encountering a shop selling shortbread, Edinburgh rock, handkerchiefs embroidered with thistles, toy bagpipes, clan badges of cast aluminum, letter-openers shaped like claymores, coin purses shaped like sporrans (some with an anatomically correct "Scotchman" attached underneath), and an eye-jangling assortment of spurious clan tartans, adorning every conceivable object made of fabric, from caps, neckties, and serviettes down to a particularly horrid yellow "Buchanan" sett used to make men's nylon Y-front underpants.
>
> Looking over an assortment of tea towels stenciled with a wildly inaccurate depiction of the Loch Ness monster singing "Auld Lang Syne," I thought Victoria had a lot to answer for. (*Dragonfly in Amber*, ch. 3)

Sir Walter Scott romanticized Scotland for the Victorians, and Victoria herself sealed the matter by gushing after a visit there. Around this time, heavy tourism and souvenirs came into play, including the individualized clan tartan patterns. Later, Roger notes, "nothing could be less like Scotland than this mix of tourist claptrap and the bald-  faced selling of half-faked traditions. At the same time, she was right, it was uniquely Scottish; an example of the Scots' age-old talent for survival – the ability to adapt to anything, and make a profit from it" (*The Drums of Autumn,* ch. 3).

Waulking Wool

On the rent-collecting trip of the show. a group of women were supposed to invite Claire for tea and cards – Gabaldon pointed out that in the remote highlands neither of these were present, and suggested waulking wool, which was then added to the scene, complete with authentic songs from the Highland Folkways Museum (Loughlin).

Writer/producer Toni Graphia said, "The wool waulking song that Claire sings with the ladies is an old traditional wool waulking song called 'Mo Nighean Donn.' It translates to 'My brown-haired lass,' a term which Jamie later uses an endearment for Claire. We chose that song not only because it was beautiful and we loved it, but we thought it might be a nice little 'Easter egg' for the fans" (McCreary, "Outlander: The Way Out, The Gathering and Rent"). In the books, Claire learns about wool waulking somewhat later:

> "Hot piss sets the dye fast," one of the women had
> explained to me as I blinked, eyes watering, on my first
> entrance to the shed. The other women had watched at
> first, to see if I would shrink back from the work, but wool-
> waulking was no great shock, after the things I had seen
> and done in France, both in the war of 1944 and the
> hospital of 1744. Time makes very little difference to the
> basic realities of life. And smell aside, the waulking shed
> was a warm, cozy place, where the women of Lallybroch
> visited and joked between bolts of cloth, and sang together
> in the working, hands moving rhythmically across a table, or
> bare feet sinking deep into the steaming fabric as we sat on
> the floor, thrusting against a partner thrusting back.
> (*Dragonfly in Amber*, ch. 34)

As such, the both waulking scenes introduce a
delightful women's community of camaraderie and
shared labor. Waulking was a typical treatment of
fabric in the north. In the rain, Jaime thinks to
himself that "nothing shed water like the waulked
wool of a Highland plaid" (*The Scottish Prisoner,* ch.
25). As a historian of the time notes:

> They use the same tone, or a piper, when they thicken the
> newly-woven plaiding, instead of a fulling-mill. This is done
> by six or eight women sitting upon the ground, near some
> river or rivulet, in two opposite ranks. With the wet cloth
> between them; their coats are tucked up, and with their
> naked feet they strike one against another's, keeping exact
> time as above mentioned. – Burt's Letters.] (Keltie)

Weddings

> We drew apart, both a little steadier, and smiled nervously. I
> saw Dougal draw Jamie's dirk from its sheath and
> wondered why. Still looking at me, Jamie held out his right
> hand, palm up. I gasped as the point of the dirk scored
> deeply across his wrist, leaving a dark line of welling blood.
> There was not time to jerk away before my own hand was
> seized and I felt the burning slice of the blade. Swiftly,
> Dougal pressed my wrist to Jamie's and bound the two
> together with a strip of white linen.

I must have swayed a bit, because Jamie gripped my elbow with his free left hand.

"Bear up, lass," he urged softly. "It's not long now. Say the words after me." It was a short bit of Gaelic, two or three sentences. The words meant nothing to me, but I obediently repeated them after Jamie, stumbling on the slippery vowels. The linen was untied, the wounds blotted clean, and we were married.

...

"I thought it might have been that that made ye faint," he said, watching. "I should have thought to warn ye about it; I didna realize you weren't expecting it until I saw your face."

"What was it, exactly?" I asked, trying to tuck in the ends of the cloth.

"It's a bit pagan, but it's customary hereabouts to have a blood vow, along with the regular marriage service. Some priests won't have it, but I don't suppose this one was likely to object to anything. He looked almost as scared as I felt," he said, smiling.

"A blood vow? What do the words mean?"

Jamie took my right hand and gently tucked in the last end of the makeshift bandage.

"It rhymes, more or less, when ye say it in English. It says:

'Ye are Blood of my Blood, and Bone of my Bone.
I give ye my Body, that we Two might be One.
I give ye my Spirit, 'til our Life shall be Done.' "

He shrugged. "About the same as the regular vows, just a bit more... ah, primitive." (*Outlander,* ch. 15)

Gabaldon appears to have created this vow herself. Ceremonies of the time did mix Pagan and Christian traditions, but for the wedding ceremony, a Catholic church service seems to have been the preference. Only the superstitions of how to proceed to church and the celebrations before and after seem to have older roots.

Traditionally, the bans were posted weeks in advance (Dougal uses bribery instead). A day of games and practical jokes preceded the festivities. On the wedding day, a party of bagpipers would escort the bridegroom and his friends on morning

147

calls, until the entire village had joined the procession. The bride made a similar round among her friends. After separate dinners, the parties advanced on the priest's house or the church "so that, with streamers flying, pipers playing, the constant firing from all sides, and the shouts of the young men, the whole had the appearance of a military army passing, with all the noise of warfare, through a hostile country" ("A Social History," ch. 7). After the ceremony, came a great celebration with fiddlers and pipers and feasting.

When a priest was not available, young people would handfast, making a solemn pledge for a year and a day and then beginning their lives together until a priest might arrive. This is a Celtic ceremony dating from at least the Middle Ages. Jaime insists on wedding Claire properly, with a priest and a church, and a fine gown for the bride. On the show, a scavenger hunt ensues, as he insists his friends must also have a ring made (in the book, he uses his father's as a temporary measure) and find him a Fraser plaid as well. In the episode, Jaime insists he'll wed "in a way that would make my mother proud." All this preparation emphasizes his determination to marry Claire permanently – he emphasizes several times in the books that he believes they'll spend eternity together in heaven. As such, a pagan handfast will not do.

Witchcraft
Gabaldon comments:

> I wanted to have a witch trial, but looking into it, I could see that the last witch trial in Scotland took place in 1722. So I was telling my husband that I'd really like a witch trial, but it doesn't fit. He looked at me and said, "You start right off with a book in which you expect people to believe that Stonehenge is a time machine, and you're worried that your witches are 20 years too late?" [Laughs] So I did stretch that point. I figured that possibly this witch trial was an ad

hoc affair that didn't make it into the record. That's the only place where I can remember I deliberately moved something that I knew was not quite there. (DeLuca)

In the 17th and 18th centuries, Scotland executed over 4,000 alleged witches, possibly more than any other country. The last of these took place in 1728. King James VI had a terrible fear of witches, dating back to a storm that nearly sank his ship. He assembled mass hunts to eliminate any possible threat, and explained his methods in a book titled *Daemonologie*. In 1735, a new law overturned the hysteria of witchcraft: it proclaimed anyone found practicing guilty of being a vagrant or con artist, but not of consorting with the devil. Condemned for witchcraft, Claire comments that she "had thought it a practice common to the seventeenth century, not this one. On the other hand, I thought wryly, Cranesmuir was not exactly a hotbed of civilization" (ch. 25).

With her knowledge of the future as well as germs, contagion, and other medical information Claire runs a serious risk of condemnation for witchcraft. This is foreshadowed in episode three, when she fantasizes about telling Mrs. Fitz she comes from the future and when she mixes an herbal antidote for a child believed to be possessed by the devil. Historically, all outspoken women who defied the church and patriarchy risked arrest, torture, and death for witchcraft. "I've yet to see the auld woman believes in witches, nor the young one, neither. It's men think there must be ill-wishes and magic in women, when it's only the natural way of the creatures," Murtagh notes (*Outlander,* ch. 31).

The trial itself is a mix of flimsy circumstantial evidence proving that Claire uses herbs and has different beliefs from the villagers. One man insists, "'Tis right ye are to call her witch, my lords! Wi' my own eyes I saw this woman call up a waterhorse from the waters of the Evil Loch, to do her bidding! A great fearsome creature, sirs, tall as a pine tree, wi' a neck like a great blue snake, an' eyes big as apples, wi' a look in them as would steal the soul from a man" (ch. 25). As Ned Gowan explains it, "the worst of these trials take place in a climate of hysteria, when the soundness of evidence may be disregarded for the sake of satisfyin' blood-hunger" (ch. 25).

"Ye still dinna understand, do ye?" Geillis tells Claire. "They mean to kill us. And it doesna matter much what the charge is, or what the evidence shows. We'll burn, all the same" (ch. 25).

While the meaning of the term is debatable (modern wiccans for instance worship pagan gods but not the devil), Geillis self-identifies as a witch. This is the origin of her name, as well. Gabaldon writes in her FAQ that "There's a 'real' female witch (late 16th century) named Geilis Duncane in *Daemonologie,* a treatise on witches by King James of Scotland (later James I of England." She adds:

> Geillis Duncan was a conscious choice, though. ... I liked the name – and had also seen a passing reference in one of Dorothy Dunnett's novels (which I much admire) to Geillis as "a witch's name." Little did I realize that the woman who bore it in *Outlander* had also chosen it deliberately, and for the same reason! She so informed me, sometime later, when she chose to reveal her real name – or what I must presently assume to be her real name – Gillian Edgars. (*Outlandish Companion* 137)

As revealed in her diary, Geillis has chosen this name for herself because of its heritage. She writes, "This is the grimoire of the witch, Geillis. It is a witch's name, and I take it for my own; what I was born does not matter, only what I will make of myself, only what I will become" (*The Drums of Autumn,* ch. 40). Geillis also calls Claire another witch, insisting the ability to use the stones is a hereditary power. Citing the infamous *Witch's*

Hammer, she adds, "Some people can leave their bodies and travel miles away....Other people see them out wandering, and recognize them, and ye can bloody prove they were really tucked up safe in bed at the time ... some people have stigmata ye can see and touch – I've seen one. But not everybody. Only certain people" (*Voyager,* ch. 60). Claire and Geillis both seem to be among their number.

Women's Clothes

Claire wears an arisaid, "a warm tartan shawl," on occasion. Geillis has a far more interesting one, as it's gauzy like a filmy Greek tunic. As Dresbach notes in her blog (August 2014):

> Geillis is wearing an Arisaid, a Scottish woman's plaid. It is purely an ornamental garment, obviously, as it is made of sheer fabric, and clasped at the shoulder with a Lovers Eye brooch.
>
> I used a man's leather belt, with a jeweled buckle, at her waist, as both a nod to Highland men, and as a way to provide contrast to her delicate, translucent costume. Feminine, but dangerous.

The painted eye of the brooch belongs to Charles Stuart. Geillis can thus parade her loyalties around Castle Leoch without anyone understanding. It also carries a tinge of the occult.

Women's garments are shown in the dressing scene of episode two, as Mrs. Fitz dresses Claire in all the layers of the time – chemise, wool petticoats, bum roll, bodice, and outer garments. Moore comments that it took twenty minutes to dress Claire for each take, but considers the scene vital in showing "Part of her transformation from a twentieth-century woman to an eighteenth-century woman" ("Inside the World," 102). The book shows Claire receiving two brown overskirts, a pale yellow bodice, and a pair of yellow leather slippers with no differentiation between left foot and right foot (*Outlander*, ch. 6).

> Till marriage, or till they arrived at a certain age, they went with the head bare, the hair being tied with bandages or some slight ornament, after which they wore a head-dress, called the curch, made of linen, which was tied under the chin; but when a woman lost her virtue and character she was obliged to wear a cap, and never afterwards to appear bare-headed. Martin's observations on the dress of the females of the western islands may be taken as giving a pretty correct idea of that worn by those of the Highlands. "The women wore sleeves of scarlet cloth, closed at the end as men's vests, with gold lace round them, having plate buttons set with fine stones. The head-dress was a fine kerchief of linen, start about the head. The plaid was tied before on the breast, with a buckle of silver or brass, according to the quality of the person. I have seen some of the former of one hundred merks value; the whole curiously engraved with various animals. There was a lesser buckle which was worn in the middle of the larger. It had in the centre a large piece of crystal. or some finer stone, of a lesser size." The plaid, which, with the exception of a few stripes of red, black or blue, was white, reached from the neck almost to the feet; it was plaited, and was tied round the waist by a belt of leather, studded with small pieces of silver. ("A Social History," ch. 2)

These garments appear in the books, though Claire generally refuses to wear headscarves or the dreaded Betsy-Ross-style mob cap. This last had "a puffed up crown worn high on the head and a frilled border" (Nunn 94). On the show, Claire has collars of fur or knitted bits at neck and sleeves. She and other women wear the fichu, or kerchief, around the neck.

Corsets were fundamental; "they were laced either at the center front or back; front lacing might form a feature of the design of the dress or gown, or be covered by a decorated stomacher" (Nunn 84). Claire wears this last in early episodes. French paniers, a type of whalebone hoop skirt, appeared fully circular in 1709 or so, and were soon flattened "reaching a fantastic width by the middle of the century in spite of male ridicule and opposition" (Nunn 86). They were obligatory for full court dress in England as late as 1820. Claire wears these under her wedding dress to give it the distinctive shape, and will likely don them again at the French court.

Terry Dresbach designs a stunning wedding gown for Claire on the show: silver and white with a pattern of acorns and oak leaves, a symbol of strength and fidelity in a marriage (Podcast, 107). "It was as if I stepped outside on a cloudy day and suddenly the sun came out," Jaime says sweetly. Glittering mica and silver embroidery indeed set the dress shining. As Dresbach describes the wedding gown in further detail, she notes:

> I had really had gotten directions from Ron that this needed to be a fairy tale; a beautiful moment that cements and entire book series and an entire television series. It's a series about a marriage and the foundation is this moment, but it's two people who didn't know each other and who didn't plan to be married and are being forced into this. And yet, we had to make it so impossibly romantic that we could believe that our heroine and our hero could just fall in love so completely at that moment.
>
> So, I wanted a dress that would be incredible in candlelight. And in the 18th century, metallic fabrics were made with actual metal woven into the fabrics. When you put them in a room filled with candles, they just glow. They're quite remarkable. There are museum exhibits that actually show the dresses in candlelight so you can see the effect...But that dress took us – we calculated it out at about, I think if one person had done it, it would have been about 3,000 hours' worth of work. We did a technique of embroidery that was done hundreds of years and is no longer used. The embroidery is done with metal.
> (Friedlander)

When Claire weds Jamie in the books, she wears a "low-necked gown of heavy cream-colored satin, with a separate bodice that buttoned with dozens of tiny cloth-covered buttons, each embroidered with a gold fleur-de-lis. The neckline and the belled sleeves were heavily ruched with lace" (*Outlander,* ch. 14).

After Claire arrives at Lallybroch, Jenny and Mrs. Crook make her a dress for important occasions of "primrose yellow silk" that fits her like a glove, "with deep folds rolling back over the shoulders and falling behind in panels that flowed into the luxuriant drape of the full skirt" (*Outlander,* ch. 31). They sew stays into the upper bodice, as Claire refuses to wear a real corset.

Caricature of 18th Century hairstyles

Sun Feasts, Fire Feasts, and Holidays

Frank describes "the ancient feasts ... Hogmanay, that's New Year's, Midsummer Day, Beltane, and All Hallows. Druids, Beaker Folk, early Picts, everybody kept the sun feats and the fire feasts" (*Outlander* 12). Frank comments on the show that Yule and Halloween come from the earlier Pagan festivals, appropriated by the church. "In druidical times four great fire-festivals were held at different periods of the year; namely, on the eve of May day, or Spring; on Midsummer's eve; on Hallowe'en, hence our Hallowe'en bonfires; and at Yule, the mid-winter feast" (Guthrie, ch. 1). The fire feasts were celebrated with great bonfires, possibly once used for human sacrifice. Ancient peoples believed they could stop the sun's decline by lighting these as the year turned dark (Henderson 587). Claire and Roger speculate that the solar festivals may correspond with ley lines and earth's orbit:

> The observation that sites seem to be "open" on the dates that correspond to the sun feasts and fire feasts of the ancient world (or at least more open than at other times) may – if this hypothesis is right – have something to do with the gravitational pull of the sun and moon. This seems reasonable, given that those bodies really do affect the behavior of the earth with respect to tides, weather, and the like – why not time vortices, too, after all?
> (*An Echo in the Bone,* ch. 46)

Other sacred days, the solstices and equinoxes, roughly correspond with the "quarter days" on which servants were hired, rents due or leases begun: Lady Day (March 25th), Midsummer (June 24th), Michaelmas (September 29th) and Christmas (December 25th). Claire and Jaime celebrate one of these occasions at Lallybroch. Here are the pagan festivals and solstices, still celebrated in some cultures today:

- Imbolc ~ Spring Festival of the Goddess Brigit, held on Feb 1st or 2nd
- Alban Eilir ~ Spring Equinox also known as The Light of the Earth or Ostara, Mar 21st/22nd
- Beltane ~ Celtic Fertility and Fire Festival, May 1st
- Litha or Midsummer's Eve ~ Summer Solstice on or around June 21st/22nd
- Lughnassadh or Lammas ~ First Harvest, July 31st/Aug 1st
- Alban Elfed or Mabon ~ Autumn Equinox and Second Harvest, Sept 21st/22nd
- Samhain ~ Day of the Dead, October 31st/November 1st
- Alban Arthuan or Yule ~ Winter Solstice and Festival of Light, December 21st

Imbolc

Imbolc was a festival of the mysteries of motherhood, carried out by the priestesses. It was at the start of the lambing season, derived from the Gaelic "oimelc" meaning "ewes milk." Thus blessings of lambs appear with the holiday. It was dedicated to Brigid the triple goddess. Brigid's snake emerges from the earth to test the weather (the origin of Groundhog Day), and in many places the first crocuses begin to appear, heralding spring. As this holiday merged into the Christianized Saint Brigit's day, girls in white dresses would carry corn dollies called Brideo'gas or Bridie dolls door to door and call out, "Let Bride come in!" Special cakes, or bannocks, were presented to the image.

Alban Eilir/Easter and St. Columba's Day

The Celtic Saint Columba has his festival on Maundy Thursday, the Thursday before Easter. A bannock of oats or rye was baked on a special fire built of oak, yew or rowan (all sacred woods). On the holiday, the children would divide it, seeking the silver coin within.

Di-Domhnuich-caisg, Easter Sunday, featured dyed eggs, and special blessings for lambs, to protect them from evil. Carefully saved food – eggs, milk, and flour – was made into pancakes, which could be totally consumed without waste. A remnant from earlier times, the holiday celebrates the Saxon goddess Ostarra or Estre, the personification of east and the spring. Claire travels to the future around this time, in a moment of loss, sacrifice and resurrection that parallels Easter itself.

Beltane

Beltane may come from "beautiful fire" in the Latin or the god Ba'al (Henderson 83). It was a celebration of an ancient pagan pastoral festival, "a time of year when witches and fairies were said to be out in great numbers" (Henderson 83). Sacrifices were made to Belinus, with cakes of oatmeal replacing animals. On the holiday, oatmeal cakes were served, or sometimes rolled down a hillside on May Day – whoever's cake broke would have bad luck.

Some believe the bonfires come from bone-fires, named for human sacrifices. Since fire symbolized the life-giving sun, many would leap through the flames to cure bad luck or barenness. Farmers drove their livestock between two fires to ensure prosperity.

157

In book one, Claire watches the circle dancers celebrate the season of sun and warmth, then travels into the past on Beltane. In her youth, she symbolically seeks her true love on this the festival of new beginnings and passion. Young, life-filled Brianna travels on this sacred day as well.

Midsummer

"On Midsummer's Eve in Scotland, the sun hangs in the sky with the moon. Summer solstice, the feast of Litha, Alban Eilir. Nearly midnight, and the light was dim and milky white, but light nonetheless" (*The Drums of Autumn,* ch. 33). On this day, all natural waters were said to have medicinal power, so many would bathe in them. This became St. John's Day after the Christian influence, dedicated to John the Baptist and his springs. The herbs and bonfires were renamed after him as well (Henderson 586).

Sometimes straw was attached to a wheel and burned. It would be rolled downhill to extinguish in the river, a symbol for the "falling" sun. The word "Solstice" comes from the Latin words, *sol sistere* – "sun stand still," on this the longest day of the year. Commemorating this time of courtship and fertility rituals, Roger travels through the stones, seeking his lover.

Lughnassadh

This comes from the name of the ancient sun god Lugh and the Celtic *nasadh,* commemoration. (Henderson 522). This was the warm summer of the year, a time for games, feasts, and magic shows. Originally connected with oats, wheat or barley, it later extended to cover the potato harvest when that vegetable became a staple crop. The family went out to the field dressed in their best clothes to hail the god of the harvest. The father took up a handful of grain and circled it sunwise three times about his head, with the salutation *Iolach Buan.*

After Christianity, the festival was called Lammas, probably from Loaf-mass or Lamb-mass since loaves and livestock were blessed in church. This was also a Quarter-day, when rent was due.

In the Highlands, people sprinkled blood to ward off evil. Funerals were common at this time, in the tradition of mourning Lugh. Finally, people would carry effigies in procession and bury them in symbolic graves with eulogies and poems. The year king may have died at this time in Celtic prehistory.

Alban Elfed

For the ancient Druids, the fall equinox was *Alban Elfed,* a time of balance. The Catholic correspondence is Michaelmas, the feast of St. Michael, the patron saint of the sea. On September 29, the Michael's Cake is served on a lambskin and moistened with sheep's milk. The day is spent in horseracing along the shore to honor the saint of the sea, frequently on borrowed horses with whips made of seaweed. The *Ceilidh,* or festival dance, follows long into the night.

Samhain

> This is the first of the feasts of the dead. Long before Christ and his resurrection, on the night of Samhain, the souls of heroes rose from their graves. They are rare, these heroes. Who is born when the stars are right? Not all who are born to it have the courage to take hold of the power that is their right. (*The Drums of Autumn,* ch. 32)

Samhain (pronounced sah-win) is an Irish word meaning "summer's end." This was the Celtic new year, a time of transition between old and new (Henderson 788). The souls who had died the previous year would come visit when the gates to the underworld opened. Bobbing for apples likely is part of the holiday because of its timing with the Roman festival to the goddess Pomona. All fires were extinguished and relit from the main bonfire. Special lanterns from gourds or turnips symbolized the sun's energy and encouraged reincarnation as the days grew shorter.

Today in Scotland and Ireland, some extinguish the peat fires and relight them from the bonfires on the hilltops. Using pumpkins for lanterns is of course the American variation for Samhain's descendent, Halloween. All Saint's Day is the Christian derivation (Henderson 788).

On the show, Claire travels on Samhain, after watching the circle dancers and getting her palm read. The ghost of Jaime also appears to her this night, a time when the beloved dead could reappear. While filming had to take place in winter, this change from Beltane in the books also allows a whiff of ghostly creepiness as the locals spill cockerel blood and dance among the stones (Episode Podcasts 101).

In the autumn of Claire's life, she travels once again, seeking the ghosts of her past. She notes:

> THE DARK CAME DOWN on All Hallows' Eve. We went to sleep to the sound of howling wind and pelting rain, and woke on the Feast of All Saints to whiteness and large soft flakes falling down and down in absolute silence. There is no more perfect stillness than the solitude in the heart of a snowstorm. This is the thin time, when the beloved dead draw near. The world turns inward, and the chilling air grows thick with dreams and mystery. (*A Breath of Snow and Ashes*, ch. 38)

On November first, Brianna and Roger return through the stones with their children, after a tearful parting. In the future, their long-dead loved ones continue to watch over them, emphasizing the ghostly connection. Gabaldon's short story "A Leaf on the Wind of All Hallows" sees Roger questing for his long-dead father, also on this festival.

VALERIE ESTELLE FRANKEL

Yule

This winter festival of light and renewal may come from 'Iul' meaning 'wheel,' as the wheel of the year concludes. Brianna, Jem, and Mandy find Roger in the past around this time of year, as they celebrate being reunited in love and renewal. On the show, Claire and Frank run to the standing stones at this time, but their mutual hope is suddenly dashed by the redcoats ("Both Sides Now").

Christmas was a minor celebration in the Highlands, with New Year as the larger festival. In England, Jaime witnesses a great celebration during *The Scottish Prisoner*.

> They'd brought down the Yule log to the house that afternoon, all the household taking part, the women bundled to the eyebrows, the men ruddy, flushed with the labor, staggering, singing, dragging the monstrous log with ropes, its rough skin packed with snow, a great furrow left where it passed, the snow plowed high on either side.
> Willie rode atop the log, screeching with excitement, clinging to the rope. Once back at the house, Isobel had tried to teach him to sing "Good King Wenceslas," but it was beyond him, and he dashed to and fro, into everything, until his grandmother declared that he would drive her to distraction and told Peggy to take him to the stable to help Jamie and Crusoe bring in the fresh-cut branches of pine and fir. (ch. 43)

Hogmanay (New Year's Eve)

Many debate the name's origin: The Scandinavian *hugunott,* "slaughter night," may be a source, as may the Greek *hagi mene,* "holy month" (Henderson 367).

> A more likely explanation is that it came from an old French epiphany carol that began, "L'Homme est né, Troi rois là" ("A Man is born, Three Kings are there") which became "Hogmanay, Troleray" in Scotland. Yet another is that it came from hagg, an old Yorkshire word for a wood or coppice. A "hagman" was a woodcutter, and "Hogmanay" was what he called out when he appealed to his customers for some kind of seasonal tip or remembrance. (Henderson 368).

Children would go to the wealthy houses, requesting an oatmeal cake and recite songs or rhymes. At each house, the Hogmanay Poem, *Duan Challuinn,* would be recited. In the ceremony known as *coullin* or *calluinn,* young Highlands men would wear cowhides and run around the house for fertility. "This was believed to protect them from diseases and other misfortunes, particularly witchcraft, during the coming year. They also gathered Hogmanay gifts, primarily food, in a bag made of animal skin"

(Henderson 369).

Workers would bring the last sheaf called the *calliagh* (from the Gaelic meaning hag, old woman, or witch) to the house. The *calliagh* was a pre-Christian crone goddess, meant to bring wisdom at the close of the year. At the end of the harvest, the *calliagh* was placed around the neck of the master or mistress of the house, who was then obligated to put on a feast. Blowing horns, beating drums, and firing shotguns are common on Hogmanay, most likely to frighten off evil spirits.

> The first visitor of the New Year was an important omen of what the coming year would be like. Many Scottish people living in rural areas still observe the old custom of opening all the doors in the house a minute or two before midnight on December 31 and leaving them open until the clocks have struck the hour – a practice known as "Letting the old year out and the new year in." The first visitor to cross the threshold after the stroke of midnight was known as a "first-foot." It was considered good luck if this first-footer was male, dark-haired, and did not have flat feet. (Henderson 368).

As Claire tells it:

> Custom held that the most fortunate "firstfoot" on a Hogmanay was a tall and handsome dark-haired man; to welcome one as the first visitor across the threshold after midnight brought good fortune to the house for the coming year. ...A red-haired man, though, was frightful ill luck as a firstfoot, and Jamie had been consigned to his study.
> ...
> A firstfoot was to bring gifts to the house: an egg, a faggot of wood, a bit of salt – and a bit of whisky, thus insuring that the household would not lack for necessities during the coming year.
> ...
> There is nothing special about January the first, save the meaning we give to it. The ancients celebrated a new year at Imbolc, at the beginning of February, when the winter slackens and the light begins to come back – or the date of the spring equinox, when the world lies in balance between

the powers of dark and light. And yet I stood there in the dark, listening to the sound of the cat chewing and slobbering in the cupboard, and felt the power of the earth shift and stir beneath my feet as the year – or something – prepared to change. There was noise and the sense of a crowd nearby, and yet I stood alone, while the feeling rose through me, hummed in my blood. (*The Fiery Cross,* ch. 35)

VALERIE ESTELLE FRANKEL

Time Travel and Magic Guide

Traveling the Stones

Gabaldon explains:

> If you're going to write time travel stories, you have to sort of figure out how does time travel work in this particular universe that I'm dealing with.
>
> There are lines of geomagnetic force running through the Earth's crust, and most of the time these run in opposing directions – forward and backward. In some places they deviate and will cross each other, and when that happens, you kind of get a geomagnetic mess going in all different directions. I call these vertices.
>
> Essentially, it could be possible to have something like this nexus of crossing lines to create a little time vortex. And if you could have a person whose sensibility to geomagnetism is sufficiently advanced so that they can not only detect this but enter into it in some way, then you have a plausible way of time travel.
>
> So if prehistoric people noticed that every so often when people crossed that particular patch of grass, they disappeared, it would cause considerable consternation, and they might think it worthwhile marking that spot. So that might be the reason why the stones are there, and why they're set up the way they are, as in, "People tended to disappear on the winter solstice when they step over here, so don't do that!" (DeLuca)

Regarding the stone circles, the show gives a clue. "The stones gather the powers and give it focus like a glass," Mrs. Graham explains ("Both Sides Now"). As Geillis describes the stones in her writings: "Something lies here older than man, and the stones keep its power. The old spells speak of 'the lines of the earth', and the power that flows through them. The purpose of the stones is to do with those lines, I am sure. But do the stones warp the lines of power, or are they only markers? ... Sacrifice is required" (*The Drums of Autumn,* ch. 40).

In her notes, Geillis records all the disappearances and all the people who failed to pass through –

likely destroyed by not having protection or not fixing on a destination. Jewels can protect travelers, as can gold and silver. There are also more disturbing forms of power. Geillis notes, "The auld ones – they always used the blood. That and the fire. They built great wicker cages, filled wi' their captives, and set them alight in the circles" (*Voyager*, ch. 60). She claims the sacrifice allows a greater range and a bit of control on travel. She makes her sacrifice by stabbing her husband and setting him on fire, though she also uses the time of year. When asked how Geillis went through the stones in 1968 but arrived much earlier, Gabaldon replies:

> We don't yet know everything there is to know about the intricacies of time travel (though I imagine we'll find out more as Claire, Roger, and Brianna put their heads together and compare experiences and make deductions). Remember that Gillian Edgars [as she once was known] used a blood sacrifice when going through the door for the first time – it may have been that she was right about this giving her power, and thus traveled farther – or the sacrifice may have been irrelevant, but some other factor was operating. (*Outlandish Companion* 383)

At one point, Claire approaches the standing stones and feels that they're sealed to her – it's not a sun feast yet. Gabaldon adds, "If the passage through the stones stands widest open on sun feasts and fire feasts, it is presumably more or less 'closed' in the periods between. As Geillis/Gillian's notes indicate, an attempted passage at the wrong time can be fatal" (*Outlandish Companion* 368).

Two hundred years appears to be the default in fairy travel (at least, according to Gabaldon). It's not clear why Claire travels from 1946 to 1743 precisely, though calendar inaccuracies and changes might account for it (and for plot purposes only those years would work – World War II has ended and the Jacobite Uprising just beginning). If travelers are drawn to loved ones, fans have speculated that it was the presence of Frank's ancestor near the stones – as close to Frank as possible. A few have also theorized that Jaime's ghost from the first episode may be providing an anchor of a sort.

There appears to be a genetic component, as specifically Claire, Geillis, their descendants and very few others can travel. The gene also appears to be dominant given how well it's lasted through the centuries. Gold and silver seem to offer some protection (Brianna has the gold-and-pearl necklace plus a silver bracelet. Claire has her two rings on all but the first journey.) Geillis insists faceted gemstones provide the most control and protection. Gabaldon adds that her gemstone hypothesis is "presumably on the basis of ancient writings she later discovered" (*Outlandish Companion* 333). According to other travelers' lore, two hundred years is standard, but "it could be changed by use of gemstones, or of blood" ("The Space Between" 234).

In the comic adaptation of the first book, Geillis's partner Kenneth follows her from 1967. He sacrifices a rabbit to open the stones and a deer to close them. As he notes, it "seemed to serve." Kenneth's blood sacrifice of the rabbit takes him from 1968 to 1743 – 225 years. He sneaks into Claire's room the night before her wedding to find out where she's from. (She's dead drunk, but her favorite expression alerts Kenneth that she's from the time of Roosevelt.) Meanwhile, Murtagh sees him and decides he's a "deamhan" or demon trying to capture Jaime's soul by using Claire. Murtagh nearly kills Claire that night, but stops himself because Jaime loves her.

Geillis is of course plotting to have the MacKenzies fight for Prince Charles – she's certain Colum will die soon and Dougal, whom she controls with her seductive wiles, will be regent for young Hamish. However, if Jaime takes over, she'll have no influence. Thus she orders Kenneth to kill Jaime while he's out hunting with the Duke of Sandringham. After the witch trial, Kenneth follows Jaime and Claire, to kill him and bring her to Geillis, but Murtagh kills Kenneth in defense of Jaime. This backstory reveals little – Kenneth is *not* the famed Brhan Seer of that name, Gabaldon has said on her website. He uses Geillis's methods but has no additional wisdom to share. And it was already clear that she and her friends appear to be demons.

Later travelers discover they can hear the standing stones making sounds, and those with the power to travel can hear ordinary gemstones as well. In France, Count St. Germain notes, "The stones. They make a buzzing sound, most of the time. If it's close to a fire-feast or sun-feast, though, they begin to sing" ("The Space Between" 237).

Roger uncovers this spell in Geillis's notes:

> I raise my athame to the North,
> where is the home of my power,
> To the West,
> where is the hearth of my soul,
> To the South,
> where is the seat of friendship and refuge,
> To the East,
> from whence rises the sun.
>
> Then lay I my blade on the altar
> I have made.
> I sit down amid three flames.
>
> Three points define a plane, and
> I am fixed.
> Four points box the earth and mine
> is the fullness thereof.
> Five is the number of protection;
> let no demon hinder me.
> My left hand is wreathed in gold,
> and holds the power of the sun.
> My right hand is sheathed in silver,
> and the moon reigns serene.

I begin.

Garnets rest in love about my neck.
I will be faithful. (*Drums in Autumn,* ch. 40)

Roger notes that the four directions are traditional Celtic. "As for the blade, the altar, and the flames, it's straight witchcraft" (*The Drums of Autumn,* ch. 40). Nonetheless, the mention of silver, gold, and gemstones also seems significant for travel.

More travelers appear through the story, as well as other portals.

There was such a group in the Caribbean, another in the Northeast, near the Canadian border. Another in the Southwestern desert – Arizona, he thought, and down through Mexico. Northern Britain and the coast of France, as far as the tip of the Iberian peninsula. Probably more, but that's all he'd mentioned. Not all of the portals were marked with stone circles, though those in places where people had lived for a long time tended to be. (*A Breath of Snow and Ashes,* ch. 55)

Brianna and Roger, speculating in a book they write together, suggest the locations and sun feasts are both tied to ley lines.

Hypothesis 1: That the time passages/vortices/whatever the bloody hell they are/ are caused by or occur at the crossing of ley lines. (Defined here as lines of geomagnetic force, rather the folkloric definition of straight map lines drawn between ancient structures like hill forts, henges, or places of ancient worship, like saints' pools. Supposition is that folkloric lines may be identical or parallel with geomagnetic lines, but no hard evidence to this effect.)

...

Hypothesis 2: That entering a time vortex with a gemstone (preferably faceted, vide remarks made by Geillis Duncan to this effect) offers some protection to the traveler in terms of physical effect.

Query: why facets? We used mostly unfaceted ones coming back through Ocracoke, and we know of other travelers using plain unfaceted ones.

Speculation: Joe Abernathy told me about one of his patients, an archaeologist who told him about some study done on standing stones up in Orkney, where they discovered that the stones have interesting tonal qualities; if you strike them with wooden sticks or other stones, you get a kind of musical note. Any kind of crystal – and all gems have a crystalline interior structure – has a characteristic vibration when struck; that's how quartz watches work.

So what if the crystal you carry has vibrations that respond to – or stimulate, for that matter – vibrations in the standing stones nearby? And if they did what might be the physical effect? D.B.K.*

...

Hypothesis 3: That traveling with a gemstone allows one better control in choosing where/when to emerge. (*Written in My Own Heart's Blood*, ch. 96)

Other Magical Powers

Several travelers manage to go to times not two hundred years in the past or to "steer." Likewise, Master Raymond helps the Count de Saint Germain to travel forward in time. Raymond himself is a mystery – while he exists in 1740s Paris, he also seems to visit 1960s America. In Paris he's called "a wizard" or "Maitre Raymond," and he has skills with gems, herbs, and slight of hand (though none of these in itself can be categorized as miraculous). In a more dramatic moment, he heals Claire by touching her and manipulating her aura. Claire glows blue him and to St. Germain, indicating her birthright and power to travel ("The Space Between," 216).

Far in the past (in fact, 1739, before Jaime meets Claire), Roger encounters a healer, Dr. Hector McEwan, who can sense how his body should work and change it with his thoughts. When he does, Roger glows blue. In Latin, the man bursts out, "*Cognosco te!*" (I know you) and acknowledges he's also a time traveler from 1841 (*Written in My Own Heart's Blood,* ch. 37). He shares skill at healing and auras with Master Raymond, though it's unclear whether he's studied with the man or has learned

170

similar skills through practice.

Time traveler siblings Jem and Amanda reveal they can hear each other's minds as well as their parents' – this is not mind reading, per se, but rather a sense of where the other person is. This skill may be linked with dowsing and ley lines (as they dowse for a person) and appears genetic. Performing a difficult surgery on Lord John's nephew Henry, Claire hears of a dowser who can feel abnormalities inside the body – she may develop a similar power herself in later books. Jaime has visions of the future suggesting he has second sight, and Jenny and Brianna show traces as well, suggesting it's a Highland gift, not a time traveler's gift.

History

History of the Stuart Kings

Under Henry VIII, much of England converted to Protestantism. For a time, his Catholic daughter Queen Mary flooded the country with purges and acts of violence. Following this, his Protestant daughter Elizabeth I managed a compromise, leading with her father's religion but refusing to persecute Catholics. When Elizabeth died without heirs, her Protestant cousin James VI of Scotland (and thereafter James I of England) assumed the throne of both countries, thus uniting them. He was succeeded by Charles I, Charles II, and then James II. Therein began a great split.

While his brother Charles II was monarch, James converted from Protestantism to Catholicism in 1668. The king began to express interest in doing the same, but Parliament, in outrage, passed acts that only Anglicans could hold positions of office, especially the throne. Catholics were denied the right to vote and sit in the Westminster Parliament for

James II

over a century; they were also denied commissions in the army, and the monarch was forbidden to be Catholic or to marry a Catholic. Soon, James took the throne and attempted to play peacemaker, refusing to persecute rebellious radicals such as Quakers.

In June 1688, his only son, James Edward Francis Stewart, was born. His birth displaced the boy's older sister, the Protestant Mary and her husband William of Orange in Holland, suggesting to the people that the Catholic dynasty would continue. Several high placed Tories invited William of Orange to invade. This he did in October that same year in what became known as the "Glorious Revolution." William and Mary took the throne in 1689 and James fled into exile with his son. He died in France in 1701. The people who remained loyal and fought to restore James and his line became known as the Jacobites.

William and Mary took the throne jointly, with William ruling alone after Mary died in 1694, until his death in 1702. After, Mary's younger sister, Anne took the throne. On May 1, 1707, under the Acts of Union, Anne's two kingdoms of England and Scotland united as a single sovereign state, the United Kingdom of Great Britain. In the wake of this, James Francis Edward Stuart attempted to land in Scotland with French aid but the invasion fleet was chased away by British ships.

Despite this early failure, a great deal of underground support for the exiled Stewarts flourished, thanks to those angry about the provisions of the 1707 Union.

Though she endured seventeen pregnancies by her husband, Prince George of Denmark, Anne lost all her children quite young and was the last monarch of the House of Stuart. When her one son to survive infancy died, the Act of Settlement 1701

VALERIE ESTELLE FRANKEL

proclaimed the heir to be her second cousin George of the House of Hanover (later George I), a descendant of the Stuarts through his grandmother, Elizabeth, daughter of James I.

When Queen Anne died in 1714, many thought James II's son James Edward Francis Stewart, a more direct heir with loud support, should be offered the throne. Meanwhile, his antagonists called him the "Old Pretender" (while his son Bonnie Prince Charlie was the Young Pretender).

In 1715, the First Jacobite Rebellion commenced. John Erskine, Earl of Mar, raised the Jacobite standard in Braemar and drew huge support. With twelve thousand men, he took Inverness, and soon conquered as far as Perth. Meanwhile, the second Duke of Argyll, John Campbell, assembled four thousand pro-Hanovarians. In France, James Edward Francis Stewart appealed to Catholic allies like the Pope as well as France and Spain for aid in restoring a Catholic Britain. The English Jacobites rose as well but were defeated by English reinforcements at the Battle of Preston, on November 12-14.

Meanwhile up North, the Jacobite army outnumbered Argyll's forces three-to-one and Mar marched on Stirling Castle. On November 13, the Battle of Sheriffmuir was fought to a draw, but after, the Jacobites numbered 4,000 men, compared to Argyll's 1,000. When the French and Spanish heard Mar had failed to destroy the enemy, they lost faith and withdrew support. On December 22, James landed in Scotland at Peterhead, but by the time he reached the Jacobite army on January 9, 1716, little army remained and he lacked all foreign support. He fled back to France and the rebellion failed.

The French and British were clashing, on opposite sides of a European war, and in 1744, France offered James's energetic son a fleet with

7,000 soldiers to help him take the British throne. However, many of the ships were lost in a storm and wrecked on the Dunkirk coast.

In 1745, Charles Edward Stuart, commonly known as "Bonnie Prince Charlie," sailed to Scotland and raised the Jacobite standard at Glenfinnan in the Scottish Highlands. Instead of the thousands of French troops, he had only brought seven followers. Nonetheless, his enthusiasm and charm won him a great deal of support, and many romanticized their "Bonnie Prince." Many Highland clans supported him, and they began marching South.

They won a victory at Prestonpans and occupied Edinburgh. While the Jacobite army rode into England as far south as Derby, they were soon defeated and more importantly, failed to have many of the English join their ranks.

Reluctantly, Prince Charlie retreated north to Inverness, though George II was reportedly packing his valuables in daily expectancy of an attack on London. Heading away from their target, Charlie found himself losing disheartened men, until he was left with only about four thousand fighting troops. The Duke of Cumberland, now leading the Hanovarian army of nine thousand, was implacable and well-armed with cannon and cavalry. On a moor near Inverness on April 16, 1746, the Battle of Culloden saw the clans slaughtered, and Charles Edward Stuart fled. The Duke of Cumberland famously slaughtered the Jacobite survivors and rounded up more, killing the locals for weeks following. The second rebellion had failed.

Prince Charlie fled through the heather, running from crofter's hut to island, barely ahead of the English. The Highlanders hid him, rather than turning him over for the substantial reward. At last, Charles reached France. "His life grew increasingly wretched, again he was a wanderer – no longer pursued by redcoats but beset by spies and informers" (Linklater 148). He wed Princess Louise of Stolberg and had a daughter Charlotte by his Scottish mistress Clementina Walkinshaw, but finally died, heartbroken, in 1788 after a stroke. "His life – all of it that amounted to anything – was lived in Scotland between the 25th of July 1745 and the 19th of September 1746" (Linklater 149).

Prince Charlie, with Order of the Garter and the Jacobite blue bonnet with a white cockade by William Mosman

To further punish Scotland, Parliament issued imperious Acts to destroy the clans' soul as well as their way of life. The heritable jurisdictions were dissolved with many estates claimed by the crown. The playing of bagpipes, the wearing of tartans and Highland dress were forbidden for all except government troops, and the possession of weapons was restricted. The exact wording of the act follows:

> "That from and after the First Day of August 1747, no man or boy within that part of Great Britain called Scotland, other than such as shall be employed as Officers and Soldiers of His Majesty's Forces, shall on any pretext whatsoever,

wear or put on the clothes, commonly called Highland clothes (that is to say) the Plaid, Philabeg, or little kilt, Trowes, Shoulder-Belts, or any part whatever of what peculiarly belongs to the Highland Garb; and that no tartan or party-coloured plaid or stuff shall be used for Great coats or upper coats, and if any such person shall presume after the first said day of August, to wear or put on the aforesaid garments or any part of them, every person so offending.... shall be liable to be transported to any of His Majesty's plantations beyond the seas, there to remain for the space of seven years."

Historical Figures

Now, Mother Hildegarde was a real historical person, though she lived in the 12th century, rather than the 18th. Likewise, M. Forez, the hangman of *DRAGONFLY IN AMBER*, was a real public hangman in the Paris of the 18th century. Bonnie Prince Charlie and many of the Jacobite lords were naturally real people {cough}, as were Benedict Arnold, General Burgoyne, and George III. But most of the historical people are treated as historical people; i.e., I haven't messed around with the facts of their lives or personalities – with one minor exception. Simon, Lord Lovat, aka "The Old Fox" was certainly a real person, and a very colorful one, too. I made no alterations to his life or persona, save for grafting an illegitimate and totally fictional branch onto his family tree by making him Jamie Fraser's grandfather. Given Old Simon's persona as recorded, attributing an illegitimate son to him would in no way be character assassination. (FAQ)

Claire meets Bonnie Prince Charlie and the King of France. Later in America, she and Jaime encounter figures of the Revolutionary War. She's startled and disturbed when she meets someone famous, whose final fate she knows:

Mr. Smith laughed and said that, in fact, Mr. Benedict Arnold is a colonel in the Continental army, and a very gallant officer he is, too. The boxes are bound for delivery to his sister, Miss Hannah Arnold, who minds both his three small sons and his importing and dry-goods store in Connecticut, while he is about the business of the war.

I must say that a goose walked across my grave when I heard that. I've met men whose history I knew before – and at least one of those I knew to carry a doom with him. You don't get used to the feeling, though. I looked at those boxes and wondered – ought I to write to Miss Hannah? Get off the ship in New Haven and go to see her? And tell her what, exactly?

All our experience to date suggests that there is absolutely nothing I could do to alter what's going to happen. And looking at the situation objectively, I don't see any way ... and yet. And yet!

And yet, I've come close to so many people whose actions have a noticeable effect, whether or not they end up making history as such. How can it not be so? your father says. Everyone's actions have some effect upon the future. And plainly he's right. And yet, to brush so close to a name like Benedict Arnold gives one a right turn, as Captain Roberts is fond of saying. (No doubt a situation that gave one a left turn would be very shocking indeed.) (*An Echo in the Bone,* ch. 25).

Charles Edward Stuart/Bonnie Prince Charlie

"Bonnie Prince Charlie," I said softly to myself, looking over my reflection in the large pier glass. He was here, now, in the same city, perhaps not too far away. What would he be like? I could think of him only in terms of his usual historical portrait, which showed a handsome, slightly effeminate youth of sixteen or so, with soft pink lips and powdered hair, in the fashion of the times. Or the imagined paintings, showing a more robust version of the same thing, brandishing a broadsword as he stepped out of a boat onto the shore of Scotland.

A Scotland he would ruin and lay waste in the effort to reclaim it for his father and himself. Doomed to failure, he would attract enough support to cleave the country, and lead his followers through civil war to a bloody end on the field of Culloden. Then he would flee back to safety in France, but the retribution of his enemies would be exacted upon those he left behind. (*Dragonfly in Amber,* ch. 7)

In fact, Prince Charlie "ran off so fast at the end of the battle that he left behind his sterling silver picnic set" (*Dragonfly in Amber,* ch 4). He's gone down in history as a beloved romantic figure, but not a great conqueror or successful leader.

> "D'ye know why they called him 'Prince Charlie'?" Roger asked. "English people always think it was a nickname, showing how much his men loved him."
>
> "It wasn't?"
>
> Roger shook his head. "No, indeed. His men called him Prince Tcharlach" – he spelled it carefully – "which is the Gaelic for Charles. Tcharlach mac Seamus, 'Charles, son of James.' Very formal and respectful indeed. It's only that Tcharlach in Gaelic sounds the hell of a lot like 'Charlie' in English."
>
> Brianna grinned. "So he never was 'Bonnie Prince Charlie'?"
>
> "Not then." Roger shrugged. "Now he is, of course. One of those little historical mistakes that get passed on for fact. There are a lot of them." (*Dragonfly in Amber,* ch 4)

The Bonnie Prince, figurehead and leader of the Second Jacobite Uprising, appears in the second book, when Jaime and Claire visit France. His first appearance is, in Claire's mind, less than impressive:

> The visitor caught his foot on the sill and landed clumsily, sprawling on the floor. He scrambled up at once, though, and bowed to me, snatching off his slouch hat.
>
> "Madame," he said, in thickly accented French. "I must beg your pardon, I arrive so without ceremony. I intrude, but it is of necessity that I call upon my friend James at such an unsocial hour."
>
> He was a sturdy, good-looking lad, with thick, light-brown hair curling loose upon his shoulders, and a fair face, cheeks flushed red with cold and exertion. His nose was running slightly, and he wiped it with the back of his wrapped hand, wincing slightly as he did so.
>
> Jamie, both eyebrows raised, bowed politely to the visitor.
>
> "My house is at your service, Your Highness," he said, with a glance that took in the general disorder of the visitor's attire. His stock was undone and hung loosely around his neck, half his buttons were done up awry, and the flies of his breeches flopped partially open. I saw Jamie

frown slightly at this, and he moved unobtrusively in front of the boy, to screen me from the indelicate sight.

…

Feeling the chill of the room seep through gown and robe, I crawled back into bed and drew the quilts up under my chin. So this was Prince Charles! Bonnie enough, to be

sure; at least to look at. He seemed very young – much younger than Jamie, though I knew Jamie was only a year or two older. His Highness did have considerable charm of manner, though, and quite a bit of self-important dignity, despite his disordered dress. Was that really enough to take him to Scotland, at the head of an army of restoration? As I drifted off, I wondered exactly what the heir to the throne of Scotland had been doing, wandering over the Paris rooftops in the middle of the night, with a monkey bite on one hand. (*Dragonfly in Amber,* 168-169)

In fact, the prince has been visiting his married mistress and her monkey has bitten him severely on the hand. With this ridiculous scene, Gabaldon introduces Charles Stuart, calling him "a person about whom much has been written – most of it glamorized, inaccurate, and wildly misleading" (*Outlandish Companion* 138). As she adds, "The chief difficulty in these instances is to do justice to the actions and personality of the dead (or at least to treat them with such respect as they seem to deserve), while still ruthlessly subverting them to the purposes of the story" (*Outlandish Companion* 138).

While the incident of the rooftop excursion and the monkey bite (in *Dragonfly in Amber*) is invented, the affair with Louise de Rohan was not. The affair of the cargo ship full of port is invented; the negotiations with Manzetti the banker and the purchase of the Dutch broadswords were not. (*Outlandish Companion* 138)

Charles was born in Rome on 31 December 1720. He lived in Rome and Bologna, a guest of the Pope along with his mother, Maria Clementina Sobieska, and his father, James Francis Edward Stuart, the son of the deposed Catholic monarch, James II. Charles had numerous affairs, famously with his married cousin Marie Louise de La Tour d'Auvergne, As an eyewitness account describes him:

> In person Charles appeared to great advantage. His figure and presence are described by Mr Home, an eye-witness, as not ill-suited to his lofty pretensions. He was in the bloom of youth, tall and handsome, and of a fair and ruddy complexion. His face, which in its contour exhibited a perfect oval, was remarkable for the regularity of its features. His forehead was full and high, and characteristic of his family. His eyes, which were large, and of a light blue colour, were shaded by beautifully arched eye-brows, and his nose, which was finely formed, approached nearer to the Roman than the Grecian model. A pointed chin, and a mouth rather small, gave him, however, rather an effeminate appearance; but on the whole, his exterior was extremely prepossessing, and his deportment was so graceful and winning, that few persons could resist his attractions. The dress which he wore on the present occasion was also calculated to set off the graces of his person to the greatest advantage in the eyes of the vulgar. He wore a light-coloured peruke, with his hair combed over the front. This was surmounted by a blue velvet bonnet, encircled with a band of gold lace, and ornamented at top with a Jacobite badge, a white satin cockade. He wore a tartan short coat, and on his breast the star of the order of St Andrews. Instead of a plaid, which would have covered the star, he wore a blue sash wrought with gold. His small clothes were of red velvet. To complete his costume, he wore a pair of military boots, and a silver-hilted broadsword. (Bell, ch. 20)

In December 1743, Charles's father named him Prince Regent, and thus a ruler in fact, Charles accepted money from France and reached Scotland on 23 July 1745. The French fleet he'd expected never arrived, and he was only able to gather some soldiers from the Highland Clans. He took Edinburgh and some of England, before a final defeat on Culloden Field. He finally fled through the Highlands and returned to France, never to return. Abroad, he had several affairs and a number of children, but neither they nor his brother, the next heir, ever took the throne.

Charles was beloved for his romantic image – the handsome young prince evading the English troops and hiding in the heather – but he was an ineffective general. By taking bad advice and insisting on a straightforward battle on the moors instead of guerrilla warfare, he lost his cause. In France, after, several politicians considered an alliance but were put off by his ineffective manner and refused to support him further. As Claire comments:

> But do you know what's really funny? That poor, silly sot and his greedy, stupid helpers; and the foolish, honorable men who couldn't bring themselves to turn back…they had the one tiny virtue among them; they believed. And the odd thing is, that that's all that's endured of them – all the silliness, the incompetence, the cowardice and drunken vainglory; that's all gone. All that's left now of Charles Stuart and his men is the glory that they sought for and never found. (*Dragonfly in Amber*, ch. 47)

Lord Charles Grey

Major General Lord Charles Grey (1729-1807), a real historical figure, is briefly grafted onto Lord John Grey's family tree in *An Echo in the Bone*. This man's eldest son is the namesake of Earl Grey tea.

> One of Howe's commanders, Major General Lord Charles Grey – a distant cousin of Grey's – attacked the Americans at Paoli at night, with orders to his troops to remove the flints from their muskets. This prevented discovery from the accidental discharge of a weapon, but also obliged the men to use bayonets. A number of Americans were bayoneted in their beds, their tents burned, a hundred or so made captive

– and Howe marched into the city of Philadelphia, triumphant, on September 21.

Grey watched them, rank upon rank of redcoats, marching to drum music, from the porch of Mrs. Woodcock's house. Dottie had feared that the rebels, forced to abandon the city, might fire the houses or kill their British prisoners outright. (ch. 71)

Clan Fraser and Simon Fraser, Lord Lovat

The name Fraser originated in Anjou, France (originally de Freselière). In Lothian, the name became Fraissier (strawberry bearer) with the flower of the *fraisse* or strawberry as part of their armorial bearings. The book *Clans and Families of Scotland: A History of the Scottish Tartan* by Alexander Fulton elaborates:

> The first known Fraser in Scotland was Simon Fraser, who in about 1160 donated the church of Keith to Kelso Abbey. The name came from the lordship of La Fraseliere in Anjou, and a descendant of Simon Fraser, Sir Gilbert Fraser, established the main line of the family in about 1250 at Touch-Fraser, Stirlingshire. His direct descendant, Alexander Fraser (d. 1332), was knighted by King Robert I (the Bruce) before the Battle of Bannockburn in 1314. After the battle he married the Bruce's sister, Lady Mary - who had been strung up in a cage for four years by King Edward I of England in reprisal for the Bruce's coronation - and he was later Chamberlain of Scotland. Their grandson gained the lands of Philorth in Buchan by his marriage in 1375.

Sir Alexander Fraser (1537-1623), 8th Laird of Philorth, founded Fraserburgh and built Fraserburgh Castle. The 9th Laird married the daughter and heiress of Lord Saltoun; their son succeeded to the Saltoun title and chiefship of Clan Fraser together.

The Frasers of Lovat (one of whom is reportedly Jaime's grandfather) are descended from Sir Alexander Fraser's younger brother, Simon, and each chief of Clan Fraser of Lovat is known as MacShimi (son of Simon). When Jaime's distant cousin Simon Fraser dies, Jaime thus addresses him.

Simon Fraser (1667 - 1747), 11th Lord Lovat and Jaime's grandfather, had several sons historically, but his bastard son, Jaime's father, was added to his family tree by Gabaldon. He was quite a famous figure in Scottish history, before and during the Rising. Gabaldon reports:

> With Simon Fraser, Lord Lovat (the Old Fox), I played somewhat more loosely. Though I saddled him with a thoroughly fictitious illegitimate grandson, the general depiction of his personality as wily, sensual, and politically astute is based soundly on a good many accounts of his life and behavior – even though those accounts vary considerably in detail and reliability. At the same time, the prostatitis that served as his ostensible excuse for not joining Charles Stuart was purely my invention. (*Outlandish Companion* 138)

> The memoirs and letters of the day abound with anecdotes respecting his villanies, his hardihood, and his wit, which did not forsake him even on the scaffold. The incidents of his life would be thought highly coloured if they had been narrated in a romance. He alternated between the lowest depths of poverty and misery, and the summit of high rank and immense power. He had been by turns an outlaw from his own country, a proscribed traitor, a prisoner for years in the Bastille, in France, a Roman Catholic priest, a peer, and the chief of one of the most powerful Highland clans. (Taylor)

In this, he sounds somewhat like Jaime himself, who is imprisoned many times, including in the Bastille, and considers becoming a monk and clan leader.

On the death of Lord Lovat, Simon Fraser of Beaufort laid claim to the Lovat title and estates. The late lord, however, had left a daughter only eleven years of age, and Simon schemed to strengthen his claim by marrying the young girl. As his character was notoriously bad, her mother and friends were strongly opposed to the match, and another was planned for her, with the Master of Saltoun, son of the 11th Lord Saltoun, head of the senior line of the Frasers, and descendent of Sir Alexander Fraser.

Meanwhile, Simon had tried to kidnap the girl, conducting her out of the house one winter night in such haste that she is said to have gone barefooted. After recovering her, Lord Saltoun and Lord Mungo Murray, the dowager Lady Lovat's brother, tried to take her to safety in the north. But Simon and a body of his clansmen seized Lord Saltoun, the father of the intended bridegroom, and carried them as prisoners to the house of Fanellan.

Simon advanced on the castle of his intended, with five hundred men and his prisoners alongside. The heiress, however, had by this time been transferred to a secure place of refuge in her uncle's country of Athole, where she was afterwards married to Mr. Mackenzie of Prestonhall, who assumed the designation of Fraser of Fraserdale. With the heiress having escaped him, Simon found her mother, the dowager Lady Lovat, in the family mansion and brutally married her by force "while the bagpipes played in the apartment adjacent to her bedroom to drown her screams. Her attendant found her, next morning, speechless and apparently out of her senses."

In September, 1698, he and nineteen of his chief accomplices were tried for rape and treason and condemned to death. Simon fled to England or possibly the continent to avoid charges and was in consequence outlawed. However, a year later, he was living in his own country again "to the contempt of all authority and justice." Upon levying Lady Lovat's tenants, he was excommunicated and fled to France. There he pledged his allegiance to the Jacobite cause and returned to Scotland with a colonel's commission in the Jacobite service.

After he got caught lying too many times, he

returned to Paris only to be arrested and sent to the Bastille. He passed ten years in prison, partly in the castle of Angoulême, partly in Saumur, where he is alleged to have taken priest's orders. He finally escaped with a kinsman's assistance and reached England, but was arrested in London, only freed when the Earl of Sutherland, John Forbes of Culloden, and some other gentlemen offered bail for him.

When the Jacobite insurrection of 1715 broke out, Simon Fraser set out for Scotland and ordered all the Fraser troops to abandon the Jacobite cause. By leading them from battle, he received a royal pardon for his crimes. His adversary, Mackenzie of Fraserdale, fled the country before he could be arrested for his part in the failed rebellion, and his forfeited estate of Lovat was bestowed on Simon by a grant from the Crown on 23rd August, 1716.

Simon was twice married after his return to Scotland in 1715, first to Margaret, fourth daughter of Ludovic Grant of Grant, by whom he had two sons, Simon and Alexander, and two daughters. His wife died in 1729, and in 1733 he married Primrose, niece of the Duke of Argyll, who bore him one son, Archibald. This marriage was rocky to put it mildly – Lovat locked her in a tower, and she had some difficulty in finally escaping.

> Having thus obtained the family titles, property, and chieftainship, Simon had full scope to indulge his evil passions, and to pursue his own selfish ends. 'He was indeed,' says Sir Walter Scott, 'a most singular person, such as could only have arisen in a time and situation where there was a mixture of savage and civilized life. The wild and desperate passions of his youth were now matured into a character at once bold, cautious, and crafty; loving command, yet full of flattery and dissimulation, and accomplished in all points of policy excepting that which is proverbially considered the best, he was at all times profuse of oaths and protestations, but chiefly, as was observed of

Charles IX of France, when he had determined in his own mind to infringe them." (Taylor)

Lovat was put in charge of a company of the Black Watch, organized at this time to put down robbery and theft, which afforded him the means, without suspicion, of training his clansmen in arms. He was the first of the seven influential Jacobite leaders who invited Bonnie Prince Charlie to invade in 1740; but when he finally arrived in 1745 without troops, money or arms, Lovat hesitated, excusing himself from joining the campaign by reason of age and infirmities.

With his usual double-dealing, he continued to profess to President Forbes his determination to support King George II, who ruled England at the time. On the 23rd of August he wrote:

> Your lordship judges right when you believe that no hardship, or ill-usage that I meet with, can alter or diminish my zeal and attachment for his Majesty's person and Government. I am as ready this day (as far as I am able) to serve the King and Government as I was in the year 1715, when I had the good fortune to serve the King in suppressing that great Rebellion, more than any one of my rank in the island of Britain. But my clan and I have been so neglected these many years past, that I have not twelve stand of arms in my country, though I thank God I could bring twelve hundred good men to the field for the King's service, if I had arms and other accoutrements for them. Therefore, my good lord, I earnestly entreat that, as you wish that I would do good service to the Government on this critical occasion, you may order immediately a thousand stand of arms to be delivered to me and my clan at Inverness. (Taylor)

Under heavy pressure from Prince Charlie, he finally sent his clan to join the rebels, under his nineteen-year-old son, Simon, Master of Lovat, while he himself remained at home. To the English, he insisted his son had disobeyed him and joined against orders. The English, however, were unconvinced, and when Prince Charlie fled, Lovat did so as well.

He was discovered by a detachment from the garrison of Fort William (where the fictitious Jonathan Randall sends for Claire). He was promptly imprisoned in the Tower of London, though his trial did not take place until the 9th of March, 1747, to afford time to collect evidence. Though he defended himself with wily wrangling over the seven-day trial, he was found guilty and sentenced to death.

When sentence was pronounced upon him he said, 'Farewell, my lords, we shall not all meet again in the same place. I am sure of that.' ... In curious keeping with his character, he remarked in the words of an old Scottish adage, 'The more mischief the better sport.' He professed to die in the Roman Catholic religion, and, after spending a short time in devotion, he repeated the well-known line of Horace, singularly inappropriate to his character and fate: 'Dulce et decorum est pro patria mori,' and laying his head upon the block, he received the fatal blow with unabated courage. (Taylor)

It must be admitted that he managed to save his lands for his son, a fact Jaime admires on several occasions. In the early books, this son, Jaime's half-uncle, appears, but doesn't play a large role. Gabaldon adds:

> Young Simon (the Young Fox) is also a real historical character, about whom a fair amount is known. Most of the actions for which he was known, though, took place in the latter years of his life – a span that falls outside the constraints of the story so far. However, I rather think we haven't seen the last of Young Simon. (*Outlandish Companion* 139)

Fraser is the 23rd most common name in Scotland – but is one of the 6th most common around Inverness. The motto of the clan is "All my hope is God," though Jaime's motto "I am ready" might belong to his smaller family branch. The Fraser coat of arms is azure: three silver strawberries quartered with three antique crowns gules (red).

Gabaldon chose to attach Jaime to the Lord Simon's family because of a quote she found in *The Prince in the Heather,* reproduced in her third book, *Voyager,* as Roger researches from "a white volume, entitled *The Prince in the Heather*":

> 'Following the battle, eighteen wounded Jacobite officers took refuge in the farmhouse near the moor. Here they lay in pain, their wounds untended, for two days. At the end of that time, they were taken out and shot. One man, a Fraser of the Master of Lovat's regiment, escaped the slaughter. The rest are buried at the edge of the domestic park. (Linklater 14)

Gabaldon knew she wanted Jaime to escape Culloden, so making him a Fraser related to the Master of Lovat seemed the logical choice. This excerpt, from a real history book, links the research taking place in the books with that of reality, emphasizing the connection with living history.

Mother Hildegarde

Mother Hildegarde runs the Couvent des Anges – the Convent of the Angels in Paris. She and the nuns operate L'Hopital des Anges, where Claire finds a place. Mother Hildegarde reappears in book three, as well as in the short story "The Space Between." Gabaldon describes the difficulty naming her and the surprising coincidence of the name:

> Mother Hildegarde was another who named herself. Having decided upon her profession and avocation, I set out to write her, and found the name "Hildegarde" being insistently shoved under my nose. Nonsense, I said, I don't think Hildegarde is even a French name. Surely she ought to be Berthe or Matilde or something. But no, it was "Hildegarde" and nothing else. Fine, I said, already used to

argumentative characters. Have it your way, Hildegarde.
We can always change it later, if the copy editor tells me it
isn't French. A year or two later, I found myself in London,
in a store called Past Times, which specializes in the
reproduction of art and artifacts from ... er ... past times.
They had a rack of musical recordings, compositions dating
from the tenth century to the twentieth, performed on period
instruments and according to the performance conditions
appropriate to the time of the composition. Finding this
interesting, I thumbed through the rack, only to find a tape
of songs composed by ... one Mother Hildegarde.
Hildegarde von Bingen, to be exact (as I recall, my actual
exclamation at the time was, "Ha! So it *isn't* French!"). A
mystic, a composer – and an abbess – from the twelfth
century. But Mother Hildegarde, nonetheless. (*Outlandish
Companion* 137)

Flora MacDonald

After the disastrous Battle of Culloden, Flora
MacDonald determined to assist Bonnie Prince
Charlie. The prince persuaded her to let him play her
Irish maidservant "Betty Burke," complete with frock
and bonnet. Together they sailed to the Isle of Skye
on June 27, 1746. As Charles's secretary retells the
story:

> Miss Macdonald was about twenty-four years of age, of the
> middle size, and to the attractions of a handsome figure and
> great vivacity, she added the more estimable mental
> qualities of good sense, blandness of temper, and
> humanity. ...As O'Neil recollected that Miss Macdonald had
> expressed, in his presence, an earnest desire to see the
> prince, and had offered to do any thing in her power to
> protect him, it occurred to O'Neil that, on the present
> occasion, she might render an essential service to the
> prince if, after dressing him in female attire, she would pass
> him off as he maid-servant, and carry him to Skye. O'Neil at
> once proposed his plan to the young lady; but she thought it
> fantastical and dangerous, and at first positively refused to
> engage in it. As parties of the Macdonald, Macleod, and
> Campbell militia were roaming over the island of South Uist
> in quest of Charles, as no person could leave the island
> without a passport, and as there was a guard posted at

every ferry, and the channel between Uist and Skye
covered with ships of war, the utter hopelessness of such
an attempt appeared evident. Bent, however, upon his plan,
O'Neil was resolved to try what effect Charles's own
presence would have upon the young lady in inducing her
to yield, and he accordingly introduced her to the prince.
Miss Macdonald was so strongly impressed with his critical
and forlorn state, that, on seeing Charles, she almost
instantly consented to conduct him to Skye. She describes
the prince at this time as in a bad state of health; and
though of a thin and weak habit of body, and greatly worn
out by fatigue, yet exhibiting a cheerfulness, magnanimity,
and fortitude, which those only who saw him could have
credited. (Bell, ch. 84)

Charles traveled in "a flowered linen gown, a light-coloured quilted petticoat, a white apron, and a mantle of dun camlet made after the Irish fashion, with a hood" (Bell, ch. 84). Over the next few days, they traveled overland to Portree, until the prince might sail for the island of Raasay and a ship to take him back to France. Upon parting from her, the Prince gave Flora a locket with his portrait, saying, "I hope, madam, that we may meet in St James's yet" but she never saw him again.

Flora was arrested and imprisoned in the Tower of London but was released in 1747 under a general amnesty. She married Allan Macdonald of Kingsburgh and emigrated with him to North Carolina (where she meets Gabaldon's characters). Her husband fought for the loyalists in the American Revolution, like many Scots, and he and his wife were exiled to Nova Scotia as a result. They finally returned to Skye. Flora died at Kingsburgh on Skye in 1790, in the same bed in which Bonnie Prince Charlie (and Samuel Johnson) had slept.

Samuel Johnson described her as "a woman of middle stature, soft features, elegant manners and gentle presence" and added, "Her name will be mentioned in history, and if courage and fidelity be virtues, mentioned with honour."

George VI

King George VI visits troops during the Battle of Britain, Sept. 26, 1940.

Claire mentions in *An Echo in the Bone* that she once met King George VI in World War II. "He came to Pembroke Hospital, to visit the soldiers there. He came and spoke separately to us – the nurses and doctors. He was a quiet man, very dignified, but warm in his manner. I couldn't tell you a thing that he said. But it was ... remarkably inspiring. Just that he was there, you know" (ch. 21).

Jenny Cameron

As the Battle of Culloden approaches, Claire discovers the legendary Jenny Cameron of Glendessary has arrived and eagerly writes to her.

> It was she who had led three hundred Cameron clansmen across the mountains to join Prince Charles, when he had raised his banner at Glenfinnan on the coast. Her brother Hugh, arriving home belatedly and hearing what had happened, had ridden posthaste to Glenfinnan to take the chieftain's place at the head of his men, but Jenny had declined to go home and miss the fun. She had thoroughly enjoyed the brief stop in Edinburgh, where Charles received

193

the plaudits of his loyal subjects, but she had been equally
willing to accompany her Prince on his way to battle.
(*Dragonfly in Amber*, ch. 36)

Historically, she is a romanticized figure, much like
Charles himself, as she's pictured riding with skirts
blowing and sword aloft to defend her chosen king.
In the books a practical woman, Jenny Cameron
quickly organizes medical facilities for Claire,
agreeing that they should do everything possible to
prepare for battle.

King Louis XV of France

"Louis XV was – obviously – a real historical person.
The descriptions of his levee and Court customs, his
sexual behavior (exchanging political patronage for
the favors of the wives of those seeking advantage),
and his deep interest in the occult were taken from
various historical sources," Gabaldon explains
(*Outlandish Companion* 139). For those trying to put
him in context, Louis XIII ruled at the time of *The
Three Musketeers*, his son Louis XIV was the Sun
King (ruling during *The Man in the Iron Mask*), and
the latter's great-grandson Louis XV had the famous
mistress Madame de Pompadour (though not during
Dragonfly in Amber). Louis XVI, the former king's
grandson, and his wife Marie Antoinette were
executed in the French revolution.

Louis XV was born on February 15, 1710. His
grandfather and father died young, leaving him to
inherit his great-grandfather's title. On September 1,
1715, Louis XIV died, leaving a Regency Council to
supervise his great-grandson's throne. With excellent
tutors, Louis XV learned a great deal, setting the
stage to later create departments in physics (1769)
and mechanics (1773) at the Collège de France. He
was reportedly "a noble and elegant figure, regular
features, a reserved but subtle and witty style of
conversation, an exquisite politeness, and a very

great care of his person" (Saint-Armand 86). He was second cousin once removed to Bonnie Prince Charlie and a supporter of the Jacobite cause.

Louis ruled for many years, and took a series of mistresses in the 1730s after his wife only bore a few children. The most famous mistress was the Marquise de Pompadour, who met Louis XV in February 1745. In 1740, Louis became embroiled in the War of the Austrian Succession after the death of Emperor Charles VI. France supported King Frederick the Great of Prussia and his claim over the emperor's daughter's. The war lasted seven years with dramatic sieges and lavish expenditures. Louis was in favor of Charles Stuart and a Catholic king of England, but had limited resources, busy as he was with Austria. Claire meets him at his palace at Versailles:

> I had forgotten the red dress; His Majesty halted directly in front of me and bowed extravagantly, hand over his waist.
> "Chère Madame!" he said. "We are enchanted!"
> I heard a deep intake of breath from Jamie, and then he stepped forward and bowed to the King.
> "May I present my wife, Your Majesty – my lady Broch Tuarach." He rose and stepped back. Attracted by a quick flutter of Jamie's fingers, I stared at him for a moment of incomprehension, before suddenly realizing that he was signaling me to curtsy.
> I dipped automatically, struggling to keep my eyes on the floor and wondering where I would look when I bobbed up again. Madame Nesle de la Tourelle was standing just behind Louis, watching the introduction with a slightly bored look on her face. Gossip said that "Nesle" was Louis's current favorite. She was, in current vogue, wearing a gown cut below both breasts, with a bit of supercedent gauze which was clearly meant for the sake of fashion, as it couldn't possibly function for either warmth or concealment. (*Dragonfly in Amber*, ch. 9)

He observes the custom of kings before and after him – on his waking, the room was filled with petitioners and others receiving a mark of special favor by being invited to attend. Those of the highest rank were entrusted to bring him his shirt or slippers, shave him, and so forth. Jaime is honored by attending the *lever* in the books, though he finds it a ridiculous custom.

Louis XV grew depressed and suspicious in his later days. "One might say he had a dual reign, with two policies and two diplomacies, a private treasury and an occult government in opposition to the official one" (Saint-Armand 82). Louis invites Claire to view his shadow cabinet and render judgments there, showing her the secret side of his reign. He died shortly before the American Revolution, and his grandson, Louis XVI, ruled during the upheaval of this and the French Revolution.

Clan MacKenzie

The Mackenzies were of Celtic stock rather than Norman, descending from the 12th century Gilleoin of the Aird. The first castle to be associated with the Mackenzie clan is Eilean Donan on Loch Duich in Kintail, and there were additional strongholds at Kilcoy Castle and Brahan Castle. The Mackenzies of Tarbat had their seat at Castle Leod, in Strathpeffer in the 17th century.

It's said that the name comes from the first chief's grandson, Coinneach MacChoinneach (Kenneth son of Kenneth), 3rd Baron of Kintail, whose name was corrupted in English into Mackenzie. "MacCoinneach" means "Son of the Fair One," and indeed, MacKenzies are described as beautiful as well as charming.

The Clan Mackenzie fought on the side of King Robert the Bruce at the Battle of Inverurie (1308) and Chief Ian Mackenzie led five hundred Mackenzies at the Battle of Bannockburn in 1314, defeating the English. In 1362, Murdoch Mackenzie was granted lands of Kintail by King David II. By good marriages and further service to King James IV, the clan extended further, with extended lands in the northwest and eventually parts of the island of Lewis. In 1715, Clan MacKenzie supported the Jacobites during the uprisings, while their longtime rival, the Munros, took the English side. In the battles of the time, the MacKenzie Jacobite garrison at Inverness soon surrendered to Simon Fraser of Lovat. The MacKenzie leader's position as Earl of Seaforth ended abruptly in 1716, with the political position going to the Munros.

Here Gabaldon inserts her fictional branch:

> Jacob MacKenzie, who is thought to have been related to the MacKenzies of Torridon, seized Castle Leoch by force in 1690, while the previous Lord of that Castle, Donald MacKenzie of Leoch, was absent from home. Donald died under mysterious circumstances before he could return to defend his property, and Jacob married Donald's widow, Anne Grant, the daughter of Malcolm Grant of Glenmoriston, by whom he had issue (*Outlandish Companion*)

These are Colum and Dougal, Ellen (mother of Jaime), Flora and Janet (no issue, though Jaime's sister is named for the latter), and Jocasta (married to three successive Camerons, seen in book four).

Historically, in the Second Jacobite Rising, George Mackenzie, 3rd Earl of Cromartie, led the Clan MacKenzie to victory at the Battle of Falkirk (1746). The MacKenzies then went on to lay waste to the lands of the Clan Munro and Clan Sutherland. As the Earl of Cromartie and his forces were travelling south to meet Charles Edward Stuart they were attacked in reprisal and prevented from joining the final Battle of Culloden. George Mackenzie and his son were surprised and captured at Dunrobin Castle, their titles forfeit.

Passing through the centuries into recent

history, in 1979, Roderick Grant Francis Blunt-Mackenzie, 4th Earl of Cromartie, and great-great-great-great-great-grandson of George Mackenzie through the female line, legally changed his surname to *Mackenzie* and was appointed chief of Clan Mackenzie by the Lord Lyon King of Arms. On his death in 1990, his son John Ruaridh Mackenzie, 5th Earl of Cromartie succeeded as chief of Clan Mackenzie. While Gabaldon invented Colum and Dougal, Castle Leod still stands today, run by the MacKenzie.

The Clan Mackenzie heraldic crest, as shown at the Gathering of Castle Leoch is a mountain in flames, with the motto in Latin "I shine not burn." The clan slogan is *Tulach Àrd* (Gaelic for "The high hill"). The slogan is derived from the mountain which was the Mackenzie rallying point or gathering place in Kintail. Their coat of arms is a golden stag's head cabossed (cleanly severed) on azure. (Cairney 57)

Mayer Rothschild

Claire and Jaime do business with a rare coin dealer, a Jew named Mayer whose only last name is the red shield hanging by his shop.

> "Well, Godspeed to ye, Mayer Red-Shield," he said, smiling.
> "Jamie," I said, suddenly thinking of something, "do you speak German?"
> "Eh? Oh, aye," he said vaguely, his attention still fixed on the window and the noises outside.
> "What is 'red shield' in German?" I asked.
> He looked blank for a moment, then his eyes cleared as his brain made the proper connection.
> "Rothschild, Sassenach," he said. "Why?"
> "Just a thought," I said. I looked toward the window, where the clatter of wooden shoes was long since lost in the noises of the street. "I suppose everyone has to start somewhere" (*Voyager,* ch. 40)

Mayer Amschel Rothschild (1744-1812) founded the Rothschild banking family, which is believed to have become the wealthiest family in human history. He's often referred to as the "founding father of international finance." He became a dealer in rare coins and managed many international loans, winning the patronage of Crown Prince Wilhelm of Hesse and other royal families. He would have been in his early twenties when Jamie and Claire met him.

St. Germain

Paul Rakoczy, Comte de Saint-Germain, features in the second book and in the short story "The Space Between." Geillis also owns *Le Grimoire d'le Comte St Germain* – a handbook of magic (*Outlander*, ch. 24). It's later revealed that she met Saint-Germain while calling herself Melisande Robicheau and staying in Paris.

The historical St. Germain may have been a son of Francis Racoczi II, Prince of Transylvania. He is said to have spent his childhood with the last of the powerful Medici family of Italy, known for mysticism and the occult. Prince Karl of Hesse says:

> He told me that he was eighty-eight years of age when he came here, and that he was the son of Prince Ragoczy of Transylvania by his first wife, a Tékéli. He was placed, when quite young, under the care of the last Duc de Medici (Gian Gastone), who made him sleep while still a child in his own room. When M. de St. Germain learned that his two brothers, sons of the Princess of Hesse-Wahnfried (Rheinfels), had become subject to the Emperor Charles VI., and had received the titles and names of St. Karl and St. Elizabeth, he said to himself: 'Very well, I will call myself Sanctus Germano, the Holy Brother.' I cannot in truth guarantee his birth, but that he was tremendously protected by the Duc de Medici I have learnt from another source. (Cooper-Oakley 11-12)

It has been said that M. de St. Germain was educated at the University of Siena. After, the Count dwelt in London for a while in 1743 to 1745, where he was briefly arrested as a Jacobite spy, then released. St. Germain was a gifted musician and several of his compositions were performed in the Little Haymarket Theatre in early February 1745. (Admittedly Claire and Jaime meet St. Germain around this time in Paris, but for such an interesting character, a bit of leeway may be forgiven).

He had an extreme love of jewels, which he had painted all over him in portraits and constantly carried about in a casket. "His only luxury consists of a large number of diamonds, with which he is fairly covered; he wears them on every finger, and they are set in his snuffboxes and his watches. One evening he appeared at court with shoebuckles, which Herr v. Gontaut, an expert on precious stones, estimated at 200,000 Francs" (Cooper-Oakley 29). Jewels of course are eventually revealed to be useful in Gabaldon's time travel.

"A man who knows everything and who never dies," said Voltaire of him. Saint-Germain created a great mystique around himself, so much so that he never ate in public. With his uncertain origins and unchanging appearance, along with boasts that he had lived for centuries, many suspected him of occult powers. Rumors of Saint-Germain sightings followed over many years – Baron de Gleichen says:

"I have heard Rameau and an old relative of a French ambassador at Venice testify to having known M. de St. Germain in 1710, when he had the appearance of a man of fifty years of age." The second date is mentioned by Mme. d'Adhémar in her most interesting *Souvenirs sur Marie Antoinette*. During this time we have M. de St. Germain as the Marquis de Montferrat, Comte Bellamarre or Aymar at Venice, Chevalier Schoening at Pisa, Chevalier Weldon at Milan and Leipzig, Comte Soltikoff at Genoa and Leghorn, Graf Tzarogy at Schwalbach and Triesdorf, Prinz Ragoczy at Dresden, and Comte de St. Germain at Paris, the Hague, London, and St. Petersburg. (Cooper-Oakley 17)

As an adult, he offered his great learning to Louis XV, which was eagerly accepted.

Louis XV was quite friendly with him, offering him rooms in the Chateau of Chambord and spending long evenings shut up with him and his own mistress, Madame de Pompadour. He also sent him on diplomatic missions. In Paris, 1750-1760, he appeared between forty and fifty. He was known for his great power, with many potions and ointments of great effectiveness. A skilled alchemist as well as a gifted pianist, singer and violinist, he spoke Spanish, Greek, Italian, French, English, Russian, Portuguese, Chinese, Arabic, and Sanskrit, according to some sources. He also wrote sonnets and painted portraits.

In the second book, a servant says the Comte St. Germain "has a very bad reputation."

> "He has sold his soul to the Devil, you know," she confided, lowering her voice and glancing around as though that gentleman might be lurking behind the chimney breast. "He celebrates the Black Mass, at which the blood and flesh of innocent children are shared amongst the wicked!"
>
> A fine specimen you picked to make an enemy of, I thought to myself.
>
> "Oh, everyone knows, Madame," Marguerite assured me. "But it does not matter; the women are mad for him, anyway; wherever he goes, they throw themselves at his head. But then, he is rich." Plainly this last qualification was at least sufficient to balance, if not to outweigh, the blood-drinking and flesh-eating. (*Dragonfly in Amber,* ch. 7)

"I'll set Murtagh to follow the Comte St. Germain. That'll give the Comte a real demon to play with," Jaime smirks (ch. 16).

Unsurprisingly, in the short story "The Space

Between," he reappears after his death and reveals he is a traveler like Claire and others in the series. Other fantasy writers have linked Saint-Germain's longevity and knowledge with the fantastical. Gabaldon notes:

> The Comte St. Germain was a real character of the times, and one with a reputation for being involved in occult matters – but very little else seemed known for sure about him. I consequently took nothing but his name and his unsavory associations, and beyond that, invented wholesale. (I note in passing that another author – Chelsea Quinn Yarbro – evidently took the Comte and used him fictionally; as a vampire, whose immortality allows him to live in various interesting time periods.) (*Outlandish Companion* 139)

The historical Saint-Germain went on to visit Russia and played a significant part in the revolution of 1762. Later he was said to have met Marie Antoinette and warned her of the upcoming French Revolution. He added, "A century will pass before I come here again." Official documents of Freemasonry say that in 1785 the French masons chose him as their representative at the great convention that took place in that year. By this point he must have been a century old, but the records always show him looking the same.

An Englishman, Albert Vandam, in his memoirs, which he calls *An Englishman in Paris,* speaks of a certain person whom he knew in 1821 whose manners and history echoed the Comte de Saint-Germain.

> He called himself Major Fraser, wrote Vandam, "lived alone and never alluded to his family. Moreover he was lavish with money, though the source of his fortune remained a mystery to everyone. He possessed a marvelous knowledge of all the countries in Europe at all periods. His memory was absolutely incredible and, curiously enough, he often gave his hearers to understand that he had

acquired his learning elsewhere than from books. Many is the time he has told me, with a strange smile, that he was certain he had known Nero, had spoken with Dante, and so on.

This is a delightful coincidence (presumably) as in Gabaldon's work, he is a time traveler and business rival of Jaime's, who might conceivably take the name of an old acquaintance for his future endeavors.

William, Duke of Cumberland

"What a mean little piggy face!" Brianna stooped to peer fascinated at the red-coated mannequin that stood menacingly to one side of the foyer in the Culloden Visitors Centre. He stood a few inches over five feet, powdered wig thrust belligerently forward over a low brow and pendulous, pink-tinged cheeks.

"Well, he was a fat little fellow," Roger agreed, amused. "Hell of a general, though, at least as compared to his elegant cousin over there." He waved a hand at the taller figure of Charles Edward Stuart on the other side of the foyer, gazing nobly off into the distance under his blue velvet bonnet with its white cockade, loftily ignoring the Duke of Cumberland.

"They called him 'Butcher Billy.' " Roger gestured at the Duke, stolid in white knee breeches and gold-braided coat. "For excellent reason. Aside from what they did here" – he waved toward the expanse of the spring-green moor outside, dulled by the lowering sky – "Cumberland's men were responsible for the worst reign of English terror ever seen in the Highlands. They chased the survivors of the battle back into the hills, burning and looting as they went. Women and children were turned out to starve, and the men shot down where they stood – with no effort to find out whether they'd ever fought for Charlie. One of the Duke's contemporaries said of him, 'He created a desert and called it peace' – and I'm afraid the Duke of Cumberland is still rather noticeably unpopular hereabouts." (*Dragonfly in Amber,* ch 4)

Prince William Augustus, Duke of Cumberland (April 26, 1721 – October 31, 1765), was the youngest son of King George II. He had charge of the Redcoats during the Second Jacobite Rebellion.

In 1745, Cumberland became Commander-in-Chief of the allied British, Hanoverian, Austrian and Dutch troops in Flanders against the French, though he ultimately lost. After, he led the British troops against Bonnie Prince Charlie. On April 16, 1746, he destroyed the Jacobites in the decisive Battle of Culloden. Cumberland ordered his troops to show no quarter against any remaining Jacobites, so they slaughtered the wounded. He then began a process of "pacification," killing any noncombatants he suspected of being rebels, with houses burned and livestock confiscated. Many were imprisoned and died on the ships carrying them to London or worse, the colonies.

The Duke of Cumberland doesn't feature in the books – Jaime only catches a distant glimpse. Later, upon hearing he's to meet a duke, Jaime assumes it's Cumberland and prepares to run him through even if he's executed for it. As Cumberland murdered women and children across the Highlands after the rebellion failed, he went down in history as a monster.

After, the duke was rewarded with an income of £25,000 *per annum* and Handel's oratorio *Judas Maccabaeus,* was composed especially for him, with the anthem "See the Conquering Hero Comes." Nonetheless, his title of "The Butcher Cumberland" remained. He took part in politics as a leader and advisor for his young nephew, the Prince of Wales. On 31 October 1765, he died of a stroke in London and was buried in Westminster Abbey.

Place Guide

Scotland

Ardsmuir prison

This place appears to be fictional. It's a prison and castle in one – the Scottish traitors from the uprising of '46 are imprisoned there in *Voyager* and forced to finish upgrading the castle. After, it is turned into a British military stronghold and the workers are transported. A gloomy, cold place, there is nothing for miles but empty moors and the coast.

Beaufort Castle

> We rode unchallenged into the courtyard of Beaufort Castle, a small edifice as castles went, but sufficiently imposing, for all that, built of the native stone. Not so heavily fortified as some of the castles I had seen to the south, it looked still capable of withstanding a certain amount of abrasion. Wide-mouthed gun-holes gaped at intervals along the base of the outer walls, and the keep still boasted a stable opening onto the courtyard. (*Dragonfly in Amber*, ch. 41)

This is the traditional seat of the Lord Lovat of Clan Fraser. Beaufort Castle (*Caisteal Duuaidh* in Gaelic) is located near the town of Beauly 12 miles west of Inverness. The present castle was built in 1880, but it incorporates older building work dating back to the twelfth century. Today it houses a Clan Fraser museum. The remains of Dounie Castle stand beside the house, and comprise a single wall, with a plaque stating that it is "the ruin of Castle Downie, the ancient stronghold of the Frasers of Lovat, built c. 1400, and destroyed by Cumberland after the battle of Culloden."

Broch Tuarach/ Lallybroch and Surroundings

Broch Tuarach (North Facing Tower) is the official name of the small estate Brian Fraser inherited, left to his son Jaime. Jaime notes that as an outlaw with a price on his head, it's too risky to go home. His sister Jenny continues to live there. Jaime also mentions the estate has strategic importance between MacKenzie and Fraser lands, so both clans would like to claim it, though it remains independent. It is more commonly called Lallybroch (Lazy Tower). Claire smirks on one occasion that round towers can't be said to face any direction, so the official name seems inaccurate, but the tower in fact leans North, accounting for both names.

Jamie describes it as rich ground with good fishing and some forest for hunting which supports about 60 tenants in *Cross Stitch,* or 60 crofts in *Outlander* (ch. 15). Broch Mordha is the name of the local village.

The main house, also called Lallybroch, was built in 1702 and includes modern innovations such as porcelain stoves and a great brick oven built into the kitchen wall for baking bread (*Outlander,* ch. 27). The house is "a handsome three-story house of harled white stone, windows outlined in the natural grey stone, a high slate roof with multiple chimneys, and several smaller whitewashed buildings clustered about it, like chicks about a hen." Claire identifies these buildings as a stable, shed for silage, granary, henyard, kailyard, disused chapel and brewhouse. Behind the house is its namesake, the stone tower

(*Outlander,* ch. 26). Jenny also has a priest hole built as a hiding place.

> Set into the flags of the floor was a large wooden panel, perforated with drilled holes, apparently mortared into the floorstones. Theoretically, this gave air to the root cellar below, and in fact – should any suspicious person choose to investigate, the root cellar, reached by a sunken door outside the house, did have just such a panel set into its ceiling.
>
> What was not apparent was that the panel also gave light and air to a small priest hole that had been built just behind the root cellar, which could be reached by pulling up the panel, mortared frame and all, to reveal a short ladder leading down into the tiny room. It was no more than five feet square, equipped with nothing in the way of furniture beyond a rude bench, a blanket, and a chamber pot. A large jug of water and a small box of hard biscuit completed the chamber's accoutrements. (*Voyager,* ch. 6).

By the 1960's, the property is unowned, though in good condition. The nearby Church of St. Kilda is apparently the burial place of Jack Randall, though it's unclear why this location was chosen (unless this is a false gravestone erected as a message, like another located there). Broch Tuarach appears to be entirely fictional. Nonetheless, Gabaldon says:

> Well, places like Inverness, Loch Ness and Fort William are certainly real, as are Paris, Fontainebleu, Cap Haitien, Philadelphia, etc... So far as I know, there isn't a physical basis for Lallybroch, but then again, I do repeatedly find things that really exist after I've written them, so I wouldn't be at all surprised. (FAQ)

Cape Wrath

At Cape Wrath, the most north-westerly point in Scotland, Fergus, Jaime, Claire, and Jamie's small band of smugglers board the Artemis to set sail across the Atlantic. It is a few miles from the isle of the silkies.

It was a cold, gray day – there is no other kind in Scotland in December – when the *Artemis* touched at Cape Wrath, on the northwest coast.

I peered out of the tavern window into a solid gray murk that hid the cliffs along the shore. The place was depressingly reminiscent of the landscape near the silkies' isle, with the smell of dead seaweed strong in the air, and the crashing of waves so loud as to inhibit conversation, even inside the small pothouse by the wharf. (*Voyager*, ch. 41)

Castle Leoch and Surroundings

 Historically, Castle Leoch/Leod was the seat of Clan MacKenzie. "The castle of the chief was a kind of palace, to which every man of his name was welcome, and whither all usually flocked in times or local war" (Grant). Moore describes Castle Leoch as the "home base" for season one. *The Outlandish Companion* reveals that Jacob MacKenzie seized the castle in 1690 from Donald MacKenzie, who was absent from the castle at the time, then passed it to his heir, Colum. Gabaldon notes:

> The petition of Colum MacKenzie for a matriculation of arms was disputed by the heirs of Donald MacKenzie of Leoch, and was the subject of a prolonged legal process. The petition was not granted before the Rising of 1745, and after the Rising (in which the heir of Donald MacKenzie, his son and grandson, were all killed), the emigration of the only heir and the loss of his lands left the matter of the title undecided; the property of the estate reverted to a distant heir of Donald MacKenzie: Jeremiah MacKenzie. (*Outlandish Companion*)

Claire's first impressions are that it is blunt and

solid like a fortified house (*Outlander,* ch. 4). The following statistics from Dunbar's *Social Life in Former Days,* give details of household furniture and expenses, for the Highland lairds:

"Sᴛʀ Rᴏʙᴇʀᴛ Gᴏʀᴅᴏɴ's Aʟʟᴏᴡᴀɴᴄᴇ ғᴏʀ ʜɪs Lᴀᴅʏ ᴀɴᴅ Fғᴀᴍɪʟʏ, ғʀᴏᴍ Dᴇᴄᴇᴍʙᴇʀ 14ᴛʜ 1740 ᴛᴏ Dᴇᴄᴇᴍʙᴇʀ 14ᴛʜ 1741.

	Sterling.		
	£	s.	D.
Imprimis, to 36 bolls malt, at 8 shillings and 4 pence per boll, ...	15	0	0
Item, to 36 bolls meal, at same price, . . .	15	0	0
Item, to 10 bolls wheat, at 13 shillings and 4 pence per boll, ...	6	13	4
Item, to 12 beeves at £1 per piece, . . .	12	0	0
Item, to meal to servants without doors, . . ,	9	7	6
Item, to servants' wages within and without doors,	41	5	0
Item, to cash instantly delivered, ...	50	6	2
Item, to be paid monthly, £4, 4s., . . .	50	8	0
	£200	0	0

" *Servants' Wages* 1741.

	£	s.	D.
Imprimis to gentlewomen, ...	10	0	0
Item, to five maids, ...	5	6	8
Item, to two cooks, ...	5	0	0
Item, to two porters, ...	3	0	0
Item, to Robin's servant, ...	1	0	0
Item, to the groom, ...	5	5	0
Item, to the neighbour, ...	3	6	8
Item, to three bout-servants, . .	7	0	0
Item, to two herds, ...	1	6	8
	£41	5	0

An inventory of furnishings for a few rooms in the home of the Dunbars of Thunderton, in the parish of Duffus, May 25, 1708, reveals many fine articles, as another example of castle life:

Strypt Room.
"Camlet hangings and curtains, feather bed and bolster, two pillows, five pair blankets, and an Inglish blanket, a green and white cover, a blew and white chamber-pot, a blew and white bason, a black jopand table and two looking-glasses, a jopand tee-table with a tee-pat and plate, and nine cups and nine dyshes, and a tee silver spoon, two glass sconces, two little bowles, with a leam steep and a pewter

209

head, eight black ken chairs, with eight silk cushens conform, an easie chair with a big cushen, a jopand cabinet with a walnut tree stand, a grate, shuffle, tonges, and brush; in the closet, three piece of paper hangings, a chamber box. with a pewter pan therein, and a brush for cloaths.

Closet next the Strypt Room.
Four dishes, two assiets, six broth plates, and twelve flesh plates, a quart flagon, and a pynt flagon, a pewter porenger, and a pewter flacket, a white iron jaculale pot, and a skellet pann, twenty-one timber plates, a winter for warming plates at the fire, two Highland plaids, and a sewed blanket, a bolster, and four pillows, a chamber-box, a sack with wool, and a white iron dripping pann.

In the farest Closet.
"Seventeen drinking glasses, with a glass tumbler end two decanters, a oil cruet, and a vinegar cruet, a urinal glass, a large blew and white posset pot, a white leam posset pat, a blew and white bowl, a dozen of blew and white leam plates, three milk dishes, a blew and white leam porenger, and a white leam porenger, four jelly pots, and a little butter dish, a crying chair, and a silk craddle. (qtd. in Keltie)

Castle Doune is its filming location on the show – it's in very good repair, so the 1740s images are realistic (with plenty of set dressing like tents and straw to cover present-day railings and signs). The ruins when Claire and Frank visit in the first episode are CGI effects.

Exploring the place in 1940, Claire jokes that the apothecary must have belonged to the castle hermit, and she and Frank joke flirtatiously about how lonely it must have been. In fact, it soon becomes her workroom.

Nearby are Croich Gorm – the fairy hill where Claire finds the sickly baby – and the mountain Ben Aden (*Outlander*, ch. 25). (This last is inaccurate geography). Cranesmuir, the local village, is where Geillis Duncan lives with her husband, the Procurator Fiscal, Arthur Duncan. Scenes there are filmed in the medieval village of the Royal Burgh of

Culross. The interiors of Castle Leoch and the nearby village were filmed on soundstages or at Hopetoun House.

Craigh na Dun

Craigh na Dun is a fictional stone circle said to be near Inverness. Of course, standing stone circles are perfectly real – while Stonehenge is the most famous, there are other rings across Britain, especially on the Scottish Isles. No one knows precisely why they were made or how they were used. Gabaldon comments:

> I was doing a lot of research on Scotland at that point because I'd never been there and kept coming across the standing stone circles. Every time I'd read about the stone circles, it would describe how they worked as an astronomical observance. For example, some of the circles are oriented so that at the winter solstice the sun will strike a standing stone. But all the texts speculate that nobody knows what the actual function of these stone circles was. And so I began thinking, Well, I bet I can think of one. [Laughs] (DeLuca)

Jaime translates the bard's song in episode three, and Claire discovers the local folk legends see women traveling the stones...and returning. Jaime tells her:

> Now this one is about a man out late on a fairy hill on the eve of Samhain who hears the sound of a woman singing sad and plaintive from the very rocks of the hill. "I am a woman of Balnain. The folk have stolen me over again," the stones seemed to say. "I stood upon the hill, and wind did rise, and the sound of thunder rolled across the land. I placed my hands upon the tallest stone and traveled to a far, distant land where I lived for a time among strangers

who became lovers and friends. But one day, I saw the moon came out and the wind rose once more. So I touched the stones and traveled back to my own land and took up again with the man I had left behind." (Episode 103)

CLAIRE: She came back through the stones?
JAIME: Aye, she did. They always do.
CLAIRE VOICEOVER: It was a folktale, madness to take as fact, and yet half of what Gwyllyn had described had actually happened to me. Why not the other half, the part where the woman returned home? What had Geillis said? As I told you, there's many things in this world we can't explain. My heart suddenly lightened, and I knew in that moment I could no longer wait for permission or assistance. I must escape Castle Leoch and get back to the stones as soon as possible or die trying.

She then decides to return to the stones herself. There are many stone circles in Britain, but Craigh na Dun was invented by the author. When asked for her inspiration, she responds:

Bear in mind that I had never been to Scotland when I wrote *Outlander*. When I finally did go, I found a stone circle very like the one I described, at a place called Castlerigg (which is not in the Highlands, but in the Lake District, in England). There is also a place near Inverness called the Clava Cairns, which has a stone circle, and another place called Tomnahurich, which is supposed to be a fairy's hill, but I've never been there, so I don't know how like it is. (FAQ)

Culloden

Culloden Moor.
You can see how flat and open and boggy it is. The highland army was completely exposed, and they then charged into the teeth of musket fire, cannons, mortars with nothing more than their broadswords, for the most part. It was very, very quick and very bloody. The whole thing took less than an hour. How many were killed? Jacobites lost something in the region of 2,000 men. But the interesting thing is that in the years following Culloden, the estates of the Clan Chieftains were plundered, sold. The

> government banned the wearing of tartan. They banned the
> carrying of swords, even the Gaelic language.
>   In effect, Culloden marked the end of the clans, and the
> end of the highlander way of life. 1746, three years from
> now. And what of these Mackenzie men? How many of
> them were doomed to die on that wretched battlefield?
> (Episode 105)

As Claire reminisces on the show, she emphasizes how soon the war will descend and destroy Highland culture forever. The first two books slowly expand towards the inevitable doom, as Claire and Jaime struggle to avert this horrible destiny, or at least avoid it.

The Battle of Culloden was fought on a moor near Culloden House, which Bonnie Prince Charlie requisitioned to use as his battlefield headquarters. In the second book, Roger does research at Culloden House (today a hotel), and he and Brianna visit Culloden Visitor's Centre and go to the field itself to find many Scots lay heather there (*Dragonfly in Amber*, ch. 4).

> The clan stones were large boulders of gray granite, rounded
> by weather and blotched with lichens. They sat on patches of
> smooth grass, widely scattered near the edge of the moor.
> Each one bore a single name, the carving so faded by weather
> as to be nearly illegible in some cases. MacGillivray.
> MacDonald. Fraser. Grant. Chisolm. MacKenzie. (*Dragonfly in
> Amber,* ch. 4)

Roger comments, "So many of the Highland clansmen who followed Prince Charles were killed on Culloden Field that they weren't buried individually. They were put into mass graves, with no more than a single stone bearing the clan name as a marker" (*Dragonfly in Amber*, ch. 1).

Ghostly soldiers are supposed to appear here on the 16th of April, the anniversary of the battle, and the cries of battle and the clash of steel have also been reported. The specter of one of the Highlanders is also said to frequent the area – tall with drawn features, he is supposed to whisper, "defeated" when people encounter him. Another tradition is that birds do not sing there, hushed by the ominous atmosphere.

Edinburgh

The Jacobites won the Battle of Prestonpans, to the east of Edinburgh, and soon captured the city. Thus, Bonnie Prince Charlie lived in the Palace of Holyrood House during the Jacobite Rebellion, along with Claire and Jaime. The royal palace of Holyrood was the place where Charles's grandfather, James II, had, almost 60 years before, exercised the functions of royalty, as the representative of his brother Charles II. As Claire describes the palace in the book:

> The long, high-ceilinged room with its two vast fireplaces and towering windows had been the scene of frequent balls and parties since Charles's triumphant entry into Edinburgh in September. Now, crowded with the luminaries of Edinburgh's upper class, all anxious to do honor to their Prince – once it appeared that he might actually win – the room positively glittered. (*Dragonfly in Amber*, ch. 37)

Prince Charlie's secretary describes his triumphal entrance:

> Exulting as he must have done, at the near prospect which such fortuitous events seemed to afford him of realising his most ardent expectations, his feelings received a new impulse, when, on coming within sight of the palace, he beheld the park crowded with people, who had assembled to welcome his arrival. Attended by the Duke of Perth and Lord Elcho, and followed by a train of gentlemen, Charles rode down the Hunter's bog, on his way to the palace. On reaching the eminence below St. Anthony's well, he alighted from his horse for the purpose of descending on foot into the park below. On dismounting he was surrounded by many persons who knelt down and kissed his hand. He made suitable acknowledgements for these marks of attachment, and after surveying for a short time

the palace and the assembled multitude which covered the intervening grounds, he descended into the park, which, from its having been much frequented by the Duke of York, afterwards James II, when he resided at Holyrood, obtained the name of the Duke's walk, Charles stopped for a few minutes to exhibit himself to the people. (Bell, ch. 20)

Holyrood House 1745

Jamie and Claire meet Colum MacKenzie outside the Kirk of the Canongate, located near the Palace of Holyroodhouse. In the kirkyard graveyard lie, among others, David Rizzio, the murdered private secretary of Mary, Queen of Scots, and the poet Robert Fergusson. Claire says:

> We found Colum in the kirkyard, sitting on a stone bench where the late afternoon sun could warm his back. His blackthorn stick lay on the bench beside him, and his short, bowed legs dangled a few inches above the ground. Shoulders hunched and head bowed in thought, at a distance he looked like a gnome, a natural inhabitant of this man-made rock garden, with its tilted stones and creeping lichens. (*Dragonfly in Amber*, ch. 37)

The city itself bustles with shops and imported goods, though on Claire's first visit, war has descended. Jaime returns to Edinburgh for a time in book three, and he and Claire visit in book seven. Important locations include the taverns, the print shop, and a particular house of ill repute. Claire also visits the historic World's End Tavern:

> Besides the row of casks, there were a number of wooden crates stacked near the center of the room, against an odd little chunk of wall that stood by itself, rising some five feet out of the cellar floor, running back into the darkness.
>
> I had heard of this feature of the tavern when we had stayed in Edinburgh twenty years before with His Highness Prince Charles, but what with one thing and another, I had never actually seen it before. It was the remnant of a wall constructed by the city fathers of Edinburgh, following the disastrous Battle of Flodden Field in 1513. Concluding – with some justice – that no good was likely to come of association with the English to the south, they had built a wall defining both the city limits and the limit of the civilized world of Scotland. Hence "The World's End," and the name had stuck through several versions of the tavern that had eventually been built upon the remnants of the old Scots' wishful thinking. (*Voyager,* ch. 25)

In modern times, the Scottish National Portrait Gallery is here, apparently displaying Jaime's mother's self-portrait wearing Claire's pearls.

Fort William

The post-Reformation fort was constructed by Oliver Cromwell's forces in 1654 to control the local population. It was originally known as the Garrison of Inverlochy. Its Gaelic name is *An Gearasdan,* meaning "The Garrison" (an unusual name in Gaelic as it's a French cognate). It was named Fort William after William of Orange – the surrounding town was *Maryburgh,* after his wife. This settlement changed names later, from *Gordonsburgh* and then *Duncansburgh* to *Fort William,* this time after Prince William, Duke of Cumberland. Since he was known as the Butcher Cumberland, some Scots are in favor of changing the name once more. This area of Lochaber was strongly Clan Cameron country. In the Rising of 1745, Fort William was besieged for two weeks by the Jacobites, from March 20 to April 3, 1746. However, they failed to take it.

Movies and shows filmed in or near Fort William include *Being Human, Braveheart, Highlander, Restless Natives, the Harry Potter series* and *Rob Roy.* Blackness Castle, a former garrison and prison, is Fort William on *Outlander.*

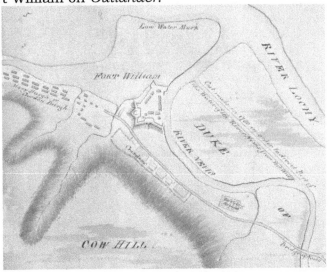

Inverness

Claire and Frank were married in a small chapel near here, and come to Inverness for a second honeymoon after the war. The Reverend Wakefield lives here as do the Circle Dancers. There's a mystery surrounding Mountgerald, a big house at the end of the High Street allegedly haunted by the ghost of a workman. Craig na Dun stands nearby, and while exploring, Claire disappears through the stones.

On the show, episodes one and eight have significant scenes here. Most subsequent books include scenes here as well, as it's the closest town to the standing stones. This is also the largest town of the Highlands in the eighteenth century, not far from Lallybroch. Nearby is Cocknammon Rock, a fictional rock formation the Redcoats used for ambushes. In *An Echo in the Bone*, a Traveler finds his way to the Old High St. Stephen's Church, visitable today. As he adds:

> After a bit, I found my way to Inverness and was sittin' on the curb of the street, quite dazed by the huge great roaring things goin' by me – I'd seen the cars on the road north, of course, but it's different when they're whizzin' past your shins. Anyway, I'd sat down outside the High Street Church, for I knew that place, at least, and thought I'd go and ask the minister for a bite of bread when I'd got myself a bit more in hand. (ch. 72)

Loch Ness

From Inverness, Frank and Claire take a day trip to Loch Ness and the nearby settlement of Lochend (*Outlander*, ch. 2). Claire and the MacKenzies stop here on the way back to Castle Leoch after the rent collecting and Claire sees the Loch Ness Monster (*Outlander*, ch. 19). Claire also takes Brianna here in the second book (*Dragonfly in Amber*, ch. 1). It's a popular tourist destination, though the monster has never been concretely proven to exist.

Perth

Claire observes that metropolitan areas such as Perth in central Scotland have newspapers, whereas the Highlands do not (*Outlander*, ch. 34). In the Rising, the Highland army reached Perth in September 1945 and the Prince stayed at the Salutation Hotel there, which still functions as a hotel today. While in Perth, Charles is said to have visited Scone, where so many of his ancestors had been crowned, though the Stone of Scone, signifying kingship, was in London at the time.

Sherriffmuir

Sherriffmuir was the site of the Battle of Sherriffmuir during the first Jacobite Rising in 1715 – Jaime's father was a soldier in it. In September of 1715, the Earl of Mar raised the Royal standard at Braemar and gathered 12,000 in what became known as the First Jacobite Rising or "The '15." They wanted the return of King James and his descendants, rather than the Hanoverian George I. Opposing Mar's further passage into Lowland Scotland were 6,000 of King George's troops, under the command of the Chief of Clan Campbell, the Duke of Argyll. The Battle of Sherriffmuir ended the Jacobite cause for a generation.

Wentworth

The fictional Wentworth Prison is located in the town of Wentworth, near MacRannoch's home – called Eldridge Hall in *Cross Stitch* and Eldridge Manor in *Outlander*. Claire, Murtagh, Rupert and the others stay here while planning a rescue (*Outlander,* ch. 35)

England

Helwater

Jaime is paroled after prison and stays at the fictional grand estate of Helwater in the Lake District for years. It's in the sparsely-populated Northwest corner of England, surrounded by hills and valleys. Today, the Lake District National Park covers much of the area, preserving the natural beauty. Of course, Jaime is most concerned with the wide acreage (the bounds of his parole) and the stables, where he works with the horses. Lord and Lady Dunsany own the estate, with two daughters, Isobel and Geneva, and finally a grandson. It's likely the estate will pass to the grandson in time.

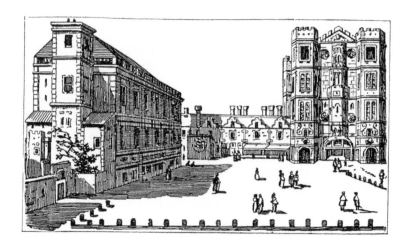

London

Lord John and his family are generally found in London with its coffee houses like White's and Boodle's. John attends society parties, literary salons, the theater, and particularly his club the Society for the Appreciation of the English Beefsteak. This last appears to be fictional, unlike the other clubs mentioned. Several of the *Lord John* novels center on his activities in London, from the notorious Lavender House to George III's coronation.

Jaime is taken to London in *The Scottish Prisoner*.

> So this was London. It had the stink of any city, the narrow alleys, the smell of slops and chimney smoke. But any large city has its own soul, and London was quite different from either Paris or Edinburgh. Paris was secretive, self-satisfied; Edinburgh solidly busy, a merchants' town. But this ... It was rowdy, churning like an anthill, and gave off a sense of pushing, as though the energy of the place would burst its bonds and spill out over the countryside, spill out into the world at large. His blood stirred, despite his fears and the tooth-jolting ride.
>
> The Jacobite soldiers would talk about London, early in the campaign, when they were victorious and London seemed a plum within their grasp. Wild tales – almost none of them had ever seen a city, before they came to

> Edinburgh. Talk of gold plates in the taverns, streets with gilded carriages thick as lice.

Driving through the city, he notes that his Fraser grandfather was executed at the Tower after Culloden, a fact which is historically true. London was not just a city of exotic civilization for the Highlanders, but also one of English brutality towards all traitors, a place where Mary, Queen of Scots, and many others lost their heads.

> As the campaign had turned, withering in the cold, when the army camped at Derby, shivering while the commanders argued whether to push on or not, the soldiers had still talked of London. But they talked in whispers then, and not of gold plates and Holland gin. They talked of the gallows, of the famous Bridge, where the heads of traitors were displayed. Of the Tower.
>
> That thought sent a qualm through him. Christ, could they be taking him there? He was a convicted traitor, though paroled these past four years. And he was the grandson of Lord Lovat, who had met his death on the block at that same Tower. He hadn't been fond of his grandfather, but crossed himself and murmured *"Fois air Anam ..."* under his breath. Peace on his soul. (ch. 7)

London is culturally important to the twentieth-century English characters, but few scenes occur there. In the 1940's Claire's beloved Uncle Lamb was killed during the Blitz (ch. 2). In *Cross Stitch* she says this happened when he was on his way to the British Museum, but in *Outlander* he was in the auditorium there. Roger's mother also died in the Blitz, at a famous collapse of a tube station. In book two, Claire dreams of Frank giving a lecture at London University (*Dragonfly in Amber*, ch. 10).

Oxford

Frank was a professor at Oxford before the war. When book one starts, he's accepted a teaching position there, and he and Claire plan to settle. On the show, Reverend Wakefield encourages Frank to return there after his wife's disappearance. Meanwhile, Claire pretends to be a widow from Oxfordshire when questioned by Colum – mostly because she's trying to keep thing simple and believable (*Outlander,* ch. 5).

Salisbury Plain/Stonehenge

This is the location of Stonehenge, most famous of the stone circles. Claire remembers visiting there with Frank soon after they were married (*Outlander,* ch. 2). There's another stone circle at nearby Avesbury.

> Stonehenge was likely built in 3200 BC as a chalk bank and a ditch. Inside the bank was a ring of 56 pits, in which cremated human remains have been found" about a thousand years later, 82 blocks of bluestone, weighing four tons each, were carried to the spot and assembled in a double circle. Around 2000 BC, the bluestone was removes, and blocks of sandstone weighting 25 to 50 tons apiece were dragged from 20 miles away. These were heaved into a ring with massive lintels to make horseshoe shapes. After 1650 BC, the bluestones were brought back and added inside. The monument was still used in 1100 BC, giving it an active life of over 20 centuries. The burial barrows of great chieftans stand nearby. (Atkinson 2487)

Folklore varyingly suggests the stones were constructed by giants or Merlin or Druids. Mystics and modern druids visit there for ceremonies, though the stones' original purpose is unknown.

Sussex

Jack Randall is from here, though he's spent some effort losing his accent. Frank notes that Jack was given the middle name Wolverton after his mother's uncle, a "minor knight from Sussex" (*Outlander*, ch. 1).

France

Abbey of St. Anne de Beaupre

This Benedictine abbey near the French coast is headed by Jamie's uncle Alexander Fraser. It is described as a twelfth-century walled edifice made of stone. The stunning high-roofed library has soaring columns that join in the multi-chambered roof and admit natural light through full-length windows (*Outlander*, ch. 38). There are several hot mineral springs under the abbey with great healing powers, a sacred spring long before the building's construction (*Outlander*, ch. 40).

Amiens

Claire was based in a field hospital in Amiens during the war (*Outlander*, ch. 1). The Germans captured the city in 1940, arresting a number of British troops. In February 1944, British aircraft bombed the prison in Amiens to allow these troops, along with political prisoners and members of the French Resistance, to escape. The Alliance liberated Amiens in August 1944, presumably bringing Claire and her medical division along with them.

Argentan

In 1714, Louis IV charged his staff with finding a proper location for horse breeding. François Gédéon de Garsault, the King's first horseman, decided on the *Buisson d'Exmes*, near Argentan, and accordingly bought the estate in 1715.

Jamie, Claire and Fergus travel here at the Duke of Sandringham's invitation to visit the royal stables. Claire comments, "The barns and stables were of quarried stone, stone-floored, slate-roofed, and maintained in a condition of cleanliness that surpassed that of L'Hopital des Anges by a fair degree" (*Dragonfly in Amber*, ch. 22).

Calais

Jaime and Claire sail from Scotland to Calais several times, as this is the closest port to Britain. Jaime is always seasick.

Compiegne

Claire tells Colum her French relatives are from Compiegne though she's never been there.

Fontainebleu

Louise de la Tour's country house is here and contains a number of decorations of dubious taste (*Dragonfly in Amber*, ch. 26). Fontainebleu is 55km south of Paris.

Le Havre

Jaime's cousin Jared lives here on the River Seine in northwestern France. He runs his shipping business from this popular Normandy port. While the area was inhabited by Neolithic builders and ancient Celts, the more modern city was founded in 1517 by François I, who named his new royal port Le Havre-de-Grâce ("Harbour of Grace"). In the 17th century, many exotic products from America appeared there (sugar, tobacco, cotton, coffee, and spices).

Paris

Paris offers Jared Fraser's townhouse on the affluent Rue Tremoulins, while Charles Stuart is living in a house in Montmartre, at the time, just outside Paris (*Dragonfly in Amber*, ch. 7). Claire visits Master Raymond's apothecary shop and Les Halles, the central market. This last, made famous by Emile Zola's famous novel by this title, was a central meeting place and shopping area for 800 years. Mother Hildegarde and the nuns work in the Couvent des Anges – the Convent of the Angels and its L'Hopital des Anges. When there is an explosion in the Royal Armory in May 1744, Claire says it startled the pigeons off the famed Notre Dame Cathedral (*Dragonfly in Amber*, ch. 18). Later, Claire and Dougal go to Quai des Orfevres – the French equivalent of Scotland Yard and still in use today – so they can report an attack (*Dragonfly in Amber*, ch. 21). Jaime fought a duel at Bois de Boulogne as a young man (a forest at the time, but now a public park), and returns there for another duel in *Dragonfly in Amber*. He subsequently finds his way to the dreaded Bastille.

Versailles

The Royal Palace of Versailles was home to the King, Louis XV. Jamie attends the King's *lever* (ceremonial wake up ceremony) here (ch. 7) and he and Claire attend a ball (ch. 9).

Louis IV wanted Versailles to "show his supremacy by conquering and reworking the natural landscape so that his surroundings reflected his own status. The grand scale of Versailles was a conscious symbol of the power of absolute monarchy" (Bruce-Mitford 43).

For an example of French court fashion of the time, here is a portrait of Madame de Pompadour (mistress of Louis XV), dated 1748-1755, by Maurice Quentin de la Tour.

Ireland

With a Jacobite plot, Jaime finds himself traveling to Ireland in *The Scottish Prisoner*. The priest Michael FitzGibbons, abbot of an ancient Irish church and Murtagh's cousin, takes him up to the druids' ancient seat and offers him the *Cupán Druid riogh*, the Cup of the Druid King. "This is the High Seat – the *6rd chnoc* – where the kings of this place were confirmed before the old gods," he says. Jaime is quite impressed. As he thinks, "It was a very old place, and the stone seemed to hold a deep silence; even the wind over the bog had died, and he could hear his heart beating in his chest, slow and steady" (*The Scottish Prisoner*, ch. 19).

The ancient kings were crowned on the Hill of Tara (*Cnoc na Teamhrach*). Today, Iron Age ruins stand there, including a stone circle and the *Forradh* or Royal Seat. Roman artifacts dating from the 1st–3rd centuries have been found here, by a ring-fort known as *Ráith Laoghaire* (coincidentally named King Laoghaire's Fort). Nearby, stands Saint Patrick's church, built in 1822 on the site of others that date back to the 1190s, or possibly earlier.

Rome

Bonnie Prince Charlie was raised here, and the pope is known to have an interest in him (though historically the pope crowned his father but not him). Jaime writes to Rome and the Jacobite conspirators there in *Lord John and the Brotherhood of the Blade*.

New World

The books travel to the West Indies, North Carolina, and (in the *Lord John* books) Canada. However, these locations are mysterious wilderness and fictional private homes for the most part – only by the final books have our heroes taken up residence in cities. Philadelphia appears as the site of Lord John's townhouse and Fergus's print shop, with occasional visits to New York and Charleston. Brianna, of course, is a native of Boston.

One significant location is Old Tennent Church near Monmouth Battlefield, in present-day Manalapan, NJ. In history and in *Written in My Own Heart's Blood,* this Presbyterian church was used as a soldiers' hospital during the Battle of Monmouth, June 28, 1778. Claire sees the actual gravestone of Gilbert Tennent (1742-1770) there with its inscription: "O READER HAD YOU HEARD HIS LAST TESTIMONY YOU WOULD HAVE BEEN CONVINCED OF THE EXTREME MADNESS OF DELAYING REPENTANCE." She even treats someone lying on the long stone (ch. 74).

About Gabaldon

My ancestry is both English (with one German branch) and Mexican-American (Latina, Hispanic, Chicana, whatever you want to call it); one of my maternal great-grandfathers emigrated from England (Yorkshire) to Arizona in the late 1800s, and two other branches of my maternal family arrived in New York during the American Revolution, while my father's family is from New Mexico. (*Outlandish Companion* 365)

Growing up in Flagstaff, Arizona, she holds an M.S. in marine biology from Scripps Institution of Oceanography, and a B.S. in zoology and Ph.D. in quantitative behavioral ecology from Northern Arizona University. She was a professor at Arizona State for about twelve years, in the Center for Environmental Studies. In the seventies, she briefly wrote comic books (freelance) for Walt Disney.

Gabaldon, who at the time was writing Fortran programs as an Arizona State University research professor, actually posted chapters from her first book, *Outlander*, to a CompuServe forum; positive feedback from her fellow geeks convinced her to seek a literary agent, and the book was published by Delacorte in 1991. Gabaldon's Compu-Serve fans spread the word on electronic bulletin boards, and Gabaldon (with the assistance of a friend at Caltech) built one of the first-ever author's Web sites. By the mid-1990s, when Slate was still just a twinkle in Michael Kinsley's eye, Gabaldon's site was attracting thousands of hits every day. (Koerner)

When writing *Outlander,* she had never been to Scotland. She adds, "I did take part of the advance money from the sale of *Outlander* and go to Scotland for two weeks, though, while working on *Dragonfly in Amber.* It was (luckily!) just as I'd been imagining it. I've been back several times since, for book tours and the like, and would go back like a shot, at the slightest opportunity" (*Outlandish Companion* 365).

Similar Books

- Judith McNaught's *Westmoreland Dynasty Saga* series – *Whitney, My Love* and *A Kingdom of Dreams*, credited with inventing the Regency Historical with wit and liveliness.
- Sara Donati's *Into the Wilderness* series, an American colonial era saga, with a visit from Jamie and Claire
- Dorothy Dunnett's *Lymond Chronicles* follows a Lowlander playing politics in Tudor times.
- Philippa Gregory's Tudor Court series – romance, history, magic, and the women's stories.
- Juliet Marillier, *Daughter of the Forest* series and *The Bridei Chronicles*. Historical Irish fantasy with women's magic.
- Kathleen Givens, *The Kilgannon Novels*, historical romance with a Scottish hero and English heroine in the Jacobite rising of 1715.
- Beth Anne Miller, *Into the Scottish Mist*. A Scottish time travel romance
- Deborah Harkness's All Souls Trilogy (A Discovery of Witches, Shadow of Night, Book of Life), time traveling historical fiction
- Kerry Lynne, *The Pirate Captain, Chronicles of a Legend* an assertive woman, Jacobites, and pirates.

Time Travel Romances
- Jude Devereaux's A Knight in Shining Armor

- Karen Marie Moning's Highlanders series
- Nora Roberts's Circle trilogy
- Anita Clenney's Connor Clan series

Scotland Romances
- Suzanne Enoch's Scandalous Highlanders
- Kinley MacGregor's Brotherhood/MacAllister series
- Karen Marie Moning's Highlanders series
- Julianne MacLean's Highlander trilogy
- Anita Clenney's Connor Clan
- Marsha Canham's Highlands series

Shows
- *Game of Thrones*
- *Rome*
- *Spartacus*
- *The White Queen*
- *The Borgias*
- *The Tudors*
- *Camelot*
- *Black Sails*
- *Da Vinci's Demons*

Scottishisms

'Scotticisms' are words and sentences that are more likely to be used by Scots in spoken rather than in their written language. Many appear in the series.

- Ah dinnae ken. – I don't know.
- Ain – Own
- Ane leid is ne'er enough – One language is never enough
- Arisad – Woman's plaid shawl
- A sair fecht – A difficult and troubling situation.
- Auld – Old
- "Aw hallaw! Ye'll have had yer tea" – A traditional Scottish welcome to the home.
- Awa' wi' you – Away with you
- Awa' wae the fairies – Describes a simple or strange person.
- Away ye go – No, or you're talking rubbish!
- Aye – Yes
- Ay, right! ... Expresses disbelief.
- Bahooky – Backside, bum
- Bairn – Baby
- Baw – Ball
- Baw Heid – Big headed
- Bawface – Someone with a big round face.
- Bawlikin' – Shouted at
- Ben – Mountain, or through
- Bide – Depending on the context, means wait, or stay.

- Bisom – Person
- Blether – Talkative, when referred to a person. To "have a blether" is to have a chat.
- Bonnie – Beautiful
- Bowfing – Smelly, horrible
- Braw from the Gaelic Breagh – Good, or brilliant
- Breeks – Trousers
- Broc – Tower
- brogues – Low heeled leather shoes
- Burn – Lake or other water
- Cack-handed – Left handed
- Canna – Can't
- canty – well
- Caw canny – Be careful
- Cloot – A wet cloth
- Collie Backie – Piggy back
- Coo – Cow
- Coo's lick – Quick wipe of the face with a damp cloth
- Couldna – Couldn't
- Cowp – Tip or spill
- Crabbit – Bad tempered
- Cry – Call, as in what do you call him?
- Cum intae the body o' the kirk – An invitation to an outsider to join in.
- Dae – Do
- Daft – Crazy
- Dauner – Walk – "I'm away for a dauner"
- Dicht yer neb Wipe your nose
- Didnae – Didn't
- Dinna/Dinnae – Don't
- Dinnae fasch yerself Don't worry yourself
- Dreepin' – Soaking wet.
- Dreich day – dull day
- Drookit – Soaking wet
- Dunderheid, Eejit, Galoot, Numptie – idiot
- Dunt – Bump

- Fair scunnered – Fed up
- Fair wabbit – Fairly done in.
- Fankle – For a tangled mess
- Feart – Afraid
- Feartie gowk Someone who is afraid of a challenge.
- Flashes – Men's decorative garters
- Frae – From
- Gallus – Bravado, over-confident
- Galluses – Braces (for holding up trousers).
- Gang – Go
- Gaun awa' – Going away.
- "Gaun yersel!" – A jibe at someone who is making a fool of themselves
- Gaunnae – Going to
- Geggie – Mouth, as in "shut your geggie"
- "Gen up" – Honestly.
- Gey – Very
- Ghillies/ghillie brogues – traditional Scottish leather slippers
- Gie's a shot then! – Give me a turn.
- Glaikit – Stupid, slow on the uptake
- Gomerel – Foolish person
- Goonie – Nightgown
- Greet – Cry
- Groozin – Feeling ill
- Gumption – Common sense, initiative
- Hae – Have
- Hame – Home
- Haste ye back – Return soon.
- Haud – Hold
- Haver – Talk rubbish
- Hing – Hang
- Hoachin' – Very busy
- Hokin' – Rummaging
- Honkin', Hummin', Howlin' – Bad smell
- Hoose – House
- Hunkers – Rear-end

- Hunner – Hundred
- Huvnae – Haven't
- Keek – A little look
- Ken – Know
- Kent – Knew
- Kerch – Married woman's headscarf
- Kirk – Church
- Laddie – boy
- Lassie – girl
- Loupin' – Sore body part
- Ludgin – lazy
- Lum – Chimney
- Mac – Son of
- Ma heed's burlin' My head is spinning.
- Mair – More
- Merrit – Married
- Mockit, Manky, Mingin', Boggin' – All mean dirty
- Moose – Mouse
- Muckle – Big
- Nae, Naw – No
- Neep, Tumshie – Turnip
- Nic – Daughter of
- Noo – Now
- Och, aye – Yes
- Oot – Out
- Outwith – Outside of
- Oxter – Underarm
- Peely Wally – Pale
- Poke – (to poke – to prod) (a poke – a paper bag)
- Reek – Smell, emit smoke
- Riddy – A red face, embarrassed
- Right scunner – Real nuisance
- Sair ficht – Sore fight (large effort)
- Screwball – Unhinged, mad
- Scullery – Kitchen
- Scunner – Irritating person

- Scunnered – Bored, fed up, disgusted
- Sgian dubh – Sock knife
- Shallna – Shall not
- Shoogle – Shake
- Shouldna – Shouldn't
- Shelpit – A thin, unhealthy looking person
- Simmet – Man's singlet
- Skelloch – Screech
- Skelp – Slap
- Skoosh – Lemonade (or fizzy drink)
- Sleekit – Sly
- Snib – Bolt
- Spail – Splinter
- Sporran – man's purse, worn on the belt in front
- Stookie – Plaster cast (for a broken bone)
- Stour – Dust
- Stramash – Fuss, fight
- Swithering – Undecided
- Tattie – Potato
- "There's no muckle drouth the day." – It will take the washing a long time to dry.
- Thon – That
- Twa – Two
- Verra – Very
- Wame – Stomach
- Wean – Child
- Wee – Small
- Wellies – Wellington boots
- Wha's nae – Who isn't
- Whit – What
- Willna/Willnae – Will not
- Widnae – Would not
- Windae – Window
- Wummin – Women
- Ya dobber – You silly idiot.
- Ya muckle gype!! – You stupid idiot.
- Ye – You

- Yer – Your
- Yer talkin mince – You're talking rubbish.
- Yin – One

Reading Order

Main Series
1. *Outlander* (titled *Cross Stitch* in the UK)
2. *Dragonfly in Amber*
3. *Voyager*
4. *The Drums of Autumn*
5. *The Fiery Cross*
6. *A Breath of Snow and Ashes*
7. *An Echo in the Bone*
8. *Written in My Own Heart's Blood*
9. Book Nine (untitled, TBA)

Prequel about Brian and Ellen Fraser in the first uprising (untitled, TBA)

Lord John Novels: These take place during *Voyager* between 1756 and 1761, while Jaime is at Helwater and feature Lord John Grey, who is briefly introduced in *Dragonfly in Amber* and becomes more significant in the later books. Gabaldon says: "The Lord John novellas and novels are sequential, but are built to stand alone; you don't need to read them in order. ...These books are part of the overall series, but are focused for the most part on those times in Lord John's life when he's not "onstage" in the main novels" (*The Scottish Prisoner,* Preface).

- "Lord John and the Hellfire Club" (1998), a novella. Originally published in the 1998 British anthology Past Poisons: An Ellis Peters Memorial Anthology of Historical Crime (edited by Maxim Jakubowski). Also in Lord John and the Hand of Devils (2007).

- *Lord John and the Private Matter* (2003). Published as a novel.
- "Lord John and the Succubus" (2003). Originally published in the 2003 Del Rey anthology *Legends II: New Short Novels by the Masters of Modern Fantasy* (edited by Robert Silverberg). Also in *Lord John and the Hand of Devils* (2007).
- *Lord John and the Brotherhood of the Blade* (2007). Published as a novel.
- "Lord John and the Haunted Soldier" (2007). Originally published in *Lord John and the Hand of Devils*.
- *The Custom of the Army* (2010). First published in the 2010 anthology *Warriors*, edited by George R.R. Martin and Gardner Dozois. Also available as a standalone eBook, and in Gabaldon's collection *A Trail of Fire* (United Kingdom, Australia, Germany and New Zealand only), US and Canada TBA.
- *The Scottish Prisoner* (2011). Published as a novel. This novel, unlike the others, is half-told from Jaime's perspective.
- *Lord John and the Plague of Zombies* (2011). First published in the 2011 anthology *Down These Strange Streets*, edited by George R.R. Martin and Gardner Dozois. Also available as a standalone eBook, and in *A Trail of Fire*.

Other Short Fiction
- "A Leaf on the Wind of All Hallows." The story of Roger MacKenzie's parents, in *Songs of Love and Death*, eds. George R. R. Martin and Gardner Dozois, 2010. Also available in *A Trail of Fire*. Takes place during book eight.

- "The Space Between." The story of minor characters Michael Murray and Joan MacKimmie in 1778 Paris, in *The Mad Scientist's Guide to World Domination,* ed. John Joseph Adams, 2013. Also available in *A Trail of Fire.* Takes place just after book seven.
- "Virgins." The story of Jaime and Ian's time as young mercenaries in 1740 France, before the events of *Outlander,* in *Dangerous Women,* edited by George R. R. Martin and Gardner Dozois, 2013.

Other Outlander Works
- *The Exile* (graphic novel adaptation of the first half of book one) 2010.
- *The Outlandish Companion* Vol. I (guide to books 1-4, titled Through the Stones in the UK) 1999.
- *The Outlandish Companion* Vol. II (TBA)

Other Short Stories
- "Dream a Little Dream for Me" with Laura Watkins. *Mothers and Daughters: Celebrating the Gift of Love* (1998)
- "A Silence at the Heart." Fathers and Daughters: A Celebration in Memoirs (1999)
- "Surgeon's Steel" *Excalibur* (1995)
- "Hellfire" Past Poisons: An Ellis Peters Memorial Anthology of Historical Crime (1999)
- ("Mirror Image," with Samuel Watkins) Mothers & Sons: A Celebration in Memoirs, Stories, and Photographs (Anthology) (2000)
- "The Castellan" "the story of a lonely man of mixed blood, a white raven with a sarcastic sense of humor, and a *real* dragon lady, who thinks blood is blood, and it all tastes fine" (Outlandish Companion 363) in *Out of Avalon: An Anthology of Old Magic and New Myths*

(2001) first published as *Jenseits von Avalon* (German) (1999)

- *Naked Came the Phoenix* (2001) and *Phoenix Noir* (2009), collaboration with other authors
- "Humane Killer," short story co-written with Sam Sykes, published in *The Dragon Book: Magical Tales from the Masters of Modern Fantasy* (2009)

Cast

Producer/Showrunner Ron Moore
Costume Designer Terry Dresbach
Caitriona Balfe as Claire Beauchamp Randall Fraser
Sam Heughan as James (Jamie) Alexander Malcolm MacKenzie Fraser
Tobias Menzies in the dual roles of Frank Randall and Jonathan (Black Jack) Randall.
Stephen Walters as Angus Mhor
Grant O'Rourke as Rupert MacKenzie
Annette Badland as Mrs. FitzGibbons
Graham McTavish as Dougal MacKenzie
Gary Lewis as Colum MacKenzie
Duncan Lacroix as Murtagh Fraser
Lotte Verbeek as Geillis Duncan
Bill Paterson as Ned Gowan
Finn Den Hertog as Willie
John Heffernan as Brigadier General Lord Oliver Thomas
Roderick Gilkison as Young Hamish MacKenzie
James Fleet as the Reverend Wakefield
Laura Donnelly as Jenny Fraser Murray
Steven Cree as Ian Murray
Nell Hudson as Laoghaire
Kathryn Howden as Mrs. Baird
Tracey Wilkinson as Mrs. Graham
Liam Carney as Auld Alec
Aislin McGuckin as Colum's wife, Letitia
Prentis Hancock as Uncle Lamb
Simon Callow as the Duke of Sandringham

OUTLANDER COMPANION

Works Cited

Atkinson, RJC. "Stonehenge" Cavendish 2487.

Bell, Robert Fitzroy, ed. *Memorials of John Murray of Broughton Sometime Secretary to Prince Charles Edward* Edinburgh: Edinburgh University Press, 1898. http://www.electricscotland.com/history/charles

Bethune, Brian. "Outlander Gives Game of Thrones a Run for its Money." *Maclean's* 12 June 2014. http://www.macleans.ca/culture/books/outlander-gives-game-of-thrones-a-run-for-its-money/

"Big-budget Drama Outlander Films in Scotland." *BBC* 12 March 2014. http://www.bbc.com/news/uk-scotland-tayside-central-26543451

Bruce-Mitford, Miranda. *The Illustrated Book of Signs and Symbols.* USA: DK Publishing, 1996.

Campbell, J. F. *Popular Tales of the West Highlands Volume I-IV.* London, Alexander Gardner, 1890. *The Sacred Texts Archive.* http://www.sacred-texts.com/neu/celt/pt2/pt200.htm.

Cavendish, Richard, editor. Man, Myth, and Magic: The Illustrated Encyclopedia of Mythology, Religion, and the Unknown. New York: Marshall Cavendish Corporation, 1995.

Clover, Carol J. "Her Body, Himself: Gender in the Slasher Film" *Feminist Film Theory.* Sue. Thornham, ed. Edinburgh: Edinburgh University Press, 1999. 234-250.

Comrie, John D. "General Practice in the Seventeenth and Eighteenth Centuries" *History of Scottish Medicine to 1860.* London: Bailliere Tindall and Cox, 1927. http://www.electricscotland.com/history/medical/scottish_medicinendx.htm

Cooper, Robert L. D., Curator, the Grand Lodge of Scotland Museum and Library. "Freemasonry: A Little History" http://www.electricscotland.com/history/freemasonry/little_history.htm

Dresbach, Terry. *Terry Dresbach: An 18th Century Life.* 2014. Blog. http://terrydresbach.com.

Ferguson, Brian. "Bill Paterson lands key part in Outlander TV show." *The Scotsman* 26 Oct 2014. http://www.scotsman.com/lifestyle/arts/news/bill-paterson-lands-key-part-in-outlander-tv-show-1-3438464.

Folk-Lore and Legends of Scotland. London: W. W. Gibbings, 1889. *Electronic Scotland.* http://www.electricscotland.com/etexts/17071.txt.

Friedlander, Whitney. "'Outlander' Costume Designer on Wedding Dresses, Kilts and Corsets." *Variety* 20 Sept 2014. http://variety.com/2014/artisans/news/outlander-wedding-costume-designer-1201309495.

Fulton, Alexander. Clans and Families of Scotland: The History of the Scottish Tartan. Edison, NJ: Chartwell Books, 1999.

Gabaldon, Diana. *A Breath of Snow and Ashes.* New York: Random House, 2005.

– . *Cross Stitch.* London: Arrow Books, 1994

– . "Diana Gabaldon, Author." Facebook Comment 10 Dec. 2013. https://www.facebook.com/home.php?ref=h...ed_comment

– . *Dragonfly in Amber.* New York: Random House, 1992.

– . "The Doctor's Balls." *Chicks Unravel Time: Women Journey Through Every Season of Doctor Who.* Edited by Deborah Stanish and L.M. Myles. USA: Mad Norwegian Press, 2012. Kindle Edition.

– . *The Drums of Autumn.* New York: Random House,

1996.

– . *An Echo in the Bone.* New York: Random House, 2009.

– . The Exile: An Outlander Graphic Novel. New York: Del Ray, 2010.

– . "FAQ." *Diana Gabladon's Official Webpage.* 2014. http://www.dianagabaldon.com/resources/faq

– . *The Fiery Cross.* New York: Random House, 2001.

– . "A Leaf on the Wind of All Hallows." *Songs of Love and Death,* eds. George R. R. Martin and Gardner Dozois, USA: Gallery Books, 2010. 429-468.

– . Lord John and the Brotherhood of the Blade. New York: Random House, 2011.

– . "Lord John and the Plague of Zombies" *Down These Strange Streets.* Ed. George R.R. Martin and Gardner Dozois. New York: Penguin, 2011.

– . "Lord John and the Succubus." *Lord John and the Hand of Devils.* New York: Random House, 2007. 45-156.

– . *Outlander.* New York: Bantam Dell, 1992.

– . *The Outlandish Companion.* New York: Delacorte Press, 1999.

– . *The Scottish Prisoner.* New York: Random House, 2011.

– . "The Space Between." The Mad Scientist's Guide to World Domination: Original Short Fiction for the Modern Evil Genius. John Joseph Adams, ed. New York: Tor, 2013. 161-243.

– . *Voyager.* New York: Random House, 1993.

Voyages of the Artemis. 18 July 2010. Blog. http://voyagesoftheartemis.blogspot.com/2010/07/steinkreis-11.html

"An Interview with Diana Gabaldon." *Outlander Podcast.* Episode 49. http://outlanderpod.wordpress.com/2014/08/03/episode-49-an-interview-with-diana-gabaldon.

"Gaelic Music." Electric Scotland. 1870. http://www.electricscotland.com/history/literat/

gaelicm.htm

Gunn, S.E. "Claims of Ireland." Scottish History and Celtic Studies, Glasgow University http://www.electricscotland.com/history/articles/claims.htm

Guthrie, E. J. "Old Scottish Customs." *Electronic Scotland* 1885. http://www.electricscotland.com/history/customs.

Hale, Mike. "A Highland Fling Would Not Be Unexpected Here." *The New York Times* 1 Aug 2014. http://www.nytimes.com/2014/08/02/arts/television/outlander-a-starz-series-adapted-from-the-novels.html?_r=0

Henderson, Helene, ed. *Holidays Symbols and Customs,* 4th ed. Detroit: Omnigraphics, 2009.

Keltie, John S., ed. "The Living Conditions in the Highlands." *History of the Scottish Highlands, Highland Clans and Scottish Regiments.* Edinburgh: Grange Publishing Works, 1887. http://www.electricscotland.com/history/working/index.htm.

Kirk, Robert. *The Secret Commonwealth of Elves, Fauns & Fairies.* London: David Nutt, 1893. *The Sacred Texts Archive.* http://www.sacred-texts.com/neu/celt/sce/index.htm.

Koerner, Brendan." *A Breath of Snow and Ashes*: The Romance Novel at the Top of the New York Times Best-seller List." *Slate* 2005. http://www.slate.com/articles/arts/number_1/2005/10/a_breath_of_snow_and_ashes.html

Lash, Jolie. "'Outlander': Caitriona Balfe's Journey to Claire." *Access Hollywood* 27 Sept 2014. http://www.accesshollywood.com/outlander-caitriona-balfes-journey-to-claire_article_99277.

Linklater, Eric. *The Prince in the Heather.* New York, Harcourt Brace, 1966.

Loughlin, Elenna. "Outlander TV Adaptation Won't Shy Away From Spanking." *Geek's Guide to the Galaxy. Wired.com.* 28 June 2014. http://www.wired.com/2014/06/geeks-guide-diana-gabaldon.

Maerz, Melissa. "Let's Talk about that 'Outlander' Sex Scene." *EW* 11 Aug 2014. http://insidetv.ew.com/2014/08/11/outlander-sex-scene/

McCreary, Bear. "Comic Con 2014 Highlights." *Bear McCreary Official Site* 29 July 2014. http://www.bearmccreary.com/#blog/blog/films/comic-con-2014-highlights.

– . "Outlander: The Garrison Commander, The Wedding, Both Sides Now." *Bear McCreary Official Site* 28 Sept 2014. http://www.bearmccreary.com/#blog/blog/outlander-the-garrison-commander-the-wedding-both-sides-now.

– . "Outlander: Sassenach." *Bear McCreary Official Site* 29 July 2014. http://www.bearmccreary.com/#blog/blog/outlander-sassenach.

McNamara, Mary. "HBO, You're Busted." *Los Angeles Times* 3 July 2013. http://articles.latimes.com/2011/jul/03/entertainment/la-ca-hbo-breasts-20110703.

Moore, Ron. "Inside the World of Outlander." Episodes 101-108. *Starz Extras. Starz.com.*

Ng, Philiana. "'Outlander': Caitriona Balfe on Claire and Jamie's Steamy Connection (Q&A)." *Hollywood Reporter* 16 Aug 2014. http://www.hollywoodreporter.com/live-feed/outlander-caitriona-balfe-claire-jamies-725840.

– . 'Outlander': Graham McTavish on Dougal's "Superobjective," Claire and Rewriting History." 6 Sept 2014.

http://www.hollywoodreporter.com/live-feed/outlander-graham-mctavish-dougal-729642

– . "'Outlander' Producer on Brutal Death Scene, Claire and Dougal's 'Conflicted' Rapport." *Hollywood Reporter* 30 Aug 2014. http://www.hollywoodreporter.com/live-feed/outlander-producer-geordies-death-claire-729063

– . "'Outlander': Lotte Verbeek on Geillis' Darkness and 'Ballsy' Nature." *Hollywood Reporter* 23 Aug 2014. http://www.hollywoodreporter.com/live-feed/outlander-lotte-verbeek-geillis-darkness-727197

Nunn, Joan. *Fashion in Costume 1200-2000.* Chicago: New Amsterdam Books, 2000.

Prudom, Laura "'Outlander' Postmortem: Stars Discuss Black Jack's Acts in 'The Garrison Commander'." *Variety* 13 Sept 2014. http://variety.com/2014/tv/news/outlander-106-sam-heughan-tobias-menzies-jamie-flogging-garrison-commander-1201305304.

– . "Starz's 'Outlander' Woos Women with Strong Female Protagonist." *Variety* 7 Aug 2014. http://variety.com/2014/tv/news/starz-outlander-woos-women-with-strong-female-protagonist-1201277091.

Radish, Christina. "Creator Ronald D. Moore Talks OUTLANDER, Bringing This Story to TV, Deciding on 16 Episodes, Season 1 Ending, and More." *Collider* 8 Sept 2014. http://collider.com/ronald-d-moore-outlander-interview/

Radway, Janice A. *Reading the Romance: Women, Patriarchy, and Popular Literature.* North Carolina: University of North Carolina Press, 1991.

Rakoczi, Basil Ivan. "Palmistry." Cavendish 1969.

– . "Tea-Leaf Reading." Cavendish 2586.

Saint-Amand, Imbert. *Last Years of Louis XV.* Trans. Elizabeth Gilbert Martin. New York, Charles

Scribner's Sons, 1900.
http://archive.org/stream/womenversailles00ma
rtgoog/womenversailles00martgoog_djvu.txt

Schwartz, Terri. "'Outlander' EP Ron Moore Explains why Claire and Frank Flashbacks Are Important." *ZapIt* 10 Aug 2014.
http://www.zap2it.com/blogs/outlander_frank_fl
ashbacks_explanation_ron_moore-2014-08

"A Social History of the Highlands." *Electric Scotland.*
*http://www.electricscotland.com/history/social/i
ndex.html.*

Taylor, James. "The Frasers of Lovat." *The Great Historic Families of Scotland.* 1887. *Electric Scotland.*
http://www.electricscotland.com/webclans/famil
ies/frasers_lovat.htm.

Vineyard, Jennifer. "*Outlander*'s Caitriona Balfe on Feminism, Fans, and Love Triangles." *Vulture* 28 Aug 2014.
http://www.vulture.com/2014/08/caitriona-
balfe-outlander-claire-chat.html

Index

About the Author

Valerie Estelle Frankel has won a Dream Realm Award, an Indie Excellence Award, and a *USA Book News* National Best Book Award for her *Henry Potty* parodies. She's the author of many books on pop culture, including *From Girl to Goddess: The Heroine's Journey in Myth and Legend, Buffy and the Heroine's Journey, Winning the Game of Thrones: The Host of Characters and their Agendas, Katniss the Cattail: An Unauthorized Guide to Names and Symbols in The Hunger Games, An Unexpected Parody, Teaching with Harry Potter, Harry Potter: Still Recruiting,* and *Doctor Who and the Hero's Journey.* Once a lecturer at San Jose State University, she's a frequent speaker on fantasy, myth, and pop culture. Come explore her latest research at VEFrankel.com.

CPSIA information can be obtained
at www.ICGtesting.com
Printed in the USA
FSHW020649191118
53886FS